Alexander Payne: Interviews

Conversations with Filmmakers Series
Gerald Peary, General Editor

Alexander Payne
INTERVIEWS

Edited by Julie Levinson

University Press of Mississippi / Jackson

www.upress.state.ms.us

The University Press of Mississippi is a member
of the Association of American University Presses.

Copyright © 2014 by University Press of Mississippi
All rights reserved
Manufactured in the United States of America

First printing 2014
∞

Library of Congress Cataloging-in-Publication Data

Alexander Payne: interviews / edited by Julie Levinson.
    pages cm. — (Conversations with filmmakers series)
  Includes index.
  ISBN 978-1-62846-109-1 (cloth : alk. paper) — ISBN 978-1-62846-110-7 (ebook) 1. Payne, Alexander, 1961– —Interviews. 2. Motion picture producers and directors—United States—Interviews. I. Levinson, Julie R., editor of compilation.
  PN1998.3.P39A44 2014
  791.4302'33092—dc23   2014013923

British Library Cataloging-in-Publication Data available

Contents

Introduction ix

Chronology xix

Filmography xxiii

Writing and Directing *Citizen Ruth*: A Talk with Alexander Payne and Jim Taylor 3
   Tod Lippy / 1996

An Interview with *Citizen Ruth* Director Alexander Payne 22
   Angie Drobnic / 1997

Adapting and Directing *Election*: A Talk with Alexander Payne and Jim Taylor 25
   Annie Nocenti / 1999

Bringing on the Payne 41
   Jeffrey M. Anderson and Rob Blackwelder / 1999

Fresh Air Interview with Alexander Payne 47
   Terry Gross / 2003

About Schmidt Director Alexander Payne Does Have Something Interesting to Say 55
   Walter Chaw / 2003

Interview: Alexander Payne 60
   Jeff Otto / 2004

Interview: Alexander Payne 64
   Scott Tobias / 2004

Alexander Payne: *Sideways* 71
    Adrian Hennigan / 2005

Alexander Payne 75
    Kate Donnelly / 2005

Alexander Payne: Staying Straight While Making *Sideways* 85
    Brad Balfour / 2004

Alexander Payne: *Sideways* Glance at America 90
    Kenneth Turan / 2005

Alexander Payne Talks *The Descendants*, Clooney, Next Black and White Film, New Trailer 115
    Anne Thompson / 2011

Alexander Payne on *The Descendants* and Why It's a Minor Work 123
    Eric Kohn / 2011

Director's Chair: Alexander Payne's *The Descendants* 129
    Iain Blair / 2011

Filmmaker Alexander Payne on *The Descendants* 134
    Edward Douglas / 2011

Interview: Alexander Payne 142
    Scott Tobias / 2011

Payne Find His Way to *The Descendants* 150
    Marshall Fine / 2011

An Interview with Alexander Payne 153
    Glenn Kenny / 2011

Interview: Alexander Payne 159
    Dave Davies / 2011

Alexander Payne Talks *The Descendants* and His Next Two Projects, *Nebraska* and *Wilson* 170
    Christina Radish / 2011

Interview with Alexander Payne 175
    Charlie Rose / 2011

Alexander Payne Prefers Actors Who Can Communicate 184
    Jennelle Riley / 2011

The Lei of the Land: A Few Moments with Alexander Payne 190
    Christy Grosz / 2012

Director of *The Descendants*, Alexander Payne, Talks Bristling Egos and Putting Life on Film 194
    Alanna J. Lawson / 2012

Omaha and the Perfect Ending: The Alexander Payne Interview 198
    Erich van Dussen / 2013

Film Director Alexander Payne: Greece "Energizes My DNA!" 202
    Demetrios Rhompotis / 2013

Whittling Birch Bark: A Conversation with Alexander Payne 206
    Julie Levinson / 2013

Director Alexander Payne on *Nebraska* 216
    Damian Houx / 2013

Additional Resources 221

Index 223

Introduction

Some unlikely scenarios for film comedies:

A young pregnant woman, whose favorite pastime is getting high on paint fumes, becomes an unwitting pawn in the abortion wars, as both pro-choice and anti-abortion forces compete for her sorry soul.

Out of spite, a popular high-school civics teacher rigs the election for student council president, thereby ending his career and, along the way, his marriage.

A middle-aged man whose wife is in a coma from which she will not emerge discovers that she has been cheating on him and sets off to find the man who cuckolded him.

None of these plot set-ups seems destined for laughs, let alone for success and staying power in the annals of Hollywood movies. Yet, *Citizen Ruth* (1996), *Election* (1999), and *The Descendants* (2011), along with Alexander Payne's other feature films—*About Schmidt* (2002), *Sideways* (2004), and *Nebraska* (2013)—have delighted audiences and critics alike with their omnidirectional satire, their all-too-human characters, and their refusal to submit to the bromides and bombast of so much contemporary American cinema. With six full-length films and one short segment of the omnibus movie *Paris je t'aime* (2006), Payne's output as a director is quantitatively small but qualitatively, and consistently, first-rate. As more than one critic has pointed out, his roster of movies boasts an unbroken winning streak. His half-dozen films have garnered innumerable awards and critical accolades; along with his co-writers, he has twice won the Academy Award for Best Adapted Screenplay. Payne's gimlet eye for human folly, alongside his mastery of the craft of filmmaking, marks him as a contemporary auteur of uncommon accomplishment.

This volume of interviews also marks him as an uncommonly erudite and articulate conversationalist about his own creative process and output as well as about that of several other directors. With a childhood spent accompanying his mother to Omaha's local art house cinema and with college majors in history and Spanish literature, Payne's frame of reference is broad and varied. He often speaks in metaphor and he is quick with a quip. But during interviews he is also quick to provide illustrative examples that bolster the point he is trying to make. The interviews collected here range from 1996, shortly after the release of his first feature film, *Citizen Ruth*, to the 2013 debut of his most recent film, *Nebraska*. They include the usual promotional back-and-forth with the press on the occasion of each film's release, discussions with trade publication journalists, conversations with high-profile interviewers including National Public Radio's Terry Gross and television's Charlie Rose, a talk with a writer for a magazine about Greek-American life, and an interview conducted expressly for this volume.

In his interactions with interviewers, Payne's comments are of a piece with his films: wry, incisive, and on the mark. Even his first interview—not to mention his first film—betrays a preternatural self-confidence and nimbleness of mind. He is an unfailingly gracious, if sometimes guarded, interviewee who chooses his words carefully and responds tersely if the question is not worthy of elaboration. His dry wit was evident at the press conference following the premiere of *Nebraska* at the Cannes Film Festival, where Payne was asked the inevitable question about why he chose to shoot the film in black-and-white. His deadpan rejoinder: "I wasn't expecting that question at all."

Throughout the interviews collected here, Payne crafts his responses earnestly, sometimes circling back to make certain that his thoughts have been expressed with precision. Even when asked the same things repeatedly, he doesn't default to pat answers. One of the questions posed to him most frequently by interviewers involves whether he condescends to or makes fun of his characters and why they are so often losers and failures. Although he bridles at the question, over the years he answers it carefully each time it is asked. In one interview, he admits, "Yes, we do make fun of people, but it's with a love and also a feeling that we're not any better and we're fairly pathetic in our own ways" (Hennigan). As an equal-opportunity satirist, he acknowledges to film critic Kenneth Turan, "Everyone's a target . . . even those who represent points of view with which I might agree." But he refuses to cop to condescension, insisting that his characters are not losers or failures but are, instead, recognizable human types who lose and who fail like each of us does from time to time.

Although several other questions crop up repeatedly, these interviews often read more like chats between avid film aficionados than like pro forma exchanges with journalists or critics. Unlike directors who treat the press as a necessary irritant, Payne never gives off an aura of noblesse oblige. He seems genuinely unfazed by the blandishments of fame and sincerely engaged in these conversations. As interviewer Edward Douglas observes, he "doesn't just field questions but actually will throw a couple back your way, and not in a rude way either, but simply because he really wants to know what others think."

Curiosity about what others think and do and desire is evident from his movies: deceptively small-scale character studies that radiate out to comment sardonically and, often, poignantly on the human condition—although Payne would, no doubt, balk at such a grandiose description. Any sentiment that creeps into his films is undercut by a mordant humor that deflates his characters' pretensions and reminds them, along with the audience, what fools these mortals be. Payne takes his place in a long line of satirists who ridicule their characters but nonetheless gaze fondly at them, finding their strivings and longings as touching as they are laughable. Like much of the best comedy, his is both subversive and affirmative; in film after film, although their lives and pretenses are turned upside down, his characters nonetheless persevere. In many of the following interviews, Payne refers to one or another of his films as "just a nice little comedy." But when asked directly if he thinks of comedy as a lesser form, he demurs and discusses filmmakers—Charlie Chaplin, Leo McCarey, Frank Capra, Vittorio De Sica—who are adept at combining comedy and pathos. Although he stops short of claiming a place for himself in that pantheon, blending comedy and pathos is precisely what he does skillfully in film after film.

In other interviews, Payne explains that he takes comedy seriously as a particular way of looking at life and maintaining a welcome distance from its painful aspects. He tells a journalist from the *BBC Movies* website that he and co-screenwriter Jim Taylor "like to find comedy and poignancy in that discrepancy between dreams and aspirations, and reality and limitations and who we really are. If drama is about obstacles . . . then maybe we like obstacles which are internal, because I think that's very true to life." Critics seem to have difficulty categorizing Payne's movies, alternately calling them dark comedies or comedic dramas or some other hybrid genre. Their indefinable status seems to be part of the point. As Payne tells a recent interviewer about *The Descendants*, "Of course, I feel flattered by its difficulty to pigeonhole. If it somehow achieves a unique or a thick tone, then, well, I'm sort of gratified by that" (Douglas).

There are discernible commonalities and through-lines among Payne's movies. His last five features all deal with men at various stages of midlife, each of whom undergoes some sort of crisis that forces him to come face-to-face with his foibles and to reassess the articles of faith that have carried him from day to day. For all of these protagonists, identity is revealed to be a house of cards. Their family or friends betray or disappoint them, or their work or romantic life falls apart, forcing them to question the bedrock assumptions on which they have built their lives and selves. Matthew Broderick's bee-stung eye in *Election*, Jack Nicholson's waterbed injury in *About Schmidt*, and George Clooney's much-discussed flat-footed run toward the truth of his wife's infidelity in *The Descendants* are all physical manifestations of their characters' spiritual lesions which mark these men as the walking wounded in their comic wars with themselves. By each of the movies' endings, Payne's characters are detached from any certainties that they may have had at the outset.

Those endings refuse to conform to the resolutions of traditional comedies, where characters gain self-knowledge, opposing forces are reconciled, a humane social order replaces a repressive one, and all's well that ends well. In literary critic Northrop Frye's famous dictum, classic comic endings prompt audiences to proclaim, "This should be," even as we recognize that those endings are more desirable than plausible. But like the unrepentant satirist that he is, Payne does not gratify his characters'—or his audiences'—desires by resolving things neatly. Rather than becoming enlightened, his protagonists do not learn much from their mistakes; instead, at the movies' conclusions, they generally remain bewildered about how they got where they are. Author Tom Perrotta's novel on which the film *Election* is based concludes with the tentative reconciliation of adversaries who seem to have softened and, as a result, changed for the better. Although Payne initially shot that ending, he and Taylor decided that it wasn't true to the spirit of what came before so they devised a new ending in which the comic universe does not right itself and, try though he might, the main character cannot rise above his petty impulses. As Payne says, "This was one of those rare instances of a studio financing a new ending that's more cynical than the original ending" (Nocenti).

In his conversation with interviewer Walter Chaw, Payne acknowledges "a certain unease my characters have with the world—they find themselves uncomfortable with the world into which they're born." But for the most part, he resists making any overarching statements about his characters or his movies; instead, he leaves it to others to ferret out his thematic preoccupations: "Separating myself from my work, I can see themes and elements emerging, but the act of creation is different and separate from the act of criticism and as I'm working, none of that enters into it" (Chaw). When Eric Kohn asks about the absence of heroes in his movies, he explains, "I'm not thinking about those things. I'm just working intuitively. . . . Actually, that's why I look to critics and good film writers for clues to how I work, which I hope won't hinder my creative process but might help articulate something I'm doing, or something that I could do better." Finally, with characteristic modesty and magnanimity, he expresses appreciation for the "generous urge on the part of the questioner to piece together what might be a body of work which is still finding its way" (Kohn).

Payne maintains that rather than consciously crafting an oeuvre, he simply proceeds film by film, devoting himself to his craft in a workmanlike fashion. Throughout the years of these interviews, his comments about his approach to screenwriting and directing give insight into his methods and his evolution as a filmmaker. He has screenwriting credits on all but his most recent film and, in several interviews, he speaks about his writing collaborations, the process of adapting novels into films, and his status as what is sometimes referred to in Hollywood as a hyphenate: a writer-director. Payne says his screenplays are tightly scripted with little on-set improvisation and few serendipitous discoveries or additions after the fact. In his scripts, he rejects the by-the-book structures and strictures endorsed by many screenwriting gurus. His films' rhythms and contours are his own and he describes a creative process that is more instinctual than rules-bound. In several discussions, he speaks about his fondness for voiceover as a tool for character exposition and he scoffs at the idea—widespread among film cognoscenti who quote chapter and verse from the so-called "screenwriters' bible"—that resorting to voiceover is some sort of lazy cop-out.

Payne repeatedly claims that the one skill he feels utterly confident about is his ability to cast his movies well, and the evidence suggests that he does have an unerring eye for which actor might be suitable for which role. His stated criterion for casting is simply that the actors have to be "appropriate vessels for the tone" of the movie (Turan). Although he is often spoken of as an independent director, Payne has been happy to work with big Hollywood stars, among them Matthew Broderick in *Election*, Jack Nicholson in *About Schmidt*, and George Clooney in *The Descendants*. But even though he had discussions with Clooney about appearing in his previous movie, *Sideways*, he ultimately decided that actor and role were not well-suited to each other and he instead cast the decidedly un-Clooney-like actor Paul Giamatti, who up to that point had landed only one leading movie role. In an interview broadcast on the National Public Radio show *Fresh Air*, Payne insists that casting is "the single most important element of the film that should be never compromised." In his uncompromising search for just the right fit for a role, Payne's sometimes surprising casting choices have revived (Virginia Madsen, Thomas Haden Church, Bruce Dern), or galvanized (Reese Witherspoon, Paul Giamatti), or launched (Chris Klein, Shailene Woodley) film careers.

His scripts are so dead-on funny and sharp that Payne's cinematic technique has occasionally been overlooked by critics. Although his directing style does not scream to be noticed, he is a highly precise and clever metteur en scène whose camera placements perfectly serve his finely tuned storytelling sensibility. Midway through *Election*, as the main characters pray for the fulfillment of their desires, a montage of successive crane shots gazes at them from on high, lampooning their self-importance and self-interest. Toward the beginning of *About Schmidt*, the high angle shot, static mise-en-scène, and spare composition of the eponymous character's packed-up office on his last day before retirement tells us all that we need to know about his diminishment and dissociation. The duration and camera placement of the final, lingering shot of *The Descendants*, in which we simply watch the father and two daughters sit on a couch and gaze at the television together while covering themselves with the dead mother's quilt, is ambiguous but also evocative and moving. Payne describes his directing technique to Iain Blair as follows: "My second unit director is a trained philosopher, and he says I have a phenomenological approach to film, meaning that I'm a bit like a documentarian. You go in to see what's there and then shoot that and order it. I don't have some vision I pursue. But I do have my own innate sense of rhythm which you impose on the project—in all phases, from the writing and directing to the speed of performance and number of angles shot so you can then control all that later in post and in the editing."

Payne declares editing to be his favorite part of the filmmaking process, telling interviewer Scott Tobias that, "more and more I find writing and directing a means to harvest material for editing." He has worked with the same editor, Kevin Tent, on all six of his feature films, and has, moreover, developed something of a repertory company of film technicians, working repeatedly with not just Tent and co-writer Taylor but also with the same composer, cinematographer, production designer, and casting people on many of his projects. In thinking holistically about his visual approach, Payne, as he often does, harks back to earlier directors and movies that he admires: "My goal is always what Chuck Jones wanted his Warner Bros. cartoons to be, which was if you turn down the sound, you could still tell what's going on. I think if you watch most of my films with the sound off, you could still tell what's going on" (Tobias). Although he has been roundly heralded for his artful dialogue and well-wrought screenplays, Payne refers often his intention, first and foremost, to tell his stories visually, like the movie directors of the past that he reveres.

His veneration for his cinematic predecessors is a constant refrain in these interviews and he admits that, "I'm a film buff first and foremost, and a filmmaker second" (Levinson). Payne's knowledge of film history is both wide-ranging and deep. He lights up when the conversation turns to old movies; indeed, in these interviews he is more forthcoming and effusive when talking about the movies and directors that he admires than about his own films. Payne's list of favorite directors is diverse, including, among others, Anthony Mann, Michelangelo Antonioni, Stanley Kubrick, Leo McCarey, Charlie Chaplin, and, most enduringly, Akira Kurosawa. His film enthusiasms are likewise eclectic and extensive; *Seven Samurai*, *Ikiru*, *Sunrise*, *The Last Detail*, *Five Easy Pieces*, *Unforgiven*, *City Lights*, *Make Way For Tomorrow*, *Topkapi*, *Midnight Cowboy*, *Amadeus*, *Withnail and I*, *The Girl in the Red Velvet Swing*, *McCabe and Mrs. Miller*, *To Live and Die in L.A.*, *Casino*, and *Amour* are among the motley assortment of movies that he extols.

Along with many film historians, Payne views the 1970s as the last glory days for American cinema. That decade was a formative period for him since it was then, during his teenage years, that he became steeped in not just silent and studio era movies but also in the quirky inventiveness of the then-current cinema. As he speaks about watching such movies as *Little Big Man* and *Butch Cassidy and the Sundance Kid* and *McCabe and Mrs. Miller*, he sounds wistful about the "New Hollywood" cinema of that era and its lingering effect on him: "My buddies and I were all great movie watchers, and somehow that golden period—you never know it's a golden period while you're living in it—but that period formed my idea of what a commercial, adult, American film is and it has just never changed" (Turan). Several times in these interviews, Payne makes a distinction between the personal cinema that reigned briefly in the early 1970s and the corporate cinema that monopolizes movie screens nowadays. In speaking about his own work in relation to that of thirty some-odd years ago, he tells an interviewer for the website *Indiewire*, "I'm sorry to use a cliché, but these are more the types of movies we had in the seventies, movies made in a modern cinematic vernacular that are just about life, and seeking to avoid the movie contrivances that so dominate our cinema today."

Although a few critics have suggested that Payne's character-centered, director-driven movies mark him as a rarity in contemporary Hollywood, he does not see himself as some sort of anomaly or throwback. He also resists being categorized as an independent filmmaker, claiming that the word is bandied about so freely that it has become all but meaningless. To an interviewer for the *Onion*, he explains, "Independent means one thing to me: It means that regardless of the source of financing, the director's voice is extremely present. It's such a pretentious term, but it's auteurist cinema. Director-driven, personal, auteurist . . . whatever word you want. It's where you feel the director, not a machine, at work. It doesn't matter where the money comes from. It matters how much freedom the director has to work with his or her team. That's how I personally define independent movies." In another exchange, he tries again to articulate what independent cinema means: "Regardless of the source of financing—be it a group of dentists in Akron, Ohio, or a major studio—I think independent should refer to a spirit of filmmaking. [An independent is] a film that tries to do something different, that feels like it comes from one person, that has some sense of authorial voice and doesn't seem to be pandering exclusively to commercial exigencies at the time" (Anderson and Blackwelder). Ultimately, he insists, "I don't use any label. I'm just a filmmaker. I'll take the money wherever it comes from, as long as I have creative control. I make movies for studios that turn a profit and are nominated for Oscars, which sounds fairly mainstream to me. Yet I'm referred to as an indie director. Maybe that just means I make personal films, or that the degree of creative control, which I'm lucky enough to enjoy, is evident" (Donnelly).

Whatever the critics label him, Alexander Payne is a director with a distinctive sensibility and sufficient success and clout to continue writing and directing the sorts of films that he wants to make. Although he claims that he has no idea what his next film will be, he is brimming with ideas about what his creative future may yield: a film set in Greece, a horror movie, a western, a historical epic. Or maybe he will simply continue to grace moviegoers with his singular "nice little comedies."

My thanks to the many interviewers who gave permission for their work to be included in this volume. Several expressed to me their admiration for Alexander Payne and his movies, and I am pleased to relay that enthusiasm in the form of this book. At the University Press of Mississippi, director Leila Salisbury and editorial associate Valerie Jones have been a pleasure to work with as I pulled together the manuscript. I am likewise appreciative of series editor Gerry Peary's initial encouragement to proceed with this project. At Babson College, Cathy Schaus and Rosely Mateo helped to transcribe some of the interviews. I am grateful to producer Albert Berger, who put me in touch with Alexander Payne, and to Anna Musso at Ad Hominem Enterprises for setting up my interview with him. In the midst of editing *Nebraska*, Alexander generously shared his time and thoughts with me. Phyllis Levinson, my mother, is a ceaseless font of confidence in and constancy for me. As always, my husband, Al Weinstein, and our daughters, Elena and Molly, sustain and inspire me.

JL

Chronology

1961   Born in Omaha, Nebraska, on February 10.
1979   Graduates from Creighton Preparatory School in Omaha and begins studies at Stanford University.
1983   Attends the University of Salamanca, Spain, where he studies Spanish philology.
1984   Graduates from Stanford with a degree in Spanish literature and history.
1985   Enters the University of California at Los Angeles (UCLA) master's program in film. Directs *Carmen*, a student film.
1990   Graduates from UCLA. His thesis film, *The Passion of Martin*, receives the Jack Nicholson Outstanding Student Director Award.
1991   *The Passion of Martin* screens at the Sundance Film Festival and then plays at over twenty other film festivals, including Sundance, Montreal, and USA-Dallas. Signs a deal with Universal Studios. Writes several unproduced screenplays, including *The Coward*, which later forms part of *About Schmidt*.
1992   Writes and directs *My Secret Moments*, part of the omnibus video *Inside Out I*, and directs *The House Guest*, part of *Inside Out III*, both produced by Propaganda Films and shown on the Playboy Channel.
1996   *Citizen Ruth* is released. Premieres at the Sundance Film Festival where it is nominated for the Grand Jury Prize in the dramatic category, wins first prize at the Munich Film Festival and is screened at several other festivals.
1999   *Election* is released.
2000   *Election* is nominated for an Academy Award for Best Adapted Screenplay. Wins Best Screenplay from the Writers' Guild of America and the New York Film Critics Circle and Best Director from the Independent Spirit Awards, as well as awards at several other festivals and critics associations. With Jim Taylor does an uncredited rewrite of *Meet the Parents*.

2001   *Jurassic Park III*, on which Payne and Jim Taylor have a writing credit, is released.

2002   *About Schmidt* is released. It is part of the Official Competition selection at the Cannes Film Festival in May (nominated for the Palme d'or) and opens the New York Film Festival in September

2003   *About Schmidt* is nominated for an Academy Award for Best Adapted Screenplay. Wins several awards including Best Adapted Screenplay from the Writers' Guild of America and the New York Film Critics Circle, as well as the Golden Globe Award for Best Screenplay for a Motion Picture. Publishes, with coauthor James Zemaitis, *The Coffee Table, Coffee Table Book*.

2004   *Sideways* is released. Premieres at the Toronto International Film Festival and plays as the closing night selection of the New York Film Festival. Executive produces *The Assassination of Richard Nixon*. Forms Ad Hominem Enterprises, a production company.

2005   Receives an Academy Award for Best Adapted Screenplay for *Sideways*. The film is also nominated for an Academy Award for Best Directing and for three other categories. *Sideways* wins Golden Globes for Best Picture—Musical or Comedy and Best Screenplay, Best Adapted Screenplay from the British Academy of Film and Television Arts (BAFTA), Best Director and Best Screenplay at the Independent Spirit Awards, and Best Adapted Screenplay at the Writers Guild of America. It is nominated by the Directors Guild of America for Outstanding Directorial Achievement. The film wins multiple other awards and accolades from film critics' associations. Publishes with coauthor Jim Taylor *The Sideways Guide to Wine and Life*. Becomes a member of the Board of Governors of the Academy of Motion Picture Arts and Sciences (Directors Branch). Chairs *Un Certain Regard* jury at Cannes Film Festival.

2006   Directs the "14e Arrondissement" segment and plays Oscar Wilde in the "Pere Lachaise" segment of *Paris je t'aime*. Executive produces *Gray Matters*.

2007   Co-writes with Jim Taylor a draft of the screenplay for *I Now Pronounce You Chuck and Larry*. Produces *King of California* and executive produces *The Savages*.

2009   Directs the pilot of and executive produces the HBO television

	series *Hung*. Completes the screenplay of *Downsizing*, which remains unproduced.
2011	*The Descendants* is released. It is the closing night selection of the New York Film Festival in October. Produces *Cedar Rapids*.
2012	*The Descendants* earns five Academy Award nominations, including the writing, directing, and best picture categories; it wins an Academy Award for Best Adapted Screenplay. It also wins a Golden Globe as Best Motion Picture—Drama, Best Screenplay at the Independent Spirit Awards, and Best Adapted Screenplay from the Writers Guild of America. The film is nominated for multiple awards from the British Academy of Film and Television Arts, the Broadcast Film Critics Association, the Hollywood Foreign Press Association (Golden Globes), and the Screen Actors Guild, among others. Serves on the jury for the main competition at the Cannes Film Festival.
2013	*Nebraska* is selected to screen in the main competition for the Palme d'or at the Cannes Film Festival in May. It is released theatrically in the fall.

Filmography

Directing and Writing Credits

THE PASSION OF MARTIN (1991) (short)
Producers: **Alexander Payne**, Evelyn Nussenbaum
Director: **Alexander Payne**
Screenplay: **Alexander Payne**
Cinematography: David Rudd
Editing: **Alexander Payne,** Niels Mueller
Principle Cast: Charley Hayward, Lauren Tuerk, Lisa Zane

CITIZEN RUTH (1996)
Miramax Films
Producers: Cathy Conrad, Cary Woods
Director: **Alexander Payne**
Screenplay: **Alexander Payne**, Jim Taylor
Cinematography: James Glennon
Editing: Kevin Tent
Principle Cast: Laura Dern, Swoosie Kurtz, Kurtwood Smith, Mary Kay Place, Kelly Preston

ELECTION (1999)
Paramount Pictures
Producers: Albert Berger, David Gale, Keith Samples, Ron Yerxa
Director: **Alexander Payne**
Screenplay: **Alexander Payne**, Jim Taylor
Cinematography: James Glennon
Editing: Kevin Tent
Principle Cast: Matthew Broderick, Reese Witherspoon, Chris Klein, Jessica Campbell, Delaney Driscoll, Mark Harelik

ABOUT SCHMIDT (2002)
New Line Cinema

Producers: Michael Besman, Harry Gittes
Director: **Alexander Payne**
Screenplay: **Alexander Payne**, Jim Taylor
Cinematography: James Glennon
Principle Cast: Jack Nicholson, Kathy Bates, Hope Davis, Dermot Mulroney

SIDEWAYS (2004)
Fox Searchlight Pictures
Producer: Michael London
Director: **Alexander Payne**
Screenplay: **Alexander Payne**, Jim Taylor
Cinematography: Phedon Papamichael
Editing: Kevin Tent
Principle Cast: Paul Giamatti, Thomas Haden Church, Virginia Madsen, Sandra Oh

PARIS, JE T'AIME (2006)
First Look International
Producers: Emmanuel Benbihy, Claudie Ossard
"14e arrondissement" segment:
Director: **Alexander Payne**
Screenplay: **Alexander Payne**, Nadine Eïd
Cinematography: Denis Lenoir
Editing: Simon Jacquet
Principle Cast: Margo Martindale

"Pere-Lachaise" segment:
Director: Wes Craven
Screenplay: Wes Craven
Cinematography: Maxime Alexandre
Editing: Stan Collet
Principle Cast: Emily Mortimer, Rufus Sewell, **Alexander Payne**

THE DESCENDANTS (2011)
Fox Searchlight Pictures
Producers: Jim Burke, **Alexander Payne**, Jim Taylor
Director: **Alexander Payne**
Screenplay: **Alexander Payne**, Nat Faxon, Jim Rash
Cinematography: Phedon Papamichael

Editing: Kevin Tent
Principle Cast: George Clooney, Shailene Woodley, Amara Miller, Nick Krause, Beau Bridges, Mathew Lillard, Judy Greer

NEBRASKA (2013)
Paramount Pictures
Producers: Albert Berger, Ron Yerxa
Director: **Alexander Payne**
Screenplay: Bob Nelson
Cinematography: Phedon Papamichael
Editing: Kevin Tent
Principle Cast: Bruce Dern, Will Forte, June Squibb, Bob Odenkirk, Stacy Keach, Mary Louise Wilson, Rance Howard, Tim Driscoll, Devin Ratray, Angela McEwan

Credits on Films Directed by Others

JURASSIC PARK III (2001)
Universal Pictures
Executive Producer: Steven Spielberg
Producers: Larry Franco, Kathleen Kennedy
Director: Joe Johnston
Screenplay: Peter Buchman, **Alexander Payne**, Jim Taylor
Cinematography: Shelly Johnson
Principle Cast: Sam Neill, William H. Macy, Téa Leoni, Laura Dern

THE ASSASSINATION OF RICHARD NIXON (2004)
THINKFilm
Executive Producers: Leonardo Di Caprio, Arnaud Duteil, Avram Kalpan, Kevin Kennedy, Jason Kliot, **Alexander Payne**, Frida Torresblanco, Joana Vicente
Director: Neils Mueller
Screenplay: Kevin Kennedy, Niels Mueller
Cinematography: Emmanuel Lubezki
Principle Cast: Sean Penn, Naomi Watts, Don Cheadle

GRAY MATTERS (2006)
Yari Film Group Releasing
Executive Producers: Joey Horvitz, Ted Leibowitz, Diane Nabatoff, **Alexander Payne,** Margaret Riley

Producers: Jill Footlick, John J. Hermansen, Sue Kramer, Bob Yari
Director: Sue Kramer
Screenplay: Sue Kramer
Cinematography: John S. Bartley
Principle Cast: Heather Graham, Bridget Moynahan, Tom Cavanagh, Molly Shannon

I NOW PRONOUNCE YOU CHUCK AND LARRY (2007)
Universal Pictures
Executive Producers: Barry Bernardi, Lew Gallo, Ryan Kavanaugh
Producers: Michael Bostick, Jack Giarraputo, Adam Sandler, Tom Shadyac
Director: Dennis Dugan
Screenplay: Barry Fanaro, **Alexander Payne**, Jim Taylor
Cinematography: Dean Semler
Principle Cast: Adam Sandler, Kevin James, Jessica Biel, Dan Aykroyd, Ving Rhames, Steve Buscemi, Nicholas Turturro

KING OF CALIFORNIA (2007)
First Look International
Executive Producers: Boaz Davidson, Danny Dimbort, George Furla, Vance Owen, Elisa Salinas, Trevor Short, John Thompson
Producers: Randall Emmett, Avi Lerner, Michael London, **Alexander Payne**
Director: Mike Cahill
Screenplay: Mike Cahill
Cinematography: James Whitaker
Principle Cast: Michael Douglas, Evan Rachel Wood, Willis Burks II, Laura Kachergus, Paul Lieber, Kathleen Wilhoite

THE SAVAGES (2007)
Fox Searchlight Pictures
Executive Producers: Anthony Bregman, Jim Burke, **Alexander Payne**, Jim Taylor
Producers: Anne Carey, Ted Hope, Erica Westheimer
Director: Tamara Jenkins
Screenplay: Tamara Jenkins
Cinematography: Mott Hupfel
Principle Cast: Laura Linney, Philip Seymour Hoffman, Philip Bosco

CEDAR RAPIDS (2011)
Fox Searchlight Pictures
Executive Producer: Ed Helms
Producers: Jim Burke, **Alexander Payne**, Jim Taylor
Director: Miguel Arteta
Screenplay: Phil Johnston
Cinematography: Chuy Chavez
Principle Cast: Ed Helms, John C. Reilly, Anne Heche, Stephen Root, Sigourney Weaver

Television Credits

HUNG (HBO, 2009–2011)
Executive Producers: Collette Burson, Dmitry Lipkin, **Alexander Payne** (26 episodes), Michael Rosenberg, Scott Stephens
Co-Executive Producer: Angela Robinson
Supervising Producer: Eileen Myers
Director: **Alexander Payne** (Pilot episode: Original airdate June 28, 2009)
Principle Cast: Thomas Jane, Jane Adams, Anne Heche, Charlie Saxton, Sianoa Smit-McPhee, Eddie Jemison, Rebecca Creskoff, Gregg Henry

Alexander Payne: Interviews

Writing and Directing *Citizen Ruth*: A Talk with Alexander Payne and Jim Taylor

Tod Lippy / 1996

From *Scenario: The Magazine of Screenwriting Art* 2, no. 4 (1996). Reprinted by permission of the interviewer.

Alexander Payne [director/co-screenwriter] was born and raised in Omaha, Nebraska. He studied history and Spanish literature at Stanford University, during which time he spent extended periods in Spain and Colombia, the latter with a grant to research and write a history of Medellin. Payne later attended UCLA's graduate program in film production, where he made several shorts, including his fifty-minute thesis film, *The Passion of Martin*, which played at over twenty film festivals, including Sundance, Montreal, and USA-Dallas, where it won a Special Jury prize. The film also had a theatrical run in Los Angeles and was broadcast on England's Channel Four.

Jim Taylor [co-screenwriter] grew up in Seattle and received his B.A. from Pomona College in English literature. After graduating, he worked at Cannon Films in Los Angeles as a production coordinator and development assistant. In 1987, he traveled to China with a grant to study that country's motion picture industry. Returning to L.A., Taylor worked for three years with the director Ivan Passer. In 1992, he used his winnings from an appearance on *Wheel of Fortune* to move to New York and enroll in the graduate film program at New York University, where he received his M.F.A. His short film, *Memory Lane*, played at a number of international and domestic festivals, winning several awards.

Citizen Ruth, Payne and Taylor's first feature film, premiered in the dramatic competition at the 1996 Sundance Film Festival. Currently, the two filmmakers are collaborating on a novel adaption which Payne will direct. Both are also developing their own writing and directing projects.

Tod Lippy: How did you two meet?
Alexander Payne: We met like ten or eleven years ago, but we were just acquaintances. Then, in 1989, I had a two-bedroom apartment in Silverlake and I needed a roommate, so I put the word out through friends and Jim showed up. We became friends and, then we started working together.

TL: How did you come up with the idea for *Citizen Ruth*?
Jim Taylor: We certainly weren't looking to make a film about the abortion debate, but we kept seeing these stories in the paper and on television that seemed to be great material for satire. People were getting into some pretty absurd situations.
AP: We thought there was a movie there, and the potential for a good, dense satire not just of the abortion debate but of Americana.

TL: When did you actually begin writing?
JT: In the spring of '92. We wrote a first draft in about six months.

TL: Did you do any research into Norma McCorvey, the woman better known as Jane Roe in the *Roe v. Wade* Supreme Court case? Her experiences as a working-class woman "used" by the pro-choice movement, followed by her recent defection to Operation Rescue, seem at least superficially similar to Ruth's. Did you read her autobiography, *I Am Roe*?
AP: We didn't read that, but we did a lot of research.
JT: Yeah. I have a huge file box full of articles on the subject. And we went to a bunch of protests, talked to different people—
AP: If you read the newspaper regularly, you can't avoid doing research. It's there every day.
JT: And what we found happening a lot was that the research we did actually confirmed what we'd already written. You know, we'd write speculatively about certain things, inventing very specific details, and then we'd be astonished to find that there were people who actually behaved that way.
AP: What's great about Norma McCorvey's story is that the "heroine"—like Ruth—of this epic political story is herself highly flawed, and really belongs to no side other than to herself.

JT: And her relationship to the people "helping" her is very troubled. There's no love lost between them. And despite herself, she becomes the instrument of some larger social issue.

TL: Can you talk a bit about constructing the character of Ruth?
JT: A big issue for us was she was this person who does all these things that are on the surface reprehensible, even repulsive—
AP: But she's still an innocent; you root for her.

TL: How do you manage to write an appealing character who embodies those contradictions?
AP: Appeal comes from truthful and complex characters. I hate when movie people say, "Your lead character has to be sympathetic," which for them means "likable." I don't give a shit about "liking" a lead character. I just want to be interested in him or her. You also have to make the distinction between liking a character as a person and liking a character as a character. I mean, I don't know whether I like Alex in *A Clockwork Orange* or Michael Corleone in *The Godfather* as people, but I adore them as characters. Besides, "liking" is so subjective anyway. So many American movies of the eighties and early nineties bent over backwards to make the protagonists "likable" in a completely fraudulent way, and I detested them.
JT: People would read the script and say, "How can you make a movie about this person? People won't want to watch this because they aren't going to care about her in the end." They felt like she wasn't involved enough in her story, that she wasn't present enough. And we felt very strongly that, once you actually see her "in the flesh," all of that sympathy and connection would be there.
AP: Also, Ruth was more passive in our first draft than she ended up becoming in later drafts, and our choice to make her more active was to find her self-serving qualities—her orneriness and feistiness—and the way in which she acts based on what's in front of her face in any given moment. So that evolved over several drafts. That sort of character, who's like a bull in everyone else's china shop, is really fun. It's great to have this amoral presence among all these people who think of themselves as supremely moral.
JT: Regarding Ruth's character, though, there were some very strong notes people consistently gave us that we very consciously ignored.
AP: "Show her being nice sometimes." "Maybe she could pet a dog."

"Have her give some of the money she gets at the end to a homeless person." Just horseshit. Truth is always sympathetic.

JT: We said, "Ruth is short for Truth."

TL: What about your treatment of the other characters? However extreme they may be, they still remain fairly sympathetic.

AP: Although we've been accused in some quarters of having stereotypical characters, people in real life are far more stereotypical than we presented them in the movie. Real fanatics never change the subject; we really wanted to have the characters talking about other things. To have the fanaticism be present, but not always the subject of conversation.

JT: Hopefully, you can in some way see everyone's perspective. Even if you watch the movie and come away with the feeling that it was made from a specific point of view, we didn't write it with that agenda in mind, obviously. We definitely didn't want anybody to think, "Oh, these are the villains and these are the good guys."

AP: I like everybody in the script.

JT: We personally didn't feel that judgmental about anyone.

AP: And at the same time, extremely judgmental. We don't judge them at all, yet we judge them harshly, like people in real life.

JT: There's that great line from Swift, about loving humanity and hating humans, which is really important to keep in mind when you're writing satire. Everyone is fair game, but at some point you have to have compassion.

AP: To write satire you have to take an essence of truth and then give it a little dollop of sour cream. Some people might see it as stereotypical, but it's just taking something you see in people and bringing it to the fore in order to have comic fun.

JT: We gave this script to many different people to read: men, women, pro-life, pro-choice. After reading it, a lot of people said, "Oh, you can't do that, you've taken things too far here." Well, that's exactly the kind of stuff people love when they see the movie. That's a really interesting thing, because people will say, "You can't have Blaine traveling around with this young boy," but then people love it when they see it onscreen.

AP: People don't know what the movie is. I mean, one reason this was so hard to get made is that it is such a straight-faced satire. A lot of people read this and didn't get the humor; they thought it was like a bad TV movie. Hopefully now with the other stuff we write together it will be an easier sell, because we've done the transformation to the screen for this one.

JT: And this was always written for Alexander to direct, so we didn't have to make everything really clear. I mean, we tried to make the irony, the humor, clear in the directions, but when I talked earlier about ignoring people's notes, a lot of that had to do with knowing that Alexander would direct it.

TL: How do the two of you write together?
JT: We did a little bit of work separately on this script, but most of the time we sat together in front of the computer, handing the keyboard back and forth.
AP: Now we have two keyboards.

TL: Alexander, as the director, are you constantly deciding whether a certain scene or segment will work for you visually when you're writing?
AP: During the writing process either one of us can veto anything. There were very few cases—actually, I can't think of anywhere we disagreed about something and I said, "Well, I'm going to direct it so I want it this way."
JT: A little of that happens in the last go-round but we'd just have a mild discussion/argument and come to a conclusion.
AP: But I trust Jim and his taste, and he trusts me and my taste.

TL: Your tastes are apparently quite similar, judging from the short films each of you wrote and directed previous to this.
AP: He's slightly wackier than I am.
JT: I don't know....
AP: I think you are. [both laugh]
JT: I think the way I would describe the difference is: that you have a little more of an angry edge to what you do.

TL: Alexander, your short film, *The Passion of Martin*, was certainly more extreme in its violence than Jim's was.
AP: Well, I had a lot of anger to express in that film. [both laugh]
JT: I think I'm usually voting for the—
AP: Safer route?
JT: Umm—gentler?
AP: Well, I remember when we were in the middle of writing this film, and you have so many doubts, and I hadn't directed a feature yet. "Is this script any good? Is this line any good? Is my life any good? Am I ever going to make a film?" I have to say that I never fundamentally doubted the merit of this script, and through four years of talking about it, writing it, directing it, editing it, I've never gotten bored with it and its essence. But

I remember seeing Buñuel's *Viridiana* again while we were writing this, and driving back from the theater and being so on fire from its courage and its boldness, and Buñuel's willingness to be responsibly subversive. People always say, "Young people have all this anger," yet Buñuel never lost his anger, or his belief that we don't live in the best possible world. So *Viridiana* was also an important influence on this film, for that kind of anger and subversiveness. And *Ace in the Hole*.

JT: Basically, we make each other laugh, and that's the most important thing. And we both have a similar, dry sense of humor, so the tone is consistent.

TL: How did you manage to sustain that comic tone throughout this film, which deals in fairly dark subject matter?
AP: Well, let me make a comment about the word "dark." Because American filmmaking in the eighties became so happyfaced, anything real—on a human level—is by now considered dark. I don't see this film as being dark, I see it as being real—at least real to how I perceive things. There's no true comedy that's not based in pain.

TL: Did you use any kind of structural tools—an outline, for instance—when working on this?
JT: We had the barest outline before we started, and we basically knew where we wanted the story to go.
AP: But we never make a thorough outline or use file cards or anything like that. It's hard for us to know what we're going to write before we write it

TL: Was Ruth's miscarriage something you came up with immediately as a way to resolve the story?
JT: I think it was in the first draft, but we had some other possibilities.
AP: We got criticized for that.

TL: I read somewhere that in one screening someone in the audience called it a "cop-out."
AP: Yeah, because she doesn't supposedly make a choice.
JT: But she does make up her mind, she just keeps changing it.
AP: But in basic screenwriting, you have a character with a goal, and you set up as many obstacles as possible toward the character reaching that goal. And just before the climax of the film is when most of those obstacles appear.

TL: Also, it's a logical outcome for the character of Ruth, who doesn't seem to be able to identify with either of the options presented to her.
JT: Well, we felt like it was really the only option, not because it took her decision away from her, but because it actually gave her a decision. It gave her the power to say, "Boy, I can pull something over on these people." It had to do with her, with giving her some victory in the midst of all these other people. And also to just see this huge crowd of people fighting each other when the problem had been flushed down the toilet. [Alexander groans] Since the movie was never meant to be either a pro-choice or a pro-life movie, we don't care what kind of a statement her having a miscarriage makes, we're making a statement about something else—
AP: Something larger, for me.

TL: You've talked about Buñuel and Wilder as influences: what about Preston Sturges? His name keeps being invoked in reviews of the film.
AP: I don't know why. I mean, I guess I'm flattered, but I'm not that big a student of Preston Sturges's films. I like some of them, but some of them tire me.
JT: By the way, regarding your question about the writing process, and whether we used an outline: one thing is that we never tried to cram this story into some kind of a Syd Field notion of how a script should be, how a story should be told. It had more to do with whether it felt right or not; that was really our only criterion—that it had some shape to it, however small. And when Ruth is sitting in her chair and makes her decision to not tell them she's had this miscarriage, that's her tiny change. That's it. She hasn't changed that much. A lot of people asked us about that.
AP: And many people ask us what happens after the film ends.
JT: Yeah, there's been a lot of pressure to say that she turned her life around after the last scene. We never felt like that was what we were interested in showing. She might have, but probably not.

TL: This script feels like it was written as much to be read as to be filmed. I'm thinking of some of your lines of direction like, "Ruth is beside herself, and beside the two Ruths is Gail's purse."
JT: Well, it's supposed to be a fun story, so putting in stuff like that sustains the tone. I mean, there are some writers who write very specifically to readers—like Shane Black—but we never thought about that.
AP: We write it so that we enjoy reading it.
JT: But that kind of thing did get us into trouble, because some people

didn't know how to read it. There's a danger to writing this kind of a film, because you're not making it really clear that something is funny—I mean, you're not giving people cues like having someone bash their head into a ladder—

AP: Well, I think stylistically having things, even in the final film, be ambiguous as to tone—unsureness as to whether to laugh or scream—is great.

JT: Another of our influences is the radio monologist Joe Frank; we're both avid fans of the way he infuses the humor with so much pain. It's unsettling.

AP: And the script, I think, suggests a harsher film. When you're finally shooting, you tend to mitigate a lot of that harshness because you become aware of how much you want to entertain every single minute, however unsettling it is. I mean, the biggest laugh in the film is probably also the most suggestive of her pain, when she tells her mother that if she'd had an abortion at least she wouldn't have to "suck her boyfriend's cock." The audience goes wild, but what it suggests is really painful. That's her whole backstory in one line.

JT: That's the whole movie, in that one line: Sometimes people's lives are really hard. As much as you can judge them for what they do, it's just so hard to make it from point A to point B. My other favorite line in the script is at the Stoneys' house, when they admonish Ruth: "We don't really sit in those chairs." That's my vote.

AP: For me, also, it's when Gail is yelling "Baby killer! Baby killer!" and then asks somebody to save her a jelly doughnut.

JT: We hope that people who are involved on either side of this issue will at least recognize that setting: the mundanity of a lot of it, like standing outside of the clinic, waiting around.

TL: You finished your first draft in six months?

JT: Yeah, but I had a day job during a lot of that, so it was a little difficult for us to get together. And then after the first draft, I moved to New York, so Alexander came to New York twice and I went to L.A. twice.

AP: We kept rewriting and rewriting all the time. We went through one dead-end producer, so there was a lot of dead time—a year and a half—before another producer, Cary Woods, signed on. It still took another year and a half before actual production, and we kept rewriting, unpaid. Just to make it better and better

TL: How many drafts?

JT: Five or six. Even though it was frustrating taking so long to get the movie made—I mean, many scripts never get made, so we're not complaining—but there was this long tease, so it was in a way a big luxury for us to continually be able to rewrite and tighten it up. So when we got out to Omaha, we were comfortable with it before going into production.

AP: It was great, also, because Jim was there the whole time, doing second-unit direction and doing a lot of support work, so that when, for instance, we could only get a location for one day instead of two, he could make some changes during the day and then show them to me later that night.

TL: So you were there the whole time, Jim?

JT: Yeah, it was great. It was like a writer's dream. I was never surprised by what he did because we'd talked about it so much. In this case, I was able to be so involved with it, even in postproduction.

TL: Who did you approach for financing once you had the script?

JT: Well, it was all driven by the fact that Alexander had some cachet as a first-time director after his short film, so there was a lot of interest.

AP: Cary Woods had been with Peter Guber and Jon Peters when that film came out, and had tried to sign me to a writing/directing deal with them. Among all the people I'd met out of film school who had expressed some interest in me, he was the only one who two, three years later had remained unflagging in his interest.

JT: Cary made this movie, with very difficult subject matter, happen. And he never interfered in the creative side of things—I mean, there were a few things we weren't able to shoot because of budget concerns, but otherwise—

AP: We had disagreements about casting from time to time, which is to be expected, but we came to really trust each other, I think.

TL: Did he go to studios for financing?

AP: Well, no. Previous to him I had some other producers who took it to some studios, who all said "no."

JT: Also, people felt that it was "old news," and then all of a sudden an abortion doctor would get shot, or Norma McCorvey would join Operation Rescue—it just doesn't seem to go away as an issue.

TL: When did Miramax get involved?

AP: Cary had had these financiers from New York—who had funded

Kids—who lost interest in *Ruth* at the last minute, but by that time he had developed a relationship with Miramax, and they eventually agreed to finance it.

TL: When did Laura Dern get cast?
AP: A few months before shooting began. Somehow the screenplay had gotten to her, and she liked it and called us up.
JT: Something we hadn't thought of, but which there is a lot of discussion about, is writing an interesting female lead, because there's a tremendous advantage in getting someone of Laura Dern's stature interested. There just isn't much material out there for all of these terrific actresses.
AP: Many fine actresses expressed interest in the part.

TL: Well, you ended up with many fine actresses in the film: Swoosie Kurtz, Mary Kay Place, et al. Did you ever feel like you would be able to populate the film with such high-caliber performances?
AP: I was prepared to shoot the film in Omaha for $300,000 on 16mm with no known actors, and that would have been fine, too. But how it ended up was pretty close to ideal.

TL: How did you manage to snag Burt Reynolds, especially for the part of Blaine?
AP: Well, his name came up, and we thought that was a good, fun idea. He read it, and said that, while he liked the script very much, he was going to have to pass, because he didn't want to confuse his audience—maybe it was too risky. We called his people back and said, "Will Mr. Reynolds accept a meeting with the producer and director?" And the word came back that he would, and that he was happy to explain why he had to pass. Anyway, the producer couldn't make it, so I went alone to Burt's suite at the Bel Air Hotel. We spent ninety minutes talking, and by the end of it he had agreed to do it. I just told him, I said—what did I say?
JT: Well, you had him autograph your *Gator* soundtrack album—
AP: That was at the end. I just said, "It's kind of weird comedy, but I can't help thinking that most Americans agree with a basic point of it, which is that we're kind of sick and tired of the abortion debate." And that comedy and satire are valid forms to explore and express that. And he agreed.

TL: How long was the shoot?
AP: Seven six-day weeks. We finished in late May of '95.

TL: This draft we're publishing contains quite a bit of material which didn't make it into the film. Besides some fairly major cuts we'll talk about in a little bit, there was a lot of pruning of scenes, such as the one near the beginning when Ruth goes into a hardware store to buy patio sealant. In the script, she has an antagonistic conversation with the owner before leaving the store. That was cut out of the final film; what happened to it?
AP: That was shot, but we cut it to speed up the first reel.

TL: How long was your first assembly?
AP: The editor's very first assembly was two-and-a-half hours.
JT: It's actually an interesting thing. You probably know when you're shooting that you're going to leave the scene at a certain point. But if there's a line or two that carries the scene to some other kind of conclusion, why not shoot it? Then you have the option to keep it later on. Also, it gives the scene—if you do cut it out—that sense of momentum—it's continuing, but you're leaving it to move on to something else.

TL: In your script, Ruth has an "Environments" tape she plays on her Walkman whenever she's huffing, which results in some pretty loopy fantasy sequences. Were these too expensive to shoot?
AP: No, that was a case of getting on location and thinking that that was sort of stupid. It was better to just have her looking at the dirt—it's more banal. I kept telling the production designer I didn't want anything pretty or unreal or movie-like.

TL: You were talking earlier about the importance of emphasizing Ruth's ability to fix on whatever happens to be in front of her at any given moment. There's a scene in the courtroom where the judge is reprimanding her and she is held rapt by the vision of a fly bouncing against the window. Did you shoot that?
AP: Yeah. We cut it for time. Until you get to the point where she meets the pro-life women in jail, the film's got to fly.
JT: That's when the movie really begins.
AP: I disagree.
JT: Well, when you really feel like you understand what—
AP: Where the rest of the movie is going to go from there.
JT: By the way, that scene with the judge was the one thing during writing that I felt was too long—but too long is better than too short.
AP: But it's more in editing than in writing when you know the point has been made and you can move on, and hopefully, directorially you've

covered enough to give you the freedom to get out of anything at any time. As my editor, Kevin Tent, likes to say, editing is boot camp for a film.

JT: By the way, the fact that both of us had directed before gave us such a better sense—I can't imagine trying to write without it. It informs the process so much.

TL: But you've both also acted—did that have any influence on your writing process?

AP: Writing is like acting. You have to get inside the characters, become them.

JT: That's right. Working as a team, we'd always get up on our feet and act it out.

AP: When we were writing. I would channel one of the characters for a while, or Jim would—Jim, you were much more Norm. [Jim laughs] I remember being very Blaine.

JT: If one person can get more into the mindset of a particular character, and is just speaking and spewing away, then the other person can be crafting that into dialogue.

AP: We wrote a whole other scene, that never made it into a draft, where Harlan tortures Kirk—that was Jim's whole thing, and it was just hilarious.

JT: The line is, just before he starts torturing him—

AP: He's been gagged with jumper cables, and Harlan's coming at him with a coat hanger—

JT: "Looks to me like you locked your keys in the car." That was maybe a point at which we felt we were going too far. By the way, I have to compliment Alexander as a director for brilliantly implying that whole thing by having Harlan drag Kirk into the basement in the film, which did everything we needed to do.

TL: The scene in the jail cell near the beginning is slightly more slapsticky in the script: she struggles with a pull-down cot, which keeps snapping back up.

AP: Well, in my tour of, like, fifteen jails, I never found a bed like that.

JT: The only reason we wrote that in there was to communicate her sense of frustration with life, how nothing goes right for her. To me, without her genuine pain in that scene, the rest of the movie doesn't work. You can't get away with all of the humor unless your audience believes that the filmmakers know how painful this is for her.

TL: What about the scene with Ruth trashing the Stoneys' bathroom while they wait for her to join them for dinner?
AP: We shot it. The crosscutting just didn't work, so we simplified it.

TL: There's a very funny addition, which I'm guessing must have come to pass in the editing room, to the dinner scene that follows: when Norm is praying, the deafening noise of an airplane obscures what he's saying. That wasn't in your script. What happened there?
AP: It was two things. One is, in early drafts of the script, we had written in, because we thought it was funny, that this town—coincidentally like Omaha—was very close to a big Air Force base. We'd have characters periodically stopping conversations in mid-sentence and looking up as planes went by. Anyway, that got too complicated. In editing, the idea of the Stoneys living near the airport was added.
JT: Why we intuitively felt that would work at this point was that it sort of signaled "something bigger": you know, this powerful presence hanging over them. It also gives the sense that these people, the Stoneys, are not exactly living in the best neighborhood—they're struggling too and they've dedicated their lives to this cause.

TL: What happened to that red spot in the eggs Gail scrambles for breakfast? I couldn't find it on the screen.
JT: [laughs] Actually, that's a funny story. They were trying to throw that together on the set, and when we saw the dailies it just didn't look realistic at all. They'd squirted some kind of red dye into it, but it wasn't working. As the nominal second-unit director, I felt it was really important to make it work, so I took it on myself. I mean, I spent all of this time trying to make it look realistic, but the blood dot's so small you can't even see it.
AP: Sure looked good on paper, though.

TL: Probably the most significant series of cuts were the dream sequences, which I have to say worked beautifully in the script; they seemed like little films in themselves. Their excision must have had to do with budgetary concerns.
JT: Yeah. Absolutely. Actually what happened was interesting. With the amount of money we had to shoot this—with a great cast and real crew—they couldn't give Alexander the days he needed. From the producing perspective, the dream sequences were the thing to lose. And I fought vociferously about it—
AP: And Laura liked them a lot, also.

JT: That's true. If there was any consistent criticism of the script, it was that we didn't know her character well enough. Even though we felt strongly that if and when you saw her—even if she was just observing what's going on, being passive—you'd know her—
AP: In cinema, you see a face and you project so much onto it.
JT: —those dream sequences were our way of making her more involved in an artificial way—giving her more of an inner life, without being so contrived.
AP: A cinematic, even poetic, way of doing it. They were also important to express two other things: a longing for innocence in the first one—
JT: A longing for *La Dolce Vita*. [laughs]
AP: Yeah, that was kind of a fun homage. And then in the second one, with the bus, an evocation of death.
JT: We really fought like heck to keep them in, because with the low budget, it was suggested we drop them. The schedule was shuffled around, and those scenes were put at the very end of shooting. Then when it was clear we weren't going to get to them in Omaha—
AP: I was still planning on shooting them in L.A. We wrapped on a Friday in Omaha, and Laura Dern stayed over the weekend. There were a couple of images we wanted to get for the dream—new stuff, which happened in a cornfield—so Laura, myself, and a local Omaha cameraman went out with a little Arri and shot all day that Sunday; that's how important it was. Ultimately, however, having seen a couple of cuts of the film, we decided it wasn't necessary.
JT: The movie doesn't need them, simply because you know this person well enough from observing her onscreen.
AP: I'm sorry to say the old film cliché is true: you write a script, and then you go in thinking you're going to direct a film, and in fact the film directs you. It directs itself—your job is to support it and help it find itself.
JT: Another case in point: in our script, it's only suggested that Diane and Rachel are lovers. In fact, when we were first writing, it was just these two women living in a house together and then we thought, "Oh, that would be interesting." In production, it became such a huge issue in terms of production design, costumes, everything. It became a really significant big deal that these women were lovers, and we're not afraid of it—although we may get attacked for it—but it was interesting to see something you just barely suggested in the script grow in importance. When we were writing it, we weren't interested in their sexuality, we were interested in other things that they had going through their minds.
AP: Similarly with Blaine and Eric—

JT: [Feigns surprise] What are you talking about? No, that's true.
AP: Well, you know, you've got to make clear choices once you get into production. You've got this script by these idiot screenwriters, and now you need to know exactly what's going on because you've got to make this fucking film.

TL: Whatever happened to "King," the attack dog?
AP: King flew out from L.A. and turned out to be the German shepherd actor of the lowest bidder. He did not perform and was cut from the film. He made more money per day than the actors made. He was such a nice dog. The cinematographer was talking about his experiences with dogs on other films, where they'd have a cage within a cage, and the dog would be, like, shackled and muzzled, and the handler would have to wear a mesh suit and carry a tranquilizer gun. We had this dog that just loved being around people. Then his trainer, who spoke French—the dog was bilingual—would have to provoke him to do things he didn't want do, so it wasn't working out. After one wide shot, we shot everything else either medium shot or close-up.
JT: King was there, you just can't see him.
AP: But it sure looked good on paper.

TL: You were talking about concerns regarding Ruth's character, and whether she was fleshed out enough. Interestingly, quite a bit of her dialogue from the script was cut from the film, including her lines about "wishing she were dead" in the "Moon Mother" scene with Rachel and Diane.
AP: That also was a big loss. Her lines about wishing she were dead and hating the country—those were important lines to express her inner life.

TL: There's also the moment in which she takes out the picture of her kids and looks at it forlornly.
AP: We never shot that; that was too stupid.
JT: I didn't think it was stupid.
AP: But we shot that scene you're talking about on the porch, because the house we found didn't have a pond—which is what the characters walk around during that scene in the script—and because of the other big porch scene that precedes it, where there is the standoff and the police come. It was too radical a shift in gears to go suddenly from that big moment to her saying, "I hate the country." That was a painful loss. Boot camp! By the way, our editor was great—like a writing partner, really.

Many of the things you're mentioning were "writing" contributions by Kevin. Like the scene in which Ruth's going to sleep in the Stoneys' basement: In the script we say something about her looking over at the praying hands, but he came up with the idea of doing those corny voiceovers, which end with "Dale's out today. You collect carts." Actually, we were lucky to have a group of people—from cast to production people to post-production—who were more or less of a similar mind, a similar comic sensibility. Everyone got in the spirit of it.

TL: What happened to the scene in which Gail and Kathleen visit Tony and Cynta to get a picture of Ruth's two kids?
AP: The scene was good, nicely shot, well-acted. Time. If there's any flaw in the rising action in the script late in act two before the climax, it's from the moment when the money is offered until the miscarriage: you know, setting everything up. It's pretty tight in the finished film, but it's a little loose in the script.

TL: The scene with Blaine and Norm in Blaine's hotel room is broken up in the film by the one with Ruth and Harlan in the kitchen; in the script, the hotel scene is one long take. It worked beautifully, though, because the idea of cutting back to that scene with Blaine suddenly shirtless (and Eric applying massage oil) really punches it up.
AP: We had to speed that whole part up, and that scene seemed a little long.

TL: I'm assuming the "Choose Life Ruth" banner flying from the airplane was not shot for financial reasons.
AP: We shot it. But we cut most of the scene in which she's in the limousine with Jessica and the others and looks out the window and sees it, so we couldn't use it.
JT: To me, that trip to the clinic was the most worrisome in terms of translating from the script. It was annoying mechanics: who would get to the clinic first, how the protest would grow out front. Actually, something I'm proud of is sticking up for the use of the helicopter evoked the sense of the escalation of this war. But it did make it problematic: how does she get from the helicopter to the car?
AP: And we couldn't afford a helicopter on the tarmac when they're getting in the limousine, so we just had them duck, and used a sound effect there.

TL: That is Diane Ladd, Laura Dern's real mother, playing Ruth's mother, isn't it?
AP: Yeah. What happened was, she flew to Omaha to be with Laura on Mother's Day, and my family, who's from Omaha, took them out for brunch at the Omaha Club. I had wanted Diane to play the part and had asked Laura about it before I knew them very well, and she said that Diane probably wouldn't do it. Then Laura asked her while she was there and she said she would: she flew back the next week when we shot it. It was just perfect.

TL: What happened to the ending of the script, which has Ruth walking away from the clinic, visiting an appliance store and buying a TV, then boarding a bus for Tucson? Her last line, "What are you looking at?" seemed so apt.
AP: For me, as a director—not as an editor, mind you—they were all big losses. The scene where Ruth goes into the Nebraska Furniture Mart, we had like two hundred TVs, all showing the melee at the clinic, and she walks up to one and switches channels to a soap opera; there's a close-up of her face, and then a wide shot. Again, an image that really summarizes the whole gist of the film. A big loss. We also had a great night shot of the bus pulling away. But forgetting all of that, and thinking only of the rhythm of the film, it felt like an ending of a film when she walks away from that clinic. And, with everything else after that, it started to feel like the film had three different endings. First she leaves the clinic, then she goes to buy a TV, then she gets on the bus.
JT: We should give some credit to Laura for the ending. The day we were shooting that scene where she leaves the clinic, Laura had this instinct to just keep running and running down that road, she said, "Get some people down there to make sure there are no cars coming." She was so fired up about it. It was a really good instinct, and a valuable contribution that paid off later.
AP: I also have to give credit to Cary Woods and Cathy Konrad—the producers—who felt early on that it should end there, even though I was still trying to make the other ending work. That's part of why Cary's such a good producer: he has good popular-audience feelings.
JT: They were great producers. They never said, "You have to do this or that."
AP: They never insisted. Which is a key to getting the best out of your people. Which I try to do as a director.

TL: You've been through a sort of titular hell with this film. Can you talk about that a little bit?

AP: The working title was *The Devil Inside*. Then when we were set to show it at Sundance, we used the title *Meet Ruth Stoops*. Shortly before the Festival, however, Miramax thought *Meet Ruth Stoops* wasn't a good title—funny, but too hard to say—and at the last minute *Precious* was suggested. But that ultimately wasn't the right title, either.

JT: [laughs] And now it's *Citizen Ruth*. We've come up with hundreds of titles for this film. A title is certainly important, but my whole feeling is that as long as it's not ridiculous, and it's something that works in terms of marketing the film, then okay.

AP: If I had my druthers, I'd call it *The Little Miracle*.

JT: Or *One of Us*, which I understand is not a great title to market. The reason I like *Meet Ruth Stoops* is that it's fun. And we wanted a title that was about her, and not about the issue.

AP: *The Devil Inside* was a nice subversive title while we were writing, but after seeing the film—

JT: I never felt that was a good title.

AP: You came up with it!

JT: I know, but I never felt that it was a good title for the movie.

TL: Any guesses as to how this film is going to be received?

JT: Well, at Sundance we got quite a few positive reviews, and only a few that were negative, for instance, the guy in *Film Comment*, who seemed genuinely offended. In a way, I was happy about that because I felt like the movie was somehow missing its mark if everyone loves it. I mean, I'm not gleeful this guy's offended, but if nobody's offended then we weren't bold enough. He called it the "prototypical apolitical political film." I mean, like, *yeah*. When people say there's no point of view to the film, I'm confused: when she has a miscarriage and runs away after taking the money from these people, that's a point of view. It's just not a pro-life or pro-choice point of view.

TL: Let's talk about that point of view for a moment. You seem to be positing that the individual is relatively impotent in an overtly politicized society....

JT: It's about an individual getting lost in politics.

AP: All of us live in society, and we're all flawed, with our specific problems, and sometimes we're asked by society, "Are you this or are you that?" Well, what if I'm neither, or what if I'm something else? Or what if I don't care? Does that make me less valuable? Is my importance or my virtue somehow lessened by my not adhering to a specific imposed model? And there are other subplots as well: What does it mean to give freedom of choice to someone who doesn't have the wherewithal to choose? That's an interesting question. I just hope that people would see the film in the spirit in which it's intended, and I also think it would be really fun if activists actually saw themselves in it and felt that their side was fairly represented and that the other side was being slammed. I don't think that anyone is being made fun of more than anyone else. I mean, I know I tried—however successfully or unsuccessfully—to understand every character in the film. I always listen to people with whom I disagree and really try to see how they think and feel. Certainly as a writer you need to do that.

JT: But it is a satire.

AP: But regardless of that, you try to get into how people think and feel. You can't deny that.

JT: Oh, no, I don't deny that, but in terms of how people are going to respond to it—

AP: Okay, but everyone is slammed equally. If we're criticizing anybody we're criticizing everybody. We're criticizing ourselves, we're criticizing society, not just people of a particular religious or political bent.

JT: Right. But to say that you're hoping that people will see themselves presented accurately in these characters is kind of insulting to those people, I think. They'd have to be awfully dim-witted to not feel attacked. So I don't know what people's reaction will be. I hope people will recognize that we're not on some vendetta. The point is that maybe it's time to have a sense of humor about this very serious issue, and to look at some of the absurdities that begin to happen when people get carried away with their political agendas. We just hope they won't feel that we don't see them as real people with real concerns and genuine pain. Just because we're having fun with it doesn't mean—

AP: —we're not serious about it.

An Interview with *Citizen Ruth* Director Alexander Payne

Angie Drobnic / 1997

From *Weekly Alibi*, May 28, 1997. Reprinted by permission of the publisher, Carl Petersen. This article originally appeared in *Weekly Alibi*, Albuquerque's free alternative newspaper: www.alibi.com.

Of all the holy cows in American culture, one of the biggest is undeniably abortion. People ponder it, fight about it and have even killed over it—which makes it the perfect topic for a sly satirist.

Enter Alexander Payne, the director and co-writer of Miramax's new film, *Citizen Ruth*. His film stars Laura Dern as the unforgettable title character Ruth Stoops, a paint huffing homeless dimwit who ends up in jail and pregnant—and not for the first time. By sheer synchronicity, Ruth shares a cell with a passel of pro-life protesters just after a judge offers her a reduced sentence if she "takes care" of her pregnancy. *Weekly Alibi* had a chance to discuss this unique film with Payne.

Angie Drobnic: Do you think the subject of abortion will affect the film commercially? Do you think you'll have a hard time getting it screened in some markets?
Alexander Payne: You know, I have no idea, but I think Miramax is appropriately trying to sell it as a movie, not an abortion movie. It's a movie that has as some of its subject matter, some of its backdrop, the world of abortion protesting. But it's about other things, I hope: homelessness, drug addiction, a woman taking some degree of self-awareness for the first time in her life, and Americana. And then it's funny, and everyone loves a comedy. There's a certain American spirit that says, "Fuck it . . . let's laugh at anything."

AD: Why do you think people want to ask what you personally think about abortion?
AP: I think people want more clues as to how to read the movie. But I think that's inappropriate because people should have their own reaction to the work and not base it on the words of the director. I have faith in viewers, and I think they should come to react to it however they want to, or can't help but to, because of their individual histories. This film is about a lot of things for me. And you know what? I may not even know why I made the movie or what it's about until I'm fifty and look back. And it may constantly change, why I think I made the film at a certain time. It's not a political thing. For me, it's a human and irrational process, the creative process.

AD: One of the film's most interesting scenes was when Harlan (a prochoice Vietnam Vet) is guarding the clinic and telling the pro-lifers when they cross the clinic's property line, "Go back . . . you know the drill."
AP: Well, that comes from real life, in observing pro-life protests against abortion clinics. Everybody gets routine, and it struck me like those Warner Bros. cartoons with the sheep dog and the coyote: You know, "Morning, Ralph," "Morning, Sam." They punch their cards and then go (try to) kill each other all day then come back and say, "See you tomorrow, Ralph," "Okey doke, Sam." And it's just like that. They all know one another's names, and say, "That's so-and-so, she's always here, does she have her baby picture today or her fetus in a jar? No, she left them at home." It's like a constant banter back and forth and a sense of the banal and the routine. I think when you get out in real life, things are much more banal-feeling than what you've seen on TV, and that's kind of what I wanted to get across in the film.

AD: Do you think Americans have a hard time with satire as a genre? The only film I can think to compare *Citizen Ruth* to is *The Player*. It's satire but not terribly broad satire. It's more pointed.
AP: I love that movie. It's fantastic. I think actually that Americans have a long tradition of satire. English letters, all the way back to Jonathan Swift, have a long tradition of satire. But somehow satire has disappeared from films recently, in the last ten or fifteen years. But there's *The Player*, and before that *Network*, before that *The Loved One* or *Dr. Strangelove*. I think this film is both maybe in that tradition, and also I hope it's a brand new movie because I really have a hard time comparing it to any single other movie I've ever seen.

AD: What do you think your next project will be?
AP: I just finished a script, also with Jim Taylor, called *Election* about a high school student council election. It's about all these people and how their lives fall apart, and these affairs between a teacher and student, and between another teacher and a guy's ex-wife. All these pathetic occurrences.

AD: Is it a comedy?
AP: A painful comedy.

Adapting and Directing *Election*: A Talk with Alexander Payne and Jim Taylor

Annie Nocenti / 1999

From *Scenario: The Magazine of Screenwriting Art* 5, no. 2 (1999). Reprinted by permission of the interviewer and editor, Annie Nocenti.

Annie Nocenti: Not many filmmakers are working in satire these days. One reviewer wrote that you two were the best of them.
Alexander Payne: David Denby said we are the "only" true social satirists working in American film today.
Jim Taylor: If we go down in a plane the nation will mourn. We always fly separately. One review said it was the first real political satire since *Shampoo*.
Payne: Manohla Dargis. Not that I read reviews or anything.
Taylor: The reviews have been embarrassingly positive. It's gratifying. And very smart reviews. Margo Jefferson opened her discussion of *Election* in the *New York Times* with the existential notion that "hell is other people."

Nocenti: Now, is there anyone there doing satire that you're influenced by?
Taylor: Harry Shearer.
Payne: Also, when we were growing up there was *That Was the Week That Was*, and *The Smothers Brothers*, and Richard Pryor. And then *National Lampoon Radio Hour*. But does it really influence us?
Taylor: I love *Firesign Theater*. But that's not really satire. Satire is one of those words where you need to pull out the dictionary and look at the definition.

Nocenti: Which brings us to that facetious question you pose in

Election—what is the difference between morals and ethics? I rocketed right back to being in school and not knowing the answer.

Taylor: We don't know the answer, either. People thought we were making a point about morals and ethics, when in fact we were making a point about apples and oranges. We love the pomposity, that a teacher would ask a question when he probably doesn't even really know the answer.

Nocenti: Tom Perrotta's novel is very topical. It opens with the Glen Ridge, New Jersey, rape case. You can decide to take references to current events out of the screenplay?

Taylor: The book was centered around the '92 election, and we wanted to move it away from that. Also, the movie took a long time to make. It's hard to be topical in a movie because so much changes while you're making it.

Payne: We're not interested in topical things. Even Elizabeth Dole, Connie Chung, and Madonna will date the movie one day.

Taylor: That's the advantage of television shows that do satire, or even Harry Shearer who has a weekly radio show. They can jump on things right away and deal with them.

Payne: I've got to say this, though—when we're making these movies, I don't think in terms of satire. We actually didn't think of the world beyond the world of the film. This just seemed like a good story, and a comedy. Early on we had the idea, how much do we want to kind of suggest things in a larger political arena, and how much is this film a microcosm? And we did say, we're not interested in that. We just like the people.

Nocenti: Even though you added scenes and changed a lot from the novel the deadpan comedic spirit of the book is still there. And there are lines in the novel that are almost like a Tex Avery cartoon. "I wanted to slow her down before she flattened the whole school," is one. I wondered if cartoons were an influence, especially scenes like when Tracy does that pogo stick jump.

Payne: I'm a big Tex Avery fan.

Taylor: He references cartoons, even in *Citizen Ruth*. And one thing for sure, whether it's a satire or not, it's a comedy. At some point in comedy you're going to exaggerate the characters. How much you exaggerate, how broad you make it, is open to question, but I guess if we're going broad, like her pogo-ing around.

Payne: Is pogo-ing in the book or did we come up with that?

Nocenti: You came up with that. In the book, it said that she won and that all she had was herself to hug.
Payne: Which we had in the film, too. There was a voiceover, "No one to hug but myself." We had that in the film up until the mix, and then she pogo-ed so well, and the music was so nice, that I thought it would be better without it.
Taylor: Did Reese Witherspoon come up with that pogo-ing?
Payne: [whispers] I showed her how to do it.

Nocenti: She was magnificent. In the book, her character wore a red dress and was supposed to have this incredible body. You made a decision to not make her a sexpot?
Taylor: Yeah, although my only disappointment in the translation from book to screenplay to film is the loss of real sexual tension between her and McAllister. Even though she is flirty with him in the film, in the book it is a powerful driving force that everybody would want to sleep with her, and it got toned down.
Payne: I just thought the teenage sexpot was a bit of a stock character. When McAllister is fantasizing about having sex with Tracy, for me it's more interesting that it's coming exclusively from him. And it's this hate-fuck he has with her. It makes it more about him and how screwed up he is.
Taylor: I guess we didn't want her to be just a femme fatale, or that that's why she was wielding all this power. It was much more about her being a focus-driven individual than that she had this great body. And, in the book, the student body knows she had that affair. We felt they would never elect her as class president if they knew she had an affair with a teacher.
Payne: It's more interesting if she's ostensibly not so sexy but has sex.
Taylor: The great thing about Reese is that she's a really attractive woman, but in portraying the character, she suppressed her sexuality and put that energy into Tracy's political ambitions.
Nocenti: She has the Lolita thing, but grim and business-like.
Payne: Denby called her a combination of Pat and Dick Nixon. If you really want to talk about the sexuality of Tracy, there was a scene where she's lying on the bed and Dave's taking his clothes off and he's got a big white pimple on his back—we shot all that and it's actually really funny and good. We cut it because of length. But I was very conscious that she be presented more like a victim and not really like a full participant. That she's really a sweet girl. And what you see visiting high schools is that

they're just kids. They're not the beautiful vixen sexpots that you see in teen movies. That's completely fake. Sure there are some oversexed kids in high school, prematurely precocious sexual stuff, but they're really kids. Tracy Flick's a kid.

Taylor: The thing about being on the cusp of adulthood is that you might be developing things that make you seem very adult, but you're really this mix of a vulnerable kid who could be taken advantage of, and someone who's learning to assert themselves.

Nocenti: There's a feeling you get from the film and from the novel, too, that no one can see themselves and that it would take a catastrophe to launch an adult out of that blindness.

Payne: That may be what's common in both *Citizen Ruth* and *Election*—somehow we come up with very unaware people, we find very unaware people interesting. Jim McAllister is constantly, unconsciously, totally creating the crisis in his own life, so that he can break out of it. And it's all in denial. "My life is great, I love teaching." And he hates teaching. He hates his life and he hates his wife. He has to break out and do something new. So he just changes his life, but he doesn't grow.

Nocenti: There are wonderful moments when the image and the words are at counterpoint. For instance, when Tracy's voiceover says something about how "Dave really understands me," but the image is often shoving her head down in the car so no one can see her.

Payne: She says, "That's the first time someone ever saw the real me." That's the beauty of voiceover.

Nocenti: Was it a big decision to go with the multiple points of view? *All About Eve* did, but very few films try a multiple narrator.

Taylor: We were lucky that the studio and the executives went for it. That could have been a huge sticking point and a battle.

Payne: But that's such a stupid point of view, that voiceover is bad. I love voiceover in film.

Taylor: Specifically because of the novelistic possibilities, to just get inside heads and hear thoughts.

Payne: Also, you can get more information in, and you can have that wonderful discrepancy and irony between what people say and what they do. I actually think that voiceover is the single greatest contribution of talking cinema, of talking pictures. More so than dialogue even.

Nocenti: You put a parallel construction at the opening—cutting between establishing McAllister and Tracy—and didn't you even give them different soundtrack songs?
Payne: It's done with score, not songs, but each is established musically, yes.
Taylor: But as far as the script goes, yes, that was very conscious. Because we were going to use four different voiceovers, we needed to set up right away the possibility that different characters were going to be able to comment on the action and that Tracy and Jim were the two principal characters. We always knew they were the principal characters, but is it Tracy's movie, is it Jim's movie, is it both their movies?

Nocenti: McAllister ends up being the dominant point of view which I thought was an interesting choice for a so-called teen movie—that the top-line point of view was an adult's.
Taylor: We couldn't really push that, because it was made for MTV Films and they have a mandate to make films for a certain age group, really, so we were encouraged to take it as far as we could in the teen direction.

Nocenti: What do you think of the teen movies that are out there now?
Taylor: Well, we haven't seen most of them.
Payne: *Election* got financed because of the teen craze.

Nocenti: But do you see *Election* as a teen movie?
Payne: Early on, I told them that I wasn't going to make a high school movie, that it was an adult movie set in a high school, and early discussions were like, well, is it going to be more like *Fast Times at Ridgemont High*, or more *Clueless*, or more like *American Graffiti*, or what? And I said the movie it's going to be most like is probably *Citizen Ruth*.

Nocenti: Even though it's a comedy, you paint a very realistic portrait of high school, with the dull hallways and the inane rituals.
Payne: That's just who we are as filmmakers. Whatever we would be exploring, we would do research and try to achieve great verisimilitude. [laughs] I just wanted to use that word.

Nocenti: Alexander, I read somewhere that your junior high school was blown away by a tornado. Was that fuel for the movie?
Payne: [laughs] May 6, 1975. Just the roof was blown off. But that changed my destiny. I ended up going to an all-boys high school.

Nocenti: Tammy is a delightful character. You desired a very eloquent solution to reduce all the business of her going to a party and meeting a girl—you just distilled it to that one beautiful scene of her looking at the Catholic school girls playing soccer.

Payne: There was one other scene that was cut, where she's pretending that she doesn't want to go to that school, while enjoying trying on the Catholic schoolgirl uniform.

Nocenti: The girls try on lingerie in the book. Is that something that just seemed to not work as well in the film as in a book?

Taylor: It's hard to remember. We read the novel three years ago and then tried to put it away. We referenced it but we really tried to reinvent it. It was given to Alexander to read first, you said you took a while to read it because . . .

Payne: Because it was set in a high school.

Taylor: [laughs] As soon as I read it, it was clear to me this was perfect for us.

Nocenti: What's the timing with the Monica Lewinksy scandal? Perrotta wrote the book years before that, and while you were finishing the film, that was unfolding?

Taylor: Yeah, and we didn't ever really think about it much. Setting the ending in Washington, D.C., was not inspired by Monica Lewinsky, it was just a natural thing for the development of the story, that Tracy would do that.

Nocenti: But it ends up having this topicality.

Payne: But ten or twenty years from now, people won't need to know about Monica at all to still get that ending.

Nocenti: You tried to keep the same ending from the book, where she goes to the used car lot and McAllister signs her yearbook?

Payne: We loved that in the book, and we shot it and it's fine. But the book is more ruminative and quiet and allowed that ending more. The movie came out too funny and too fast-paced, too cynical and that ending just felt wrong.

Taylor: Which is ironic because the ending is one of the things I love most about the book and was what convinced me that was worth making as a movie. Because in spite of all this comedy there was this beautiful moment of grace at the end of film.

Payne: Sentimentality can work better either in literature or film if the background is cold and those moments feel earned. Chekhov wrote about that. So I thought it would work in that way, but it didn't.

Nocenti: Also, in the novel, McAllister stays with his wife.
Taylor: We tried to get them back together and it just felt false.

Nocenti: He explodes his life, but ends up in the same place. "What's the difference between morals and ethics?" becomes "what's the difference between sedimentary and igneous rocks?"
Taylor: That's our cruel joke.

Nocenti: And then there's the new Tracy Flick in the audience.
Payne: That's satisfying in a traditional way because endings relate to the beginning. You find the ending at the beginning. But this was one of those rare instances of a studio financing a new ending that's more cynical than the original ending.

Nocenti: So the new ending came about late in the game.
Payne: Yeah, just after we'd cut the film and previewed it, Jim and I were then given an opportunity to come up with a new ending if we wanted to. So Jim and I just holed up in a hotel for a week and thought, if this were an original, what would we have come up with?

Nocenti: Why are endings so hard—is it because life doesn't end?
Payne: Certainly in our case, yes. The only true ending to life is to say "it continues." And even *Citizen Ruth*, while having a seemingly victorious ending, also says, quietly—but she's going to turn that corner and take drugs again. Yet usually you face the odd pressure to give hope at the end.
Taylor: I don't think that's an odd pressure. I think it's just a cultural thing. I had an opportunity to go to China for six months and study the Chinese film industry in 1987. And one of the most striking things about Chinese films is how tragic they are. The story arc was always: things start out bad and then they get worse and worse and worse and worse until they are really terrible, and then the film is over. And everybody gets to cry a lot. So happy endings say something about Americans.

Nocenti: The film *Sullivan's Travels* is about a comedy filmmaker who thinks he should be telling serious stories, and he finds out in the end that making people laugh is best.

Payne: I'm not so sure I like the message of that film. It lets American cinema off the hook in a big way if they take that message too seriously. I don't think that's a very good message.

Nocenti: Tom Perrotta told me that everyone in the novel is "either a victimizer or a destroyer."
Taylor: That sort of polarizes them, though. We think they're all victimizers and destroyers. If we ever thought about them in terms of their parallels in politics, Paul was Ronald Reagan. In a certain way, Reagan's naiveté made him a destroyer—sending all the homeless people out on the street.

Nocenti: And Tammy is any card who could upset an election?
Payne: Tammy is Perot. Well, that's who she is for Tom Perrotta.

Nocenti: You added McAllister being stung by a bee, and it made me think of a "Scarlet A," that he sinned and in the morning it was there on his face.
Payne: Also blindness, ancient ideas of blindness. The bee sting was Jim's idea.
Taylor: I'm really happy about the bee sting because it's an example of something that comes out of a pure instinct that something should happen to him at that point, but what? And then there's a brainstorm, what if he gets stung in the eye by a bee? Just a silly thing. But then it ends up working through the rest of the film as a symbol and as a comic device.
Payne: Do you like the shot in the film that establishes the bees?

Nocenti: I like it very much, because I only realized that you were establishing the bees the second time I saw the movie. Any reason for seeing bees in the foreground of that shot is just subliminal in the first viewing.
Payne: I'm still on the fence about that. One way I can justify it is that it's always springtime in Linda's backyard. The rest of the movie is like winter. But there are flowers, and you hear birds and you see bees, so "birds and bees." So it's reproduction, and his failure to reproduce. Then at the motel, it says "Welcome, Seed Dealers." Just ideas that mock his barrenness, his failure to produce a child. Even the opening sprinkler jet at the beginning of the film.

Nocenti: The lawn sprinkler was a potency symbol?

Payne: In a joking way. All of our symbols are sort of jokes. I like how they function. They don't really add something, but they add something.

Nocenti: When I saw that shot open the film, I knew I was in good hands. The lawn sprinkler is one of those suburban noises, what with the bland rhythm of it.

Payne: I like that that shot has no music on it, that it's bare. That shot was not in the script. The DP thought of that shot.

Taylor: I do have to say, though, that the script suggests it in a certain way. The school is "slumbering." It's a world about to wake up. It's quiet and even though the sprinkler is going, it's at rest.

Nocenti: I loved McAllister's establishing shot. There's the running, but when he goes through all the turns in that fence, it's like a rat maze. It says—in suburbia, this is the conveyor belt that you get on.

Payne: The school is a factory, or a prison.

Taylor: That maze, that's an example of Alexander going on location and seeing something that worked in the spirit of the script.

Payne: Actually, we constructed that, so that it would be a ridiculously rat-like maze. In fact, one of our criteria in picking the school was that it have the beginnings of a good little fence maze, one that we could build onto. You'll never see a fence like that one. And it's a direct overhead shot, as though Jim McAllister is caught like a rat in a maze.

Nocenti: It's a wonderful set-up—you get a sense of a guy who's sort of sloth-like but going through the motions and then into his world comes the gunslinger, Tracy Flick.

Taylor: That's probably the biggest difference between the novel and the film. There's more time to establish things in a novel. We really had to be serious about how, with voiceover and everything, can we quickly set up the world of the film?

Nocenti: You approached these characters as human beings, you weren't thinking of Tracy as a symbol of American politics?

Payne: Never. We're not so interested in that. We like people.

Taylor: In terms of writing, we're not interested in that. We can sit here now and be reflective about the film, but I think it's been a great benefit to us that we really don't have an agenda. In *Citizen Ruth*, we didn't have a political agenda to put forth. And when we did this film, we didn't have a metaphoric agenda.

Payne: If there's a political agenda in both of them, I'd say that it's political in that it's anti-political. I mean, to say we don't have a political agenda in *Citizen Ruth* . . . we don't have one that's defined by those sides [pro-choice, pro-life], but maybe on some level we have one that just opposes politics as defined in those ways.

Nocenti: The idea that a woman's body can become a battleground for political issues is very clear in that movie.
Payne: It's not so much about our communicating political ideas, but maybe asking some political questions. For me, a political question in *Citizen Ruth*, which is, again, not answered, is, what does freedom of choice mean for an animal who really can't choose? That's something I'm really interested in. I think Ruth is a poster child for court-ordered sterilization. Because really, she's an animal that needs to be spayed. So what does that mean, that she's a citizen and has rights? What does it mean that she has the right to choose, and she even has to learn what that means, and never really grasps it? Again, that's just what I enjoy in the film. Jim may not.

Nocenti: What you're saying sounds harsh, but when a woman is pregnant and sniffing glue, I guess you're right to put her in those terms. Getting back to *Election*, you also added McAllister's sweaty race to prepare the hotel room for his tryst. Was that just to heighten his fall?
Taylor [laughs] We just thought it was funny.
Payne: And it gets him washing his butt.
Taylor: That's your addition.
Payne: That's in the script: "carefully washing his undercarriage." But it gets mentioned a lot—on the internet, some people hate that, and other people really love it.

Nocenti: It's very funny.
Taylor: And why is it so funny? Because it's so true. People clean themselves before they think they're going to have sex, but you've never seen it in a movie, and so then just to see the truth is somehow startling.
Payne: That came from my childhood in a way, from a Redd Foxx album. He had a whole routine called "You've Got to Wash Your Ass." Before you go on a date you've got to wash your ass.

Nocenti: I'm curious about the amount of litter and garbage in the film.

It was more in the script than in the film—people picking up garbage and throwing it away—Mr. McAllister specifically.
Taylor: That's another instinctive addition, but it's also about trying to put your problems away.
Payne: I actually disagree that it's more in the script. If you look at the film and look only for garbage, it's obsessive. Any time you see a street exterior, it's garbage day. When Mr. McAllister is listening to the speeches in the gym, way in the background you see a janitor leaning on his broom. At the end, where he gets spat on, he's being pursued by a garbage truck. When Tammy is on her bike, behind her you see garbage. When he wakes up in front of Linda's house, we open the shot on a garbage truck.
Taylor: We just had a garbage truck always on call. [laughs]

Nocenti: I ended up thinking of it in terms of how people want to hide things, flush everything down the toilet.
Taylor: You think you can tidy up everything but the garbage is still around, it's just in a can somewhere, or in the landfill.

Nocenti: The janitor becomes an almost mystical character. There was a line in the novel where Tammy says of the principal, "put a broom in his hand and make him an honest man." And another line that says, "They put janitors there to remind you of what happens if you don't do your schoolwork."
Payne: We actually thought a good alternative title for the film would be *The Custodian*.
Taylor: That was a great one. It sounds like a Harold Pinter title. I'm realizing that that's where the garbage thing came from. Of course, also because he throws away the ballot. But Tracy throws away Dave's picture in the computer, she throws away the posters. People try to make things go away but they come back.
Payne: It's even foreshadowed at the beginning of the movie. Tracy says, "None of this would have happened if Mr. McAllister hadn't meddled the way he did." Just in that moment, he picks a piece of paper off the ground and throws it away. It's a very subtle foreshadowing of how he's going to meddle later in the film.

Nocenti: So the janitor becomes this male, malevolent force of judgment.

Payne: You know who he is? He's the Watcher, the comic book character. He's the Watcher who violates his code a little bit by interfering. The Watcher who only intercedes when Galactus threatens to destroy everything.

Taylor: You know what's the best thing about this interview? It's that you haven't mentioned Ferris Bueller. [laughs] Everyone talks about *Ferris Bueller's Day Off* in connection to this film because Matthew Broderick used to be an iconic high school student, and now here he is as a teacher.

Nocenti: What did you think of *Rushmore*, because there's lot of comparisons to *Rushmore*?

Payne: Why do you think those comparisons exist? I don't think they would exist if the two films didn't come out within eight months of each other.

Nocenti: They're both comedic but serious, and very intelligently written high school movies, but for adults. Was there some confusion around how to market *Election*? To adults, to teens?

Taylor: Mass confusion. But in the end, I think it found its little niche, and it certainly did better than *Citizen Ruth*. In terms of whatever strategy they had for this film, it worked. And I think the posters are evocative, they put some money into it.

Nocenti: I thought the Pepsi/Coke thing was a stroke of genius, the idea that Tracy comparing herself to Coke inspires McAllister to get "Pepsi," or Paul, to run against her. Where did that come from?

Taylor: I'd always heard that said about Coke, that it worked hard to stay number one.

Payne: I thought I came up with that.

Taylor: [laughs] Maybe you did, but at least I was familiar with it when you came up with it. But it's like apples and oranges, these fake decisions you have in your life.

Payne: I think it actually started more organically, when we were writing the scene in the parking lot. When she says "Coca-Cola's number one."

Taylor: Yeah, so we thought, what's the alternative to Coke?

Nocenti: One of the funniest things in the film is that tribal music that comes in when Tracy goes on the warpath.

Payne: It's from a 1966 spaghetti western called *Navajo Joe*. I had heard that many times, and then in the editing room it just came to me to put it in there. We thought it was just going to be temporary, but then when we could find nothing to replace it that worked as well, we got the rights to it.

Nocenti: You also added the power station.
Taylor: My brother used to watch the tollbooths near our house. When he was feeling melancholy, he would just go watch the toll takers taking money. So I was thinking, what would be an interesting thing to do if you're feeling like an alienated kid? Because teen suicide is such a big thing, those thoughts of "I just want to go away and evaporate."
Payne: It's the most poetic part of the film.

Nocenti: She's an alien. Tammy is clearly a displaced being who shouldn't be in that particular family, so it works well.
Taylor: You can say that Paul's the only nice guy in the film, and she's the only really honest person. She seems to really know herself better than anyone else.

Nocenti: She's delusional, though. You added the romantic scenes on the swings, which to me meant that she also can't see herself.
Payne: She's delusional about love, but in a way that we all are.
Taylor: That's the only forgivable delusion in life.

Nocenti: Is the "Jennifer" song an allusion to seventies movies?
Payne: I just thought that when Tammy has flashbacks, it should be like a 1960s student film, 16mm, and by the way, I'll add that that was mostly shot by Jim. The 16mm stuff.

Nocenti: You also used different footage when McAllister goes to New York. There's all that grainy pickup footage.
Payne: That's stock footage. I just like old film stuff. I like rear-screen projection, and it's fun to get the tapes of the plates, from stock houses. They have things which are shot just for rear-screen projection. There are guys who, to make a buck, stick their camera on the back of their car and just drive. They sell it to stock footage houses. And it sits and languishes there for decades, used or unused, and I love watching that stuff.

Nocenti: The Tammy/Lisa relationship is very poignant.

Payne: A lesbian friend of mine said, how did you get it right? It reminded me so much of me when I was that age trying to figure it out.

Nocenti: Lisa had an authentic moment with Tammy, but she ran from it to the big heterosexual, the football guy.

Payne: For me, Lisa's just sort of fucked up, and her sexuality is like Russell Stover candies. My mom always takes a bite of one and puts the rest back. Let me see what this one's like. First Lisa likes a woman, then she likes a man, then she likes a black guy—she's going to try everything.

Nocenti: I wanted to ask you about the process of working together. I read that you have two keyboards linked to one computer. You work on scenes together, talk and type at the same time?

Taylor: Yeah, pretty much. We hardly write anything where we're not in the same room.

Payne: Every once in a while, Jim or I will say, let me just have a half hour. Because every once in a while you have to be in a writer's place, silent, and just write and not have to say it first and explain it or justify it. But 90 percent of the time, it's together.

Nocenti: And the process of getting *Election* financed?

Payne: It was supposedly pre-financed, because we were hired by a studio to adapt it together and for me to direct. But it's funny, we had to go through some of the same hurdles as if we were looking for original financing. Putting the right cast together, and just making it seem even more appealing to the financier, in this case the studio. Even though they already owned it, there were still hurdles to jump through.

Nocenti: And what was the budget on this?

Payne: It started out at about $8 million or $8.5 but ended up at about $9 million. Although, you never really know the budget, because they don't tell you. And then my post-production went a long time and I really don't know how much the additional photography for the new ending cost. On *Citizen Ruth*, I never really knew. Maybe $4.4 to 4.5 million.

Nocenti: Was Reese Witherspoon your first choice?

Payne: After I met her she was. I still met some more actors after I met her, just to have met everyone who was around. But there was really no one else.

Nocenti: And Matthew Broderick?
Payne: He was the first one that the studio and I really agreed on that we should pursue. You know, you have to go through the huge mega-stars first, the studios always force you to. But very soon after that, it was Matthew Broderick.

Nocenti: And your idea for the rest of the cast? Were you looking for a particular kind of face, a Nebraska face?
Payne: Just real people. Just people who were people, and not actors trying to be people. A lot of them came from Omaha.

Nocenti: And what are you guys going to do next?
Taylor: We have to talk about that. Because I've been working on this script for a while, while Alexander was cutting *Election*. I don't like writing alone, but I'm getting more excited about the possibility of making the film. But just the writing process itself, of writing on my own, is very unpleasant and unproductive, and it's just no fun. So we've talked about some other things and in fact we have some deals pending, but we'd like to write on spec.
Payne: That's the only way to do it.
Taylor: This movie definitely put us in a different place, both Alexander as a director and us as a writing team, and even me thinking about doing stuff to direct. So we have to decide what we want to be both individually and together. It's interesting because we really like working together.
Payne: It's one of the most joyous parts of the process.
Taylor: So it's sort of a de facto partnership. It's not like we set out to form a company.
Payne: I have some opportunities, but I'm finding that I'm really only interested in stuff that I or we write. I'm reading scripts that other people write, but I have a hard time falling in love. I think when you're a director and you're reading a script, thinking if you want to make it, you look for certain moments. There are some scenes that are just workaday scenes, but then you get to this moment, and you think, oh, it would be great to do that. I'm lucky to see, in a script that I haven't written, three of those moments, five maybe. The two scripts that we've written, each of them has fifty moments that I couldn't wait to do.

Nocenti: Reading the novel, you saw that there were potential moments?
Payne: Potential, and then we came up with more, which is what we do.

It's really about treating all of it like writing. Which means really looking inside of yourself and pulling it out. I mean, the whole thing comes from the writing. And then directing is another form of writing, and editing is certainly another form of writing. Actually there are very few movies I look at these days and say, wow, I wish I had directed that. I wish I had had that script. Almost none, ever. Except *Unforgiven*. That was a good one.

[Both laugh]

Bringing on the Payne

Jeffrey M. Anderson and Rob Blackwelder / 1999

From *Combustible Celluloid*, April 16, 1999, and *SPLICEDwire*, April 16, 1999. Reprinted by permission of the interviewers.

"So what up? How may I help you today?" gibes thirtyish writer-director Alexander Payne as he straddles into a chair at the glass dining table in his San Francisco hotel room. "Have you seen my film?"

He's asking about *Election*, his deliriously sardonic and underhanded satire of politics and high school culture that follows trepidatious government teacher (Matthew Broderick) through increasingly bizarre attempts to sideline a senior's fanatical student body presidential campaign. The film, which opened locally last Friday, had just played the night before at the San Francisco International Film Festival.

"Oh, yes. I liked it," I reply.

"Really?" asks Payne, eyebrows akimbo. "Wow! Thanks, man. Thank you."

His voice has a practiced tinge of cynicism, but he's completely sincere in his gratitude, even though his film has been enjoying some of the best advance buzz of any movie this year not featuring Jedi knights and droids.

A ruthless, laugh-out-loud roundelay of back-stabbing and vote manipulation, *Election* is a rare breed—an intelligent high school comedy, long on acerbic wit and refreshingly devoid of clichéd, cardboard characters. Driving the story is Reese Witherspoon in an award-worthy performance as star candidate Tracy Flick, an obsessive overachiever and the perfect neurotic zealot.

Payne, whose first writing-directing effort was 1996's abortion debate farce *Citizen Ruth*, pours a can of Coke into a tumbler from the mini-bar and rubs a lime around the lip of the glass with his narrow hands he will soon be using to mold the air in front of him like clay, as if trying to physicalize his thoughts as we talk about his sophomore venture behind the camera and his deep dissatisfaction with the state of American movie-making.

Jeffrey Anderson and Rob Blackwelder: How did you get away with making an intelligent, dark satire for MTV Films?
Alexander Payne: Specifically with respect to MTV Films? Can I tell you? I haven't seen a single other MTV film.

Q: They're mostly bad John Hughes spawn.
Payne: You know what, though? To be fair—not that I really care about being fair to anyone, ever—but to be fair, I'm sure that same ratio of bad films to good probably exists in every studio. Every producing entity these days makes largely bad films and every once in a while a good one. I'm glad you happen to think *Election* was one of those good ones. But it's just that the whole country is making generally lousy films these days and has been for quite a while. That's the big problem that we all have to think about, I mean you guys on the critical side and me in terms of things I want to make. We have to think about it because we have to change it. Movies are too important. We love our cinema too much and we also have this cinema with a world-wide influence.

Q: Do you think there's more crap now than there was fifty years ago?
Payne: It's true they always made lousy pictures, but they used to have a higher number of good ones every year than we have. And I don't know where to point the finger. Movies are too expensive these days, and that sense of film as software to be used for the TV and the airplane and the foreign, [instead of being] thought about as just, what's the story we want to tell and how should it be told. They're now all owned by corporations, and everyone answers to and answers to and answers to. See? Except like Harvey Weinstein, like or dislike, or Bob Shea from New Line. Those guys get personally involved with their products.

Q: Which is another reason for the question. *Election* feels very much like an independent film, not a studio product, yet MTV Films and Paramount produced it. How much autonomy did you have?
Payne: A lot. A lot. But I think it's important to define these days what we mean by independent. Regardless of the source of financing—be it a group of dentists in Akron, Ohio, or a major studio—I think independent should refer to a spirit of filmmaking. [An independent is] a film

that tries to do something different, that feels like it comes from one person, that has some sense of authorial voice and doesn't seem to be pandering exclusively to commercial exigencies at the time. I had a lot of people I had to answer to. I had, at one point, seven producers on the film, and then all the executives at Paramount. And they all say things. So at times I had a lot of hand holding to do. But, god love 'em, in the final analysis they gave me the support and the vote of confidence to do what I wanted to do. Authorial voice. Which means the director has some autonomy.

It's funny. There's a really good book called *Show People* by Kenneth Tynan. Check it out from the library sometime. It may not be worth buying. Actually, it's worth buying to keep as a toilet book. My toilet books are generally there for three and a half to four weeks each, and then I move to another toilet book. Just something you can dip in and out of. It's a good one. And it's Kenneth Tynan's very intelligent profiles of people, done for *New Yorker* magazine. It was during the seventies. And he's profiling Mel Brooks in one of them. And in it, Mel Brooks explains his theory that when you do comedies—I don't know if this is true, but somehow it's been true for me—when you do comedies, they tend to leave you alone a little bit more. Because they somehow perceive it as something a little . . . special. That's hard to tamper with. People somehow think comedy is difficult to do. Like, everyone can sort of come in on a drama, because there's no control people laughing.

Q: Because as long as you're making somebody laugh, they're okay. Whereas with a drama there's all kinds of minefields as far as the studio is concerned—can they pimp it for an Oscar? Will the audience take the actors seriously?

Payne: The pitfall of making a comedy with a studio, it's probably an American cultural thing, but I get tired of being encouraged to always go for laughs. When you're trying to make something complex—even in *Citizen Ruth*, there's a very serious, highly critical subtext going on. At least I hope there is. Like in *Election* when you're dealing with pathetic characters, like some guy who's just making all the wrong and really pathetic choices and being a total loser in his life, or Tammy with her fragile sense of first love and this wonder that she's feeling and that huge disappointment of losing first love. When you're going for poignancy, there can be forces pulling you to go for laughs, and to abort the serious moments. And that's something that I have had to be on guard against. The apotheosis of that of course is Woody Allen, going completely into serious films and that cliché of saying, "We miss your earlier funny ones." I agree with both. Now having made two comedies, I really see the desire for making serious films, not that comedy can't be a serious form.

Q: So it wasn't the satire that drew you to the material?
Payne: I liked it not because I read it and saw a satire, but because I read it and thought, look at these interesting people doing these really pathetic and hilarious things. It was just the human landscape. I mean, I don't really look at the film as being necessarily satirical. That's something other people have called it. I just see it as this human landscape.

Q: Can you talk about the idea of working with "unlikable characters"?
Payne: I would say that they're all likable, because they're real people.

Q: As opposed to machine-made characters?
Payne: I hate those characters. I don't go to see those movies, and when I do . . . like when you can see that the script and the performance and the music and the editing are being manipulated in such a way for you to like that person, I leave the theater. I can't take that.

Q: How did you go about getting Reese Witherspoon for the role of Tracy Flick?
Payne: I didn't have anyone in mind. It was really meeting her that sold me. I didn't have her audition. I just met her and I just knew she could do it. I could believe her as being seventeen, but as an actress she's a young woman, not a girl. She's just really cute and really funny. She's much more seductive with her humor and her niceness than she is with her babeliciousness. She's just a delight.

Q: Her physical manifestation of the character is just remarkable. How much did you two talk about the character? How much of it was her creation and how much of it was what you wrote?
Payne: Well, I like physical humor in films. They're really different films and really different performances, but in *Citizen Ruth*, Laura Dern's performance relies a lot on physicality—the walk and everything. Similarly, Reese with Tracy Flick, there's a certain similarity between those two characters.

Q: I see that. But it's almost a 180 degree difference in their physical behavior.

Payne: Correct. But both have unique, kind of comic walks, ways they hold themselves, how they fight, how they screw up their faces. And the nostril-y-ness of her performance. If you ever see the film again, watch her nostrils....

Q: Oh, I noticed that. I made note of that!
Payne: It's like they're independently wired with a remote control!

Q: It was amazing to me. There were times they were so flared it looked like she'd just pulled a couple marbles out of her nose.
Payne: You know when I think she's really good in the movie is when she's making those campaign buttons. She's very Richard Nixon–like to me, kind of begrudgingly wanting this impersonal love of the masses and having no concept of the individual relationship. And how she puts all the long hours in on the yearbook "just to give them their stinking memories!" It really comes through in her performance. How she was making those buttons—that's something that she brought to it. She'd just learned that morning. The prop master told her how the button machine works. [I told her] You have to sit here and make buttons so that it looks like you've been doing it for a long time, so that you're really fast with it. She didn't really understand the machine so she kind of overdid the stamping. In fact you can do it [really lightly]. But somehow she started to do it and it comes off like she's all fucking pissed off.

Q: How much conversation did you and she have about the physical traits of the character?
Payne: Um . . . I don't remember. . . . Oh, a lot! It all comes from me! [laughs] I think a lot of it comes from her, but I think I encouraged her and urged her to go further with it and I would be there to tell her when it's too much. That's how I like to do it with actors, have them really go for it and I'll tell them when it's too much. It's always easier reeling it back than to push it further. A lot of actors are timid. Go! Try it! Do it!

Q: What advice would you give up-and-coming filmmakers?
Payne: To writers, don't read screenwriting books, and if you do, don't take them too seriously. Don't take screenwriting classes, and if you do, don't take them seriously. There's a strong tendency right now toward formula. Like this is how a screenplay is written: By page thirty this has to happen, the inciting incident, and your Act Two goes to page ninety.

That's just horse shit. I think a badly crafted, great idea for a new film with a ton of spelling mistakes is just a hundred times better than a well-crafted stale script. I mean if you can do both, like have this well-crafted thing and it's fresh and original, then you'll become a millionaire screenwriter.

For example, Scorsese talks not about three acts in a script, but rather five sequences. Or you watch Fellini films—you watch *Nights of Cabiria* or *La Dolce Vita* or *8 ½*—and you get a sense not of a three act structure, but of episodes with one character going through all these episodes. Then you get to the end of the film and there's a sudden realization or a moment that pulls a loose string suddenly taut through the whole movie you've been watching up until that point.

We need different mental models of what a film can be, and if you pay too much attention to these books, by Sid Field and Robert McKee and I don't know who else, they're only presenting one cultural paradigm, and that's really, really dangerous to the act of creation and to our cinema, which needs new ideas and new blood now more than ever. Hollywood films have become a cesspool of formula and it's up to us to try to change it.

[Suddenly laughs out loud.] I feel like a preacher!

Q: The Reverend Payne!
Payne: But it's really true. I feel personally responsible for the future of American cinema. Me personally. But so should you. Because of what we do and our generation of young guys on the creative and critical front. So anyway. There you have it.

Fresh Air Interview with Alexander Payne

Terry Gross / 2003

Transcript of *Fresh Air* radio show, February 20, 2003. Published by permission of WHYY, Inc. *Fresh Air* is produced by WHYY, Inc. and distributed by NPR.

Terry Gross: This is *Fresh Air*. I'm Terry Gross. Jack Nicholson and Kathy Bates are nominated for Academy Awards for their performances in *About Schmidt*. My guest is the director of the film, Alexander Payne. He also directed *Election* and *Citizen Ruth*. *About Schmidt* is set in Omaha, where Payne grew up. Nicholson plays an insurance actuary who is forced out of the life he knows when he retires and his wife dies suddenly. The movie is loosely based on the novel of the same name by Louis Begley. The movie also draws on the screenplay that Payne and his writing partner started about ten years earlier called *The Coward* about a retiree in crisis. *The Coward* had narrative problems Payne couldn't fix. After he was sent a copy of *About Schmidt*, he found similarities between it and *The Coward*. His movie drew from both with a generous amount of rewriting.

Alexander Payne, welcome to *Fresh Air*. In *About Schmidt*, Schmidt faces two turning points right at the start of the film, his retirement and the death of his wife. And there is this—like his life has become this big empty hole. There's no work. There's no marriage. And there's very little meaning that he can find. But he's the kind of person who doesn't have the introspective tools or the language to either express or comprehend what he's feeling. What kind of challenges does that give to you, as the screenwriter, to write about a character who's facing this kind of crisis of meaning but has no kind of tools to comprehend or speak it?
Alexander Payne: Yeah, but the point of the film is the guy who's

suddenly aware, waking up to what's missing in his life, but he lacks the tools to correct his life. And some people have said, "Oh, you know, the character doesn't change. He doesn't grow. He is just miserable through the whole film." And I say, "Well, yeah, you know, he's made his bed and he has to lie in it." But that's precisely why we used the device of his letters to the little boy in Africa to get some access to his interior life.

Gross: Yeah, this is a boy in Africa he adopts through like a TV commercial and he confides all of his thoughts in the letters to this boy and, of course, the boy is too young and too culturally distant to comprehend any of it. So had you been watching one of these commercials when you came up with the idea?

Payne: Yeah, and I think I came up with the idea a long time ago, and just because I was watching one of those ads and "Oh, soon you'll be corresponding with your foster son or daughter," and I thought "Well, I don't know. What would I say?" And you just take that thought into its most absurd extension and you just pour out your whole life and the specifics of your life, and then later thought when I was initially alone writing *The Coward* about this old guy in Omaha, older fellow in Omaha, who retires, I thought, "Well, what if he sponsors a boy in Africa, and uses him as his unseen, distant, and absurd confessor?"

Gross: Well, Jack Nicholson is nominated for an Oscar for his performance in *About Schmidt*. What do you have to do to get Nicholson to be in your movie?

Payne: Well, in this case, it was in a way alarmingly easy because *About Schmidt*—the book—had been submitted to me by two producers, one of whom is a guy named Harry Gittes, like Gittes of *Chinatown*, who is Jack Nicholson's very good old friend. And so seeking to create a film for his friend, Mr. Nicholson, Harry Gittes had found the book *About Schmidt* and had shown it to Jack Nicholson and Jack Nicholson had read it and said, "Yeah, potentially this is interesting, and if you get a decent script conjured up, show it to me, and I'll consider it."

So that's when Gittes and Michael Besman found me and then I expressed interest and then lured Jim Taylor into working with me on it. And so we knew while writing this script that Jack Nicholson would be the first actor to read it when we finished with no assurances whether he would take it or not, of course. So we finished the second draft and Nicholson read it the next week and then I met him and he said he wanted to do it. So it was fairly easy. I mean, working on the screenplay was very hard, of course, as it always is, but it just worked out very nicely that way.

Gross: Well, after Nicholson accepted the part. . . .
Payne: Yeah.

Gross: Were there questions he asked you about the character Schmidt, you know, things he wanted you to explain to him or interpretations of the character he asked about?
Payne: No, he didn't really—we spent many hours—our rehearsal process, if you can call it that, was simply my going to his house and spending many hours in conversation with him, mostly not about the work we were about to do, but about other things, so that we—you know, he's a completely enjoyable guy, and then also we were both interested in getting to know each other before beginning the film. And I had basically just two directions to give him, one of which was that I needed him to be a small man, a very mediocre unself-aware fellow, and that also he act as someone who was older than he is—older than he, Nicholson, is, because even though he's more or less the same age as Warren Schmidt, he in real life is much more youthful and vital than Warren Schmidt is. So I needed him really to be—because the older Warren Schmidt is in the movie then the more the movie's about what it's about, in terms of aging and death.

Gross: Anything you found particularly interesting about Nicholson's approach to getting into the role, and preparing for the role?
Payne: Yeah. How profoundly—I don't know if you want to call it method or what, but just how profoundly he was living the part of Warren Schmidt. In the months preceding shooting, he would tell me he would just pad around his house and become and be thinking about Warren Schmidt and even while shooting remaining in character, I mean, keeping that alive, keeping Warren Schmidt alive inside of himself all the time. And he confessed to being very depressed because he was getting into Warren Schmidt through Schmidt's depression. And he was very happy when shooting ended because he could kind of throw off that onus of a depressive man.

Gross: Yeah, and the interesting thing about Schmidt's depression is that he doesn't even know he's depressed. It's the kind of depression in someone who doesn't understand depression, isn't aware of depression.

Payne: Wouldn't admit to it, would never—very midwestern—would never consider going to a psychiatrist or a therapist. And even in his letters to Ndugu, when he's confessing how he really feels, he often just as much lies to Ndugu as well, and puts a happy face on what he's doing.

Gross: Is that an approach to living in the world, to seeing the world that you understand because you've seen that?

Payne: Yeah, I've seen—you see it a lot. You hear it a lot among Americans. I mean, it's hard for me to generalize, but I certainly have experienced that a lot. "No, no, no, I'm fine. You know, I'm a little down these days, but I'm getting by." And that's pretty much a survival mechanism.

Gross: Kathy Bates is nominated for an Oscar for best supporting actress. Can you describe her character in *About Schmidt*?

Payne: A very overbearing, garrulous, sometimes awful woman who would basically tell her life story to people at the bus stop.

Gross: Right.

Payne: That's what I would say. What would you say?

Gross: I'd also say—and we'll get to this in a moment—that she's incredibly inappropriate with her behavior . . .

Payne: Yeah, yeah.

Gross: . . . and her sexuality.

Payne: Yeah. Everything that Schmidt is not.

Gross: Now the scene that's most talked about that Kathy Bates is in is the scene in which, a little later in the movie, she has invited Schmidt to take a dip in her hot tub. And then much to his shock and dismay, she strips and climbs in with him. I've heard a lot of people talking about that scene. And I know a lot of people have interpreted it as "Isn't it wonderful to see a mature woman who has a full body being so comfortable with her sexuality?" And my take on the scene is "God, she's behaving so inappropriately." And that scene is not about . . .

Payne: Yeah.

Gross: . . . being comfortable with her sexuality.

Payne: For me, it's just what that woman would do. I mean, she has the hot tub in her own back yard. And why would she wear anything when she goes into it if she doesn't think anything of it?

Gross: Right. Right. Right. When did you break the news to Kathy Bates that she'd be naked in a scene?
Payne: Well, it's in the screenplay so she read the script even before I ever met her, so she knew it was there. And she wanted to play the part. She had some concerns about that scene so it wouldn't be exploitative in any way, so, you know, she wanted to be comfortable in the moment of doing it and then comfortable also sitting in the cinema with other people watching that scene. So we talked about exactly what would be shown and how we would shoot it and then we did it.

Gross: I guess if I were her I would want to make sure that if people laughed, they were laughing at the moment, and at the conflict of the two personalities, as opposed to laughing because she's not skinny like everybody else who we see nude in the movies.
Payne: Yeah, but I don't think about how we see everybody else in the movies. It's such a weird thing that "Oh, we're so not used to. . . ." I mean, I get so many questions about this film that are more about the context in which this film—about other films, but "Oh, how did you get Nicholson to do this?" And, "Oh, you've got a slightly older woman getting naked here and she's not thin as a rail," and I don't know. I never really know how to answer those questions. And if I'm lured into a political discussion somehow about, you know, image of woman, I really don't know what to say. All I know is it's appropriate for that character and it's funny.

Gross: Right. Right.
Payne: And it's funny. And maybe it's a problem not with my film but with other films that something like this would just cause such a—not a major fuss but I certainly get a lot of questions about it.

Gross: How did you fall in love with movies?
Payne: Oh, I fell in love with movies very early in my life. My parents, my mother, in particular, were big moviegoers and they would take me, and also I became very interested very early on in life in old movies. I liked silent comedy very much, and then movies from the thirties, particularly Warner Bros. gangster pictures and Universal horror films. And I just became kind of obsessed with older movies, particularly older

comedies. And my father had a restaurant. He was partners with his father, my grandfather, in a restaurant in downtown Omaha, and we had a—not even a Super 8, but a regular 8 projector at home, which had been a bonus from Kraft Cheese. And in those days you'd get three- or twelve-minute shortened versions of films at the camera store. So my brothers had bought some of those. And I liked . . .

Gross: Wait a minute, you had three-minute versions of films?
Payne: Yeah. Yeah.

Gross: Like what films did you see the three-minute version of?
Payne: Oh, *Frankenstein Meets the Wolf Man* and Abbott and Costello movies and mummy movies and there used to be a company called Castle Films and then later there was Blackhawk Films in Davenport, Iowa. That was much more serious because you could buy whole silent features from them as well as two-reel shorts in regular 8 and Super 8 formats as well as 16. But I was a kid. I started buying these films early on and into my teens and sending away for—because, you know, this was before video. This is in the sixties and seventies, and so there was no video, obviously, and to see old movies you had to scour the TV Guide every week, or if you were lucky enough to have any kind of revival house in town, or you had to send away for them and actually get prints. And the cheapest way to do it was regular 8.

Gross: Do you think watching so many silent films and early comedies affected your sense of what you want from a movie as a director, or what kind of performance you want from actors, what kind of look you want?
Payne: Well, I think so because even though my films are very written and the verbal aspect is very marked, I think, really what I'm more interested in is characters and space, and finding dialogue-less solutions to getting across—exposition—you know, in searching for cinema, somehow, and I'm a big sucker for gags. At the Golden Globes a couple weeks ago, people were calling *About Schmidt* a drama, which is fine. That's how the Hollywood Foreign Press and New Line decided to submit it, but I always start out making comedies. But comedy's rooted in maybe serious subjects.

Gross: Didn't Nicholson actually almost correct them when he accepted the award? He said, "Did anyone notice this is a comedy?"
Payne: Yeah, well, I don't remember exactly what he said, but he was

befuddled and a little bit ashamed because he said, "I thought we were making a comedy."

Gross: Yeah, that's right. I guess you thought so, too, right?
Payne: Yeah, well, I mean, I'm surrounded by very funny collaborators, because I work with the same team over and over again, my co-writer and composer and cinematographer and production designer and editor and casting people, and we're always looking for what's funny. I mean, hopefully—and sometimes we turn away from what's funny and let something serious be serious. You have to have that. But I kind of lament that comedies are underappreciated these days in terms of being able to treat serious subjects.

Gross: When you fell in love with movies, how did you know that what you wanted to do was direct?
Payne: Well, I didn't know. I didn't know for the longest time. As a kid I wanted to be a projectionist at first, and then—you know, as a little kid, and then, well, in college, the idea of going to film school was such a distant and far-off and seemingly unrealistic dream, but when I was a senior in college and thinking about what professional school I would attend, really all I could think of was journalism and film, and so I applied to Columbia Graduate School of Journalism and five film schools. And then I said, "Well, let me see what I get into and then I'll decide." Because I had done no film work in college at all. And then when I got my acceptance letters to film schools I thought, "Oh, I have to go. I have to try this."

Gross: Did you ever get to sit in the projectionist booth with a professional?
Payne: Yeah. Oh, yeah, I've done that a lot. It's fun.

Gross: I mean, when you were young, did you do that?
Payne: No, I didn't. I never did. I have since then, but I didn't as a kid.

Gross: What's fun about it once you're a filmmaker and an adult?
Payne: I don't know. It's just—I like the chatter of the projector. I mean, it's corny stuff. You're asking me to say corny things, but I like the smell of film and the chatter of the projector, and I don't know; just all that corny stuff.

Gross: So what is your next project? Can you talk about it at all?

Payne: Yeah, sure. It's the adaptation of a so-far unpublished novel called *Sideways*. And it's about two fairly loser guys from San Diego who go wine-tasting for a week, the week before one of them is to be married, and it's about their rather pathetic misadventures in that week.

Gross: Well, congratulations on the success of *About Schmidt*. And I want to thank you so much for talking with us.
Payne: Oh, it's been such a pleasure. Thank you.

About Schmidt Director Alexander Payne Does Have Something Interesting to Say

Walter Chaw / 2003

From *Film Freak Central*, June 8, 2003. Reprinted by permission of Bill Chambers, editor, FilmFreakCentral.net.

Eyes glowering under a shock of black hair, Alexander Payne, tall and angular, strikes a sort of middle-American Neil Gaiman figure, cutting through the crowds gathered for the twelfth Aspen Shortsfest with authority and something like diffidence. Meeting in the lobby of the Wheeler Opera House, we go off in search of a shot of espresso; along the way, he corrects that he didn't study Spanish philosophy in college, but Spanish philology; makes it a point to punctuate some statements with a companionable squeeze of my arm; and then says something sort of curious: "I don't know why you'd want to talk to me, Walter, I don't have anything interesting to say." I chuckled, of course, but he was deadly serious and would repeat the statement a couple of times. Judging it to be neither a strategy to avoid interviews nor a way to disarm a would-be interrogator, I took it as weariness with the entire junket/publicist/interview process.

The ironic thing is that Payne's films . . . there really isn't much to say about them that isn't already said by the film. One can comment on Reese Witherspoon's performance in *Election* or Laura Dern's in *Citizen Ruth* or Jack Nicholson's in *About Schmidt*, one can go through the motions of eliciting the same sound bites about "being an actor's director" or "how did you meet your writing partner" or "what made you interested in the film," yet press clips seem to do precious little in unfolding what it is about Payne's work that makes it so painful and incisive. The chief criticism of *About Schmidt*, in fact, is that it's depressing when, ultimately, the message of the film seems to me to be infinite hope for the ability of a man to find purpose at any point in his life—no matter how empty that purpose may appear to his "peers." Payne is smart enough to engage in a different kind of conversation. I took his "I don't have anything interesting to say" as a challenge.

Film Freak Central: How has Spanish literature influenced the feeling and direction of your films?
Alexander Payne: [laughs] Wow, I should have studied up for this, this is great. Well, my thesis film at UCLA was sort of a loose adaptation of an Argentine novel by Ernesto Sabato called *El Tunel*—he was to Argentine letters what Camus' *The Stranger* was to French existentialism. Kind of this terse, kind of hilarious, stark, postwar, slim novel. Beyond that it would be kind of hard for me to pinpoint influence.

FFC: And yet there seem to be many connections to French existentialism: your protagonists strive for meaning in the middle of meaningless actions and meaningless societies.
AP: I would say this, that as good an observation as that is, it's only in retrospect that I'm able to mark those things in my work. There was a discussion, it's funny, at the Museum of Modern Art a couple of weeks ago, and I told the moderators that looking at my films I find this certain unease my characters have with the world—they find themselves uncomfortable with the world into which they're born.

FFC: It's that element of the archetypical existential search of your work that is attractive, I think, whether people know it or not.
AP: Whether *I* know it or not, really, it's not something I strive for. Separating myself from my work I can see themes and elements emerging, but the act of creation is different and separate from the act of criticism and as I'm working, none of that enters into it and I think that's important. I think a lot of times that the work suffers for too much self-consciousness—that you can trace these things in my films really speaks to something like success for me in letting myself seep into my work. That's gratifying.

FFC: Tell me about your script for *Jurassic Park III*.
AP: It was a job. It was four weeks, a nice paycheck, seemed like a good challenge. [Jim Taylor and I] thought we could help them out but they

didn't end up using much of our stuff anyway. But we did enough structural changes that we got credit on it, which is good because you get residuals.

FFC: The film felt like a satire of that genre—enough so that it felt almost like a criticism of the audience.
AP: I would say that what survives of our draft—I mean, look, I love movies, not just the ones I make.... In fact, I don't like the movies I make very much. So when I was looking at the first two *Jurassic Park*s—the second one is an abortion, it has wonderful moments but you can't help but see missed opportunities, so when we were talking to [*Jurassic Park III* director Joe] Johnston, we were saying, "Give us an opportunity within this to make it different." We were hired for the character and humor, you know, because the problem with the movies isn't the dinosaurs, it's with the characters and the dialogue, the human beings. We were hired for the human beings. So I said that it should have more the feeling of *The Wages of Fear*, you know, the feeling of *King Kong* mixed with *The Wages of Fear*. The eggs are sort of like nitro-glycerine—a look at what humans should and might do. A sort of grounding in reality of what might go on if you were on an island full of dinosaurs. We had a whole thing with the problem with mosquitoes, and how they would try to salvage parts of the ship to help their survival—but they didn't want any of that, they got rid of all of that, they didn't want anything that made sense. That director, Johnston, and the studio—they're not interested in movies, they're interested in theme park rides. I know that our script—and this sounds like sour grapes and it's not—is much more interesting. All they wanted was action.

FFC: *The Wages of Fear* works not for the action scenes, but for our investment in the characters involved in the action.
AP: Exactly right. We were looking for something like that in our script and all they kept were a couple of lines. You know, recently, I caught up with *Sorcerer* for the first time.

FFC: William Friedkin's really underestimated remake of *The Wages of Fear*.
AP: Absolutely. I think [Friedkin's] *To Live and Die in L.A.* is one of the only worthwhile films of the 1980s, as well. It's hard to say that there are any great American films in the eighties, but I'd also toss something like *Amadeus* into the mix. Was *Groundhog Day* in the eighties or nineties?

FFC: Early nineties.
AP: There you have it. You know, in the eighties I was at UCLA so I was able to watch older films on nitrate prints that the film and television archive had. Even now, four out of five films I see are old films—why see new films, new American films, you know. I always keep up with Iranian films and anything that Zhang Yimou does.

FFC: What's broken in American cinema?
AP: Basically, if I can sum it up in any way, although I have a lot to say about it, those eight multi-national corporations need film consumed as reliably as McDonald's needs bad hamburgers consumed reliably. So there's no impetus at all for film to be *film*, just film to be product. Let me quote Coppola: he believes that when you're given a problem, you're given a key to the solution of that problem. He feels by extension that it's no coincidence in the same horrible century that we're given world war, the Holocaust, the Information Age—all of which pose huge problems for mankind to figure out "who are we?"—is the same century that we're given the cinema. That within this extraordinarily powerful art form lies the key to the solution to our problem. But he said that in terms of American cinema, Sir Galahad is in chains. And who has him in chains? You can point to them: Rupert Murdoch, and Sumner Redstone, and Barry Diller—these robber barons, essentially, who buy and sell our culture like it's pig's feet. Not just the cinema but news media—this ultra-conservative, super-right wing. I haven't read this book, *What Liberal Media?* but if we thought the Reagan media was on bended knee....

FFC: Dan Rather referred to the beginning of "shock and awe" as "rocket's red glare, bombs bursting in air."
AP: He said that? I think that Peter Jennings is the only decent one of the big three.

FFC: He's Canadian.
AP: [laughs] You know, you can't just blame the government, you have to blame the media. The fact that there's been no opposition, you'd think that the media would roll in and fill that vacuum, but they haven't done so.

FFC: What's next for you?
AP: We start shooting in September, a comedy, set in the world of wine tasting. Two guys go wine tasting for a week before one of them gets

married. Nothing too serious. But our cinema has to get more serious—more political again and maybe in a direct, didactic way, but certainly in a metaphorical way. Maybe the economy going to hell will help our cinema. Prices start going down, we won't spend as much which means that we might have to become more human again at the movies and I think we're seeing signs of that in the last couple of years—going back to 1999, maybe.

Interview: Alexander Payne

Jeff Otto / 2004

From IGN.com, October 19, 2004. Reprinted by permission of Peer Schneider, publisher, IGN Entertainment, Inc.

With his first three films, *Citizen Ruth*, *Election*, and *About Schmidt*, Alexander Payne has achieved the rare feat of not only avoiding the sophomore slump, but also of avoiding the trappings of success in Hollywood. Even with his largest-scale film to date, *About Schmidt*, Payne kept his very original voice and unique perspective. Payne's latest film is entitled *Sideways*, adapted from the 1999 novel by Rex Pickett. For the first time, Payne has decided to venture out of his home state of Nebraska and move to the beautiful vineyard territory of Santa Barbara County. Paul Giamatti and Thomas Haden Church star as Miles and Jack, respectively. Jack is about to get married and these two longtime friends have scheduled this final getaway together before the ceremony to have a little fun. The problem is, Miles and Jack have different visions of what the weekend will be. Miles, a wine enthusiast, is looking forward to drinking some fine wine, eating some good food, and playing golf. Jack, much to the contrary, is in pursuit of one final sex fling before tying the knot. The challenge of going four for four is now upon Payne and it seems as if he's up for the task.

In a time of remakes and movies based on TV shows, Payne is one of those select few filmmakers that is still making films with an original vision, perhaps one of the saviors of originality in Hollywood. At a press day at the gorgeous Bacara Resort in Santa Barbara, California, Alexander Payne joined the press to talk about the new film. The locale was just a few miles from where *Sideways* was shot. Miles is a character who is a wine connoisseur. Things aren't going all that great in his life, but wine is a hobby that takes him away from real life, at least briefly. As we follow Miles and Jack's adventure through Santa Barbara, Miles attempts to teach his uncultured friend Jack the proper tenets of wine tasting, giving audiences an interesting lesson along the way.

"It's not all about wine," says Payne. "It's a story of people. There's a romance, there's a buddy thing, it's a road trip, and what's wrong with learning a little something about wine?" Following *About Schmidt*, this is the second road movie Payne has directed in a row. "Yeah, I know, and I was going to be doing a third one, this thing called *Nebraska*, but I'm not gonna do that next, and I don't even like road movies all that much necessarily. It's really just, [with] *Election*, I wasn't interested in making a high school movie, I couldn't have been less interested, but it just, the characters, the situations, somehow it just happens. And I can't stand shooting in cars." Shooting on location was an added bonus for the cast and crew. "We had a really rich time making the film, and a lot of it was because of the locale. Just in the sunshine, it was harvest time, you're out in the fields and it was just so beautiful. It's so nice to be outside. I love shooting outside. I'm not so crazy about shooting inside and I hate shooting in sound stages. We had a real creative community spirit of making this film, where everyone was included, was made to feel included, contributing creative ideas. . . .

"I would want the film, by extension, also to be inclusive with the audience, inclusive with the emotions. . . . I don't like to manipulate the audience any more than you have to. . . . If they find something moving, then great. . . . Let the audience contribute to, not the construction of the narrative, [but] I don't like just clobbering the audience with things. I want to bring the audience in, and I think wine itself is an inclusive-making element."

Payne doesn't think that the wine talk will alienate those who aren't as knowledgeable, and he hopes the film can educate those who might be interested in learning more about wine. "Well, I like specificity. If elements are going to be in a film of mine, I like them to be true and specific, so both about Santa Barbara County, where we were shooting, and that it feel accurate in that way, and also about the whole wine [stuff], because I think all the wine people are going to see the movie and judge me. Did he get it right, did he not get it right? The audience is not general, I never think of it as general audience. The audience is made up of individuals who know a lot. Everyone has his or her own niche.

"I've done a few interviews with wine press and they're talking about, 'Well, how do we overcome this snobbery that's associated with wine?' I'm like, 'I know, it's so weird. Why is wine considered an exclusive or snobby undertaking? Is it because of the high prices they charge in restaurants, the high markup?' That's a problem with restaurants because, you go to other countries, Canada for example, and they don't, there's not that hideous, stupid markup. Many restaurants in New York have begun to learn that. But I want inclusiveness." Payne says that he has explored the wine world in the past, although he had not really been a part of that world in a few years before going into production on *Sideways*. "Yes, but my wine knowledge had kind of plateaued out. I had read a lot about it in the early nineties, because I was cooking a lot and was learning more about wine and bought a bunch of wine. . . ."

Coming off his highly acclaimed performance in *American Splendor*, Paul Giamatti has quickly gone from character actor to a hot commodity. The character of Miles in *Sideways* is a pretty different character, although some may draw the connection of Giamatti as a generally unhappy character in both films. "He never brought it up. I just saw Miles Raymond as so different from Harvey Pekar. The physicality, okay maybe Paul Giamatti himself has a certain connection to the tragic side of life that comes through in some of his performance, but who is funnier? I just love that guy. I just think he's such a great actor. And also, I hadn't seen a bunch of his movies; I really hadn't seen any of his movies before I cast him. I saw *American Splendor* when I had met him but not yet announced my selections or called him up to say, 'Would you please be in [my movie]?' I liked it and I liked him in it, but all I could think of is how different I thought Miles was, but I thought he'd be a good enough actor."

The on-set atmosphere was said to be a pretty relaxed one, and Payne says that the off-camera antics between Giamatti and Church were often a sight to behold. Still, Payne says that they mostly stuck to the script: "It was all pretty much the screenplay. From time to time, Tom would say something during rehearsal or practicing a scene, he just ejaculates these things constantly that incorporate into the script. But pretty much, what you see in the script is as written."

While the character of Jack is the fun-loving good buddy to Miles on the surface, beneath he is actually a pretty dark and even downright unlikable character. "To me, the most violent scene in the movie is where he calls his fiancé and says, 'We're just going out for the night. We'll probably get home late, I just thought I'd check in now, say good night. I love you.' And he's going off to f**k."

Jack is about to get married, although his exploits on the trip soon beg the question of why? "Well, it's hinted that he needs the dough. His career is floundering and he's about to marry into some money. That's part of it. Obviously, from experience, we see that many people get married for less than self-aware reasons."

One of Payne's signatures has always been his multi-faceted and colorful female characters. "I don't distinguish between the genders. I hope they're all real people, male or female. . . . We don't really think about that too much, we just hope they're all real, outrageous in some way. But there aren't enough good parts for women these days. That's true. You see old Warner Bros. pictures and movies in the forties. . . . Where's my Bette Davis, where's my Joan Crawford?"

Payne sees co-star Virginia Madsen as having the look of those stars of the past. "She's a forties Warner Bros. actress. She's a little Barbara Stanwyck-y. She's very 1940s and I love that about her. She's just really one of those gals, she's just out of time. She's one of them."

So far, Payne's three films have all been adapted from other material. We asked Payne about this and why he is more attached to novels for his source material than screenplays. "I have never read a script I've wanted to make. There's been one. At least a novel, there's often more going on in a novel than in a screenplay; it's just a richer form. And then Jim and I can find our own voice through our dialectic with the novel. . . . It's getting rid of stuff and asking questions of the novel and finding threads which were maybe presented but not elaborated on in a way that would have pleased us more. That's how we're able to work and find our own voice within an adaptation. And an example for me is, a great example is, Kubrick, and he's like Mr. Fantastic, innovative director who 95 percent of the time did adaptations."

When all is said and done, Payne says that he's really just grateful to be doing what he's doing. "I have more fun than I've ever had in the rest of my life making movies. The biggest problem, or the studio's gonna yell at me or if a set falls over, I don't care, because it's all within the context of making a movie, and I feel so lucky, then what else is there?"

Interview: Alexander Payne

Scott Tobias / 2004

From the *A.V. Club*, November 10, 2004. Reprinted with permission of THE AV CLUB. Copyright © 2004, by ONION, INC. www.avclub.com.

With only four features to his credit, writer-director Alexander Payne has established himself as one of the most reliable auteurs in American comedy, drawing comparisons to Preston Sturges and Billy Wilder for his crackling dialogue and acerbic social commentary. Originally from Nebraska, Payne returned to his hometown of Omaha for his first three comedies, which depict the Midwest without the golden gloss that plagues Hollywood films about life between the coasts. In different ways, 1996's *Citizen Ruth* and 1999's *Election* satirized the political process—the former in the tug-of-war that pro-life and pro-choice activists wage over a pregnant junkie (Laura Dern), and the latter in a story about a ruthlessly ambitious teenager (Reese Witherspoon) who runs for student-council president.

Payne's ambivalence over midwestern life got its fullest treatment in 2002's *About Schmidt*, a painfully funny portrait of a retired middle manager (Jack Nicholson) who comes to terms with his wife's death and his daughter's marriage. Payne's latest comedy, *Sideways*, switches the milieu to California wine country, where middle-aged divorcé Paul Giamatti takes a weeklong excursion with soon-to-be-married college buddy Thomas Haden Church. Their adventures lead to romantic entanglements with a couple of attractive locals, played by Virginia Madsen and Sandra Oh. Payne recently spoke to *The Onion A.V. Club* about Jim Taylor (who co-wrote all of Payne's films), modern comedies, the Midwest, unfaithful adaptations, independent cinema, and signs of a return to the director-driven films of the seventies.

Onion: In an interview, *Sideways* author Rex Pickett said that novelists should never adapt their own books, because they're too close to the material. Do you think adaptations need to be processed through a sensibility other than the writer's?
Alexander Payne: Well, I can't make a categorical statement like that.

Onion: Well, what about your sensibility when you adapt a book?
AP: I know that Jim Taylor and I have to write it, because I find it really hard to get connected to a piece of material unless I'm involved in the writing. To us, it's not about the broad strokes of the story. It's really about the little details that Jim and I put in, and that's what I've been able to connect to. We always include something that we find delightful—though we don't know if anyone else will—on every page. It really has to come from us, from the writing. So, yeah, on one hand, I feel that I have to be involved in the writing. I'm connected to it, so that I feel it's coming from something personal. And in a general sense, to convert any short story, novel, play, or opera into a movie, you have to re-rig it. Even though they're all narratives over time, they're very different forms.

Onion: Another school of thought says, "We have to be faithful to the book to do justice to it." But your films do drift away. They seem to have the spirit of the source material, but not the content, at least to the letter.
AP: The obvious point is this: A book is a book, but a movie is a movie. The more faithful you are, the more you'll come up with *Harry Potter* #1 and #2, which are like filmed books on tape. They're so petrified of turning off the readers that they make no concessions to the fact that they're trying to make a piece of cinema. I haven't seen Alfonso Cuarón's [*Harry Potter and the Prisoner of Azkaban*], but I'm sure it's far more cinematic, because he's a real director. That [Chris] Columbus guy isn't such a great director. But you have to change things. The better a novel is, in literary terms, the more you can't be faithful. The novel succeeds on terms exclusive to literature. A good film succeeds on terms exclusive to the cinema. That's why so many bad novels can become good movies, like *Jaws* or *The Godfather*.

Onion: What's the nature of your collaboration with Jim Taylor? How do you work together?
AP: We have to schedule our time together because he lives in New York and I live in Los Angeles. Some writing teams split up the tasks: They'll

outline together, then one writes the first half, the other writes the second half, and then they rewrite. We do it all together. We have a system with one monitor and two keyboards.

Onion: You were roommates, right? How did you develop similar sensibilities?
AP: It just grew. It just so happened that he took this extra room in this apartment I had in the late eighties, and we just started hanging out as roommates, and became friends. We took some tentative steps at screenwriting together with two shorts in 1991, then again a year later with *Citizen Ruth*, and it's grown from there. I don't think either of us anticipated having a co-writer in life.

Onion: What are his strengths? What in your work can be credited to him?
AP: We don't really divide up our tasks that much. We both do it all: structure, ideas, dialogue sculpting, everything. But I think he's funnier than I am. He's really funny.

Onion: Did you have total autonomy in the casting choices for *Sideways*?
AP: I did. I assumed it because we paid for casting ourselves. We didn't get connected with any studio until after we had cast the movie. Michael London and I optioned the book, Jim and I wrote the screenplay on spec, and Michael and I paid for casting. We rented an office and hired a casting director, hung out a shingle, and said, "Hey, we're casting a movie!" Then we approached the studios later and said, "Okay, here we are. Here's a script, a director, a producer, a budget, and a preferred cast."

Onion: But if you had taken it to a studio at an earlier point . . .
AP: Then I would have had to play the name game much more and fended off pressure to hire the most famous possible people.

Onion: Do you normally go about things this way?
AP: Actually, this is the first film since *Citizen Ruth* that I've cast without being attached to the studio during the casting period. With *Citizen Ruth*, even after we got connected with Miramax, they still started the name game with some of the supporting parts. It all worked out fine. But this is one where I really just wanted to cast whoever I thought was most appropriate, top to bottom. They could have been famous people, but I

didn't find any that I thought were better. Fortunately, the ones I picked were all available.

Onion: How difficult has it become to find financing for the sort of modestly budgeted comedy you seem to specialize in?
AP: Well, people say it's hard, but for me, it's grown easier. I won't say easier, but less hard. Each one of my movies becomes easier to get off the ground. This one was $16 million, which is not very much by Hollywood standards. I have to think that if it could go like that for me, then it certainly could for other people.

Onion: Maybe it's that there aren't a lot of these sorts of films being made.
AP: No, there aren't. There aren't enough.

Onion: How connected do you feel to the American independent scene, if there is such a thing?
AP: Independent means one thing to me: It means that regardless of the source of financing, the director's voice is extremely present. It's such a pretentious term, but it's auteurist cinema. Director-driven, personal, auteurist . . . whatever word you want. It's where you feel the director, not a machine, at work. It doesn't matter where the money comes from. It matters how much freedom the director has to work with his or her team. That's how I personally define independent movies.

Onion: Has it ever been defined any other way?
AP: Well, a lot of people get stuck, like, "Oh, if it's made by a studio, it can't be independent." Often they link it to the source of financing, or how it's distributed, but I don't really know how you can. A filmmaker will take his money from anywhere. It doesn't matter. I wrote an article about the state of American independent cinema for *Variety*. My lead-in to the article was that whenever I'm asked about independent cinema, I think of what Fidel Castro said during the Cold War about the league of non-aligned nations. He said that really, there were only two non-aligned nations: the U.S. and the USSR. The rest of us have to be aligned somewhere. I said similarly, in a way, Paramount, Sony, and Warner Bros. are the only true independents, because they're the only ones who can do whatever they want and have distribution for their films built in.

You asked me about what I want American independent cinema to be now. I want studios to be financing director-driven, auteurist cinema, as they did in the seventies. I think it's starting to happen now. You have the usual suspects, these young guys like Wes Anderson, Paul Thomas Anderson, myself, David O. Russell, Spike Jonze, Sofia Coppola, and whoever else you want to mention, getting our financing from studios. Then you have really great, strong directors like Sam Raimi and Alfonso Cuarón and Steven Soderbergh doing more franchise films, like *Harry Potter* and *Spider-Man* and *Ocean's Eleven*. Those are great directors doing strong work. And it's great that they have a great deal of control at that end. This year, Mike Nichols has a film coming out, James Brooks, Woody Allen. I think it's a really good year for movies. Plus, because of how our world has changed politically, I think audiences are demanding more realism. We need to have more stuff in our culture about what is really going on right now.

Onion: Do you think filmmakers, apart from documentarians, have responded on a political level as strongly as they could?
AP: You have to remember that films take time. Jon Stewart can do a show in a day. Satire—which is flourishing and in a way is our greatest form right now—is immediate. A lot of documentaries have been made very quickly, but I think they're like frogs in an ecosystem: They're harbingers. Film is always two or three years behind, because it takes so long to write a script, get financing, and get it made. It just takes a while. But I think it's coming. It has to.

Onion: You've been talking about the auteurist cinema of the seventies. Some of those films are very strongly political.
AP: Yes, but the thing is, right now the films don't need to be overtly political to be about our times. We also need films that are just human, that are about people. People need that, too. It's like we need to reconnect to what it is to be human. Not just what our political situation is. That's not what I'm thinking about exclusively. Human content is needed again, as it was in the seventies. I think films were more human than they've been since then.

Onion: Cinema's few depictions of Midwest life seem to describe it as America's Heartland. Do you consider your films a corrective to that?
AP: It's not really my job to say that, because I don't think that way. I think about what movie I would like to see. I don't think of them as a correction or palliative. I certainly am irritated by anything that's shot

in the Midwest and filled with these noble people. "Oh, they're so good, and they're so honest. . . ." I'm not interested in that. I just think of what's right for a movie.

Onion: What do you like to emphasize? What do you feel needs to be captured about the region?
AP: Well, again, not just about my films, but in general, I think the complexity. I think about what I want to shoot in Nebraska again, and one thing that most comes to mind is to make a film about Mexicans. The Midwest is crawling with Mexicans now. It's very interesting. In Omaha, there's a Mexican consulate because of the large numbers of people who work all over the state in slaughterhouses and packing houses. They're the current wave of Catholics who come from another country and take the lowest job. I think that's interesting, for example. You say the Midwest: Well, what is Detroit? Black, ghettoized Detroit? That's the Midwest. The south side of Chicago is the Midwest. North Omaha is the Midwest. To say it's all noble white people is such bullshit. I think anything that communicates a monolithic point of view about anything is wrong, certainly about a region.

Onion: Your movies are rich in a lot of incidental details, particularly in the production design. But production-design awards usually go to some frilly period piece. Do you think people are looking closely at the art of production design?
AP: I think my production designer, Jane Stewart, does work that's so good, it's invisible. We spend a lot of time scouting locations, and during those hours together in the car, we're always talking about the class of our characters and how class is reflected in the way they live and what where they live says about them as people. I always hate to say, "Oh, wine is a character in the film." It's not a character. It's a very large part of who the characters are. We're very interested in people in a place. It's not just about being in Omaha or being in wine country. What are we shooting? What's in the foreground? Obviously, the flesh. But what do we put in the background? I'm constantly interested, as a director, visually, in keeping both in focus—the background and the foreground. I admire other directors who have similarly used sets or landscape, however broadly or intimately, in depicting their story or characters. I'm a huge fan of Anthony Mann. He's a master at using landscape to depict what was going on with his characters, but not ever letting the landscape clobber the human story in front of the camera. That's really where you can

learn from the masters. Mike Leigh films, I think, are very thorough in that way.

Onion: Do you ever see yourself moving away from film comedy, or do you think this is the genre through which you work best?
AP: I don't know. I don't know yet.

Onion: Why comedy, then?
AP: Because it's so fun. I love comedies. Jim and I take comedy very seriously as a form. It's a serious form, involving a certain way of looking at life, specifically the painful aspects of life. I get asked, "How can you have such failures in your films?" Well, what else is life about? There's some sense of constant failure in something. Humor gives you a distance from it.

Alexander Payne: *Sideways*

Adrian Hennigan / 2005

From *BBC Movies*, January 14, 2005. Reprinted by permission of the interviewer and the BBC, http://www.bbc.co.uk/films.

In the space of three movies, Alexander Payne has established himself as one of America's most distinctive filmmakers. The Reese Witherspoon high school comedy *Election* (1999) was his calling card, but it was 2003's *About Schmidt*—featuring an Oscar-nominated turn by Jack Nicholson—that really made audiences sit up and take notice. Now critics worldwide are having kittens over his buddy comedy *Sideways*, in which two loser forty-something men—Paul Giamatti and Thomas Haden Church—go on a week-long wine-tasting tour of California.

Adrian Hennigan: Why are you attracted to losers in your movies?
Alexander Payne: I don't know. . . . Me and Jim Taylor—he's my co-writer—maybe we like to find comedy and poignancy in that discrepancy between dreams and aspirations, and reality and limitations, and who we really are. If drama is about obstacles—you know, setting up a goal and having obstacles toward that goal—then maybe we like obstacles which are internal, because I think that's very true to life.

Hennigan: You've said that *Withnail & I* was one of your references for *Sideways*. . . .
Payne: I admire that film very much, and it's such a classic film, a cult film. I wouldn't call it a real influence on this film, but it was a direct influence on the novelist [Rex Pickett]. When he was turning some version of his own experience into a novel, he was thinking a lot about *Withnail & I*—that kind of gonzo, two guys constantly drinking on a holiday of some sort. Jim Taylor and I did revisit the film as we were writing, but we didn't get a whole lot out of it that we could use directly.

Hennigan: How much research can you do for a film like this?

Payne: Quite a bit . . . but not a whole lot! We inherited a lot from the novel, but we did some wine research and I knew something about wine that I was able to put into the film. In fact, Virginia Madsen's speech about why she likes wine, and how it's alive: that's very personal to me and how I feel about wine. The research came later before preparing to shoot—research on the wines of the region so that our jargon was correct, and so that physically I was capturing that area and that sense of place.

Hennigan: Sense of place is integral to your movies. How important is it for you to capture the "real" America?

Payne: Very important, but it's not just about the real America, it's about the real planet and wherever I happen to be shooting—which so far has been America. You as an Englishman are seeing an America that you don't often see—at least in current American film—but then, it's an America that we're not seeing in America on film, because we don't have films, really, about Americans. Our culture is suffering as well from the abomination of the commercial American film. You know, we need national cinemas.

Hennigan: How do you make sure that the audience is laughing with your characters and not at them—that you're not being condescending?

Payne: *About Schmidt* was accused by some critics of being condescending to its characters, and I was always sorry that they took that away from the film because I didn't feel that at all. And I sometimes felt—and I don't think it's a defense mechanism—that those critics were condescending to those people by projecting such condescension onto me. Also, the fact that I'm making comedies, well, comedies do require a certain acknowledgement of type so that there's a recognizable truth that is slightly generalized, hopefully not caricaturized—which is too broad a way to depict character. How do I do it? It's just the style and the tone that occurs to me and Jim collectively as a writing team. Yes, we do make fun of people, but it's with a love and also a feeling that we're not any better and we're fairly pathetic in our own ways.

Hennigan: At one point in the movie Paul Giamatti's character talks about modern-day publishers not being interested in books which are a "hard sell." That's something that is equally true of the movies.

Payne: The key line there, which is certainly true about movies, is: "It's not about the quality of the books any more, it's about the marketing." And I see it every day in commercial American movies. It's not about the quality of the movies, it's about the presence of marketable elements. Marketing has supplanted story as the primary force behind the worthiness of making a film, and that's a very sad thing. It's film only as a function of consumerism rather than as an important component of our culture, and that's everywhere around the world.

Hennigan: You've worked within the studio system before, writing *Meet the Parents* and *Jurassic Park III*.
Payne: With *Sideways* we work within the system. These are all studio movies.

Hennigan: But they leave you alone to do your own thing, they trust you.
Payne: Correct, yes, and I'm happy we got those jobs. We wrote the last draft on *Meet the Parents*, the last draft of *Jurassic Park III*. Those were interesting jobs, but they were short. One was two weeks, the other one was four weeks. You know, it's like you're paid to take a class. The nice thing about those jobs is they give us a little more confidence that we can actually write quicker than we think we can write, because when we do a script it's about six months. And suddenly, because there's a deadline, it's like you're in school and you have to write an entire script in two and a half, or four weeks—and it's quite refreshing to work on something you don't really care that much about. We care so desperately about what we do, and then you're hired to do a job. These are broken scripts that need a little fixing, and we're ideas guys, that's all we do—come up with ideas. *Meet the Parents* was a good fit, *Jurassic Park* was not a good fit.

Hennigan: Why did they approach you for that?
Payne: Exactly! You know why? Because we had helped Universal make a lot of money previously with *Meet the Parents*. We got the call and were like, "What? *Jurassic Park III*?" But really, why they came to us was character and story, because the dinosaurs aren't the problem in those films, it's the human beings that are the problem. You've got Sam Neill and William H. Macy, and they want to have something to act. They didn't have anything to act! So we gave them things to act, and then they took it all out!

Hennigan: You obviously work very closely with Jim Taylor, but what happens when you've finished the script and you start directing?

Payne: When we're writing, we are only a writing team. It's not that I'm a director and calling the shots at all. It's one man veto power over anything. However, a last pass of the draft might be me thinking, "Am I going to be comfortable directing this?" So that's when he then does defer to me a bit, just to make it a little easier for me. He's not on the set or in the editing room, but I send him cuts and get his comments. And also, if I'm on the fence between two or three actors, I'll send him a tape and say, "Hey Jim, what do you think?" And he's always exquisite with his comments and his taste; they are impeccable. He remains a constant resource to me. I can't imagine my filmmaking without him. Absolutely. But he was not very involved in the making of *Sideways*, other than when I would call him up and ask him.

Hennigan: You're working on an ensemble project at the moment. The obvious film that comes to mind is Robert Altman's *Nashville*.

Payne: That's one film we're looking at to get some "vocabulary" that we can begin talking about. We're not that far with it yet. I just finished this film two months ago and immediately began showing it, and I just haven't stopped doing festival work and promotional work yet.

Alexander Payne

Kate Donnelly / 2005

From the *Believer*, March 2005. Reprinted by permission of the interviewer.

Alexander Payne makes films with an eye for incidental details. He circles his characters when they are at their most fragile and vulnerable. In *Citizen Ruth*, a pregnant Ruth Stoops plunges down a flight of stairs. In *Election*, Mr. McAllister washes his genitals in a hotel bathtub before an adulterous affair. In *About Schmidt*, Warren Schmidt loads up on Percodan and plunges into a hot tub with his future in-law. In *Sideways*, Miles Raymond accidentally encounters a waitress and her flabby boyfriend having wild sex to a televised (and muted) Donald Rumsfeld. With a sense of ease, he shares with us those perfectly perverse and uncomfortable moments that nevertheless make us laugh. In doing so, he helps his audiences reconnect and reflect on what it is to be human.

When talking to Payne, he is easily distracted. But when the subject is steered towards his love of film or his hometown of Omaha, he can talk on and on endlessly. He speaks five languages, plays piano, digs cats, and knows a bit about wine. Just don't ask him one of the following questions about his latest film *Sideways*: "Where did you get the idea?" "Why did you decide on this cast?" And that dark, inevitable question, "If you were a wine, which wine would you be."

Payne has just returned from a month-long tour of the Mediterranean, where he presented *Sideways* at film festivals in Turin, Thessaloniki, and Marrakesh. He's now back in Los Angeles, where he is attempting to sooth his circadian rhythms, juggle award nominations, and visit with a fellow midwesterner. This conversation took place in two parts: the first, in a telephone call to Alexander's home in Los Angeles, and the second, several days later, when he picked up an honorary doctorate from the University of Nebraska at Omaha.

Believer: Some critics have observed that you employ techniques of 1970s cinema. Are you consciously paying homage to that era in filmmaking?
Alexander Payne: I don't think I'm trying to pay homage to anything. The fact is that I was an American teenager in the 1970s and those were the movies I was watching. My idea of what an adult American film is has never changed.

Believer: Were you influenced by films like *Star Wars*?
AP: It didn't impact me at all. You know how people say, "Oh, and then I saw *Star Wars* and it just changed my life"? I saw *Star Wars* when it came out, but I don't even remember it. I probably forgot about it the next day.

Believer: So you weren't a fan of the commercially popular movies of the seventies?
AP: Well, I liked *Jaws*. But I didn't think about *Jaws* the way I thought about *One Flew Over the Cuckoo's Nest* or *Chinatown* or *Coming Home* at the time.

Believer: You were sitting in the *Cuckoo's Nest* while your friend was next door watching *Jaws*?
AP: Not at all. I remember being in high school and arguing about whether we liked *Annie Hall* or *Manhattan* better.

Believer: Wow. It sounds like Omaha was a sophisticated movie-going town in the seventies.
AP: I remember my friend Dan Cowdin saying about *Manhattan*, "They're just so neurotic and complain-y. How can you like that one?"

Believer: Martin Scorsese was on *Charlie Rose* the other night.
AP: How was he?

Believer: Really great. He's like an encyclopedia on film.
AP: What did he say?

Believer: He talked a lot about films of the thirties and forties. Those twenty years seem to be, for him at least, the golden age of cinema. He talked about *Hell's Angels* and *Scarface*. He also mentioned high-impact films like *The Searchers*, *Citizen Kane*, and *On the Waterfront*. What were your high-impact movies, beginning from the time you went to the cinema as a teenager?

AP: You have to go back to before I was even a teenager. They were largely based on movies my older brothers thought were cool, like *King Kong, One-Eyed Jacks, The Good, the Bad and the Ugly,* and *Cool Hand Luke.*

Believer: *King Kong?* The Jessica Lange version?

AP: No, no no. The 1933 movie. I probably saw it ten times as a kid because it would always be on TV. Those were the earliest movies I remember being cool. Later, on my own, without my brothers, I started getting into a lot of silent comedy. Chaplin and Keaton. I didn't see much Lloyd. It was harder to get your hands on Lloyd. And then, of course, the Universal horror movies. That's just what kids watched. Oh, and when I was nine or ten, a movie I probably saw at the movie theater three or four times with my buddies was *Little Big Man.* And *The Sting.* We were little kids, like twelve years old.

Believer: *The Sting?* Very discerning taste for a twelve-year-old kid. What was going on in Omaha?

AP: *The Sting* is a great kids' movie. *Butch Cassidy and the Sundance Kid,* I probably saw it about four times the year it came out. I remember seeing Philippe de Broca's *King of Hearts* probably three times. That's a good kids' movie, as well. And I remember it played with two animated shorts, *Bambi Meets Godzilla* and *Thank You Masked Man.*

Believer: What is the kids' movie demographic?

AP: I'm talking between eight and fourteen. And we loved Woody Allen's *Bananas* because you got to see a girl's breasts in it, which was very exciting for us. I would say *Five Easy Pieces* was a little over our heads.

Believer: That film didn't make the kid cut?

AP: I was nine when that came out and now it's one of my favorite movies. But at the time, we didn't go to see it. The big movie I saw when I was twelve, which everyone was trying to see and nobody's parents would take them to, was *The Exorcist.* I finally got a friend of my parents to take me and I was actually underwhelmed by it. I think it's scarier now than I did when I was twelve.

Believer: So you weren't sleeping with your lights on?

AP: The hype and buildup around it was so huge. It's only years later that I realize how scary it is. The scariest movie for a lot of people in my generation was *The Omen*.

Believer: And did that scare you when it came out?
AP: Oh yeah. That's a frightening movie. It doesn't completely hold up anymore, but at the time, it was terrifying.

Believer: You reference Akira Kurosawa in nearly every interview I've read. Could you talk to me about the importance of Kurosawa and why you like his films?
AP: Maybe because I've studied them. His films made a very big impact on me. There was a time period of many, many years where anytime I could see a Kurosawa movie, I would. I devoured Donald Ritchie's book about him, and read his autobiography. There wasn't a whole lot of scholarship in English about him in the eighties, which was my big Kurosawa period. But it was a time when, between San Francisco and Los Angeles, you could see his films projected. Plus, I got a chance to hear him speak in Los Angeles in 1986, when he came with *Ran*. I don't know, there's just something unbelievably great about his films. They are ferocious. He tells a good story, and he's not afraid of anything. They are deeply, deeply passionate in an unsentimental way. Only the films he made at the end of his life were more openly sentimental.

Believer: Do you consider *Ikiru* a sentimental film?
AP: I think whatever sentimentality it has is very honest and earned. I saw it for the first time projected at Stanford, and about a half an hour into the film, there's a montage about Watanabe's son Mitsuo. He's accompanying his son to have an appendectomy, cheering him on when he's a loser baseball player, sitting in the back of a car following behind the wife's hearse when the man is widowed. The motion from shot to shot often matches. And then his son calls down from upstairs, "Dad," and the father says, "Mitsuo . . . Mitsuo . . ." [Alexander employs a specific and convincing Japanese accent.]

Believer: [laughs] Perfect inflection.
AP: And then he leaves the frame and you hear him run up the stairs and the son says, "Be sure to turn off the lights. Be sure to lock the door when you go to bed." Pause. Pause. Cut. Look down and there's the actor

Takashi Shimura with his head resting on a step. He only made it two-thirds of the way up the stairs before his disappointment. I hadn't seen a movie that had me crying so early. When I was in film school, I watched Kurosawa movies. This is before I had videos of them, and I would take notes on every shot. I would write down nearly every shot and start to memorize the films.

Believer: You seem really well-organized and meticulous in that regard.
AP: Not always. There have been times in my life when I have been, but it's been harder for me now. My life is a little bigger and all. When I was in film school, I would go watch movies and write down shots. I used to see a movie, come home, write my reaction to it, and talk about cool shots and cool sequences. I still do that sometimes.

Believer: What's the last film you remember doing that for?
AP: *The Girl in the Red Velvet Swing.* I did it about three weeks ago in Turin, Italy. I couldn't believe how good that film was. Apparently, it's fairly obscure.

Believer: *Sideways* was based on a novel by Rex Pickett. What's the greatest challenge in adapting a book for film?
AP: It's no different from writing an original. In fact, the way [writing partner] Jim [Taylor] and I work, not always, but in general, is that we read the book a few times and then stop referring to it. We then write an original based on our memory of the book. That's sort of how we work. So it's as though we are always doing originals.

Believer: How do you come across books these days?
AP: I have precious little time to read. I sometimes have to dedicate that time to reading books or scripts sent to me; otherwise, I'll never get around to reading them. But then I often grow resentful of having to do that because I think about all the books I'm not reading. I've never read Proust. I've never read James Joyce other than *A Portrait of the Artist as a Young Man.* I'm woefully under-read in Faulkner. I can't even talk about keeping up with new stuff.

Believer: What about F. Scott Fitzgerald and Hemingway?
AP: I was never a very big fan of Hemingway. And Fitzgerald, yes, but mostly in high school. In college, most of the literature I read was in

Spanish. I am very well-read in Garcia Marquez, for example, and Vargas Llosa. You know, the classics along with some of the great Mexican and Argentine writers and some Spanish writers.

Believer: That makes sense. Your first thesis film was an adaptation of a novel by Ernesto Sabato, *El Túnel* [midwestern accent applied].
AP: *El Túnel* [thick Spanish tongue employed].

Believer: [laughs] Thank you. You sound like the fellow on *Jeopardy*.
AP: Did he ever lose?

Believer: He finally lost.
AP: Who beat him?

Believer: A woman. I missed his televised demise. Clearly, he's not missing any meals. He won over $2 million.
AP: Yeah, that's unbelievable.

Believer: Would you ever have auditioned for *Jeopardy*?
AP: Yeah. Except I don't know sports.

Believer: Do you enjoy sports?
AP: I like playing them, not watching. I used to play a lot of tennis and I don't anymore, but I'd like to get back to it. I used to play a lot of racquetball. Right now, I do yoga and go to the gym and throw weights around and jump on the machines. I swim when I can. I like to swim in the ocean. That's pretty much my favorite thing. And being in a stream and hopping from rock to rock. I like that a lot.

Believer: Getting back to writing, will you ever write a novel?
AP: I don't know yet. I would like to try short stories and poetry, but I'm afraid of poetry. I think filmmaking is hard but poetry is *really* hard. Good poetry. Poetry is king of the most important thing, in a way. I get a poem sent to me every day by Garrison Keillor.

Believer: How?
AP: I get the *Writer's Almanac*. Do you get that?

Believer: I don't. How does one subscribe?
AP: You subscribe to it online at Minnesota Public Radio and then every

day Garrison Keillor sends you a poem: sometimes new, sometimes classic, never too long. And biographies of writers or notes about important events that took place that day.

Believer: You just went to Washington, D.C., to pick up the annual Distinguished Nebraskan Award. What were the prerequisites for such an award?
AP: I think you have to be from Nebraska. They have given it to a wide variety of individuals, from politicians to educators to corporate leaders.

Believer: Would you ever consider running for public office?
AP: I'm not prepared to confirm or deny the possibility. But I have thought about it, yes. [*Pause*] What's making you ask? Did someone tell you that?

Believer: No. You just seem politically inclined to me. Hypothetically, how would you go about campaigning?
AP: Well, even though I can neither confirm nor deny that I do or do not intend to run for office, one day, I may or may not have a plan for that which I'm not prepared to discuss.

Believer: Do you think it's right for a film director to pursue other interests? Wouldn't a political life interrupt a film career?
AP: It would obviously interrupt a film career. But one of the reasons I wanted to be a filmmaker in the first place was that it allows me to be a generalist in life—to immerse myself in different topics, different disciplines, different cultures, different issues, different academic fields.

Believer: Growing up, which major political figures in Nebraska influenced you? Did you have any "good guys" to look up to?
AP: The neat thing about Nebraska is that even though it's a solidly Republican state, the voters tend to look at the character of the person running. For example, Nebraska has had two democratic senators at one time. In recent history, it's the first state, and I think the only state, to have two women running against each for governor. And, while it's a very conservative Republican state, it produced George Norris, a progressive—who was actually a Republican, but a progressive in the old way Robert La Follette of Wisconsin was. It produced Herbert Brownell, who was Eisenhower's attorney general and helped pioneer, and then enforce, some civil-rights legislation. There's a very comforting history of

freethinking in Nebraska that I appreciate. In fact, when I went to Washington a few weeks ago, I made a point of visiting Republican senator Chuck Hagel so I could shake his hand and tell him how encouraged I was that there was a Republican senator who was publicly and actively disagreeing with the president about how the war is being pursued. Which is not to say that I necessarily agree with his points of view on many other issues. But I respect the man, who's unlike so many politicians nowadays, who seem to have given up the idea of thinking for themselves.

Believer: Politically speaking, what kind of household did you grow up in?
AP: My father is Republican and my mother is Democrat.

Believer: That's the Midwest. Do you think the Midwest has become conservative now?
AP: It has always been so. It's so easy to talk about "red states" and "blue states," but it is not as though everyone is of a certain political bent. We know there is diversity everywhere, maybe less diversity in some places. You certainly don't find a lot of ethnic diversity in North Dakota, for instance. In spite of the trend, I think it's really hard to generalize about people. When you get to know them, you discover everyone's got a story. It's hard to generalize. There just happens to be much deeper strains of conservative attitudes ingrained in the Midwest. And obviously, in the South, there is something else again, and that's just disappointing. The problem for me is that people respond to labels like conservative, Republican, Democrat, Liberal. Bush and company do not seem to me to be real Republicans. They are virulent ideologues who have commandeered the word "Republican." Many people fall for it perhaps more than they would or should if they just thought a little bit more or read a little bit more.

Believer: Would you have any interest in directing a political film?
AP: How would you define a political film?

Believer: A political film is what's timely right now. Not necessarily the war in Iraq, but the fear and paranoia going on inside America.
AP: Yeah, I'm surprised we haven't had science fiction like we had in the fifties, because we have generalized fear. At least we're told we have fear. Are people really afraid?

Believer: I think they might be. What would a political film mean for you?
AP: The genre does not matter. It's the concerns. A political film can be a science fiction; it could be a Western. *Little Big Man* is a political film.

Believer: What about a black and white silent film?
AP: I would love that, but it might be in color. I'm going to work in black and white cinemascope in the film after next. And silent film is beautiful. At its apex, right before the talkies came in, telling a story through images had reached a sublime and sophisticated place. And many people, as you know, thought the talkies would be the end of cinema because they would just film people talking. It would be filmed theatre in a way. It would decrease cinematic beauty and it certainly did for a while. Have you seen *Sunrise*?

Believer: I have not.
AP: You have to make it the first film you see when you hang up with me. You must see *Sunrise*.

Believer: You had the benefit of a film-school education. You're like an encyclopedia.
AP: Scorsese is like an encyclopedia. I'm just a pocket guide. A stocking stuffer.

Believer: Steven Soderbergh and Martin Scorsese have recently chosen to make big-budget films. Do you feel an obligation to dabble in the mainstream?
AP: I don't know how to answer that question. It's not just a matter of how much money you spend on a film. I mean, are my films mainstream? They have always been financed by studios. This will be the third film in a row that makes a profit. This will be my third film in a row nominated for an Oscar. Am I a mainstream director? I don't know. I don't use any label. I'm just a filmmaker. I'll take the money wherever it comes from, as long as I have creative control. I make movies for studios that turn a profit and are nominated for Oscars, which sounds fairly mainstream to me. Yet I'm referred to as an indie director. Maybe that just means I make personal films, or that the degree of creative control, which I'm lucky enough to enjoy, is evident.

Believer: Critics like to gripe about veteran directors who don't evolve or adapt to audience expectations. Should a filmmaker worry about his relevance?

AP: Can you control how relevant you are? I don't know how you control that. Sometimes the more you try to do something, the more it eludes you. I think you either are or you are not. And no matter what the budget—I don't know how budget impacts relevance. Is Sophia Coppola, who made her film for $4 million, more or less relevant than Chris Columbus, who made the first two *Harry Potter* films? How do you define relevant? To my eyes, these are relative and vague terms.

Believer: Did you have creative control over the film poster for *Sideways*?
AP: Well, I told them it should be a graphic, and not photographic.

Believer: It reminds me of an old foreign-film poster.
AP: Yeah, good. That was definitely the idea.

Believer: The Santa Barbara Film Commission recently ordered a second printing of "*Sideways*, the Map." There's also a "snob-free" wine-tasting tour for $79. Have you sparked some sort of pop-cultural phenomenon in the way of a new, non–Napa Valley?
AP: It seems that way. I didn't try to do that. There are people watching the film and there's a general interest in wine anyway, at least more so than there's been in the past. Every once in a while, someone will email me something about a wine critic talking about it or how a wine store has seen its sales of certain wines go up. It's interesting.

Believer: In Rex Pickett's book, he showcases a 1982 Latour, but you chose a 1961 Château Haut-Brion that my parents bought me when I was born.
AP: Oh wow. Fuckin' A.

Believer: Yeah. It was to be opened when I got engaged, which I told my dad would be in the distant future. So we opened it, and it was great. Is life about drinking what you have when you have it?
AP: If you're smart.

Alexander Payne: Staying Straight While Making *Sideways*

Brad Balfour / 2004

From PopEntertainment.com, April 4, 2005. Reprinted by permission of the interviewer.

With *Sideways*, Alexander Payne really proves he's a true contender, not just the creator of smart, snarky idiosyncratic comedies but solid filmmaker who tackled humanity with aplomb. In this humorous on-the-road buddy flick, leads Paul Giamatti (failed writer Miles Raymond) and Thomas Haden Church (former hot actor Jack) grapple with Jack's final week of freedom before marriage. In doing so, they review their lives through their bumpy ride throughout the California's wine country. Though Payne's previous films *Citizen Ruth*, *Election*, and *About Schmidt* garnered acclaim, *Sideways* garnered him the Oscar nomination for Best Picture and Best Director because it displays a real wisdom that needs to be experienced.

Brad Balfour: When did you decide this was the project to do?
Alexander Payne: It was easy. I read it and thought it would be great. I sent it to Jim; he thought it was going to be great. And I even thought that it might be easier trying to adapt it on my own. But that's not fun, so Jim and I ended up doing it.

Balfour: So you have someone to bounce off ideas.
Payne: Writing is hideous, solo. There's something about screenwriting which lends itself to collaboration. You don't see it with novelists; you don't see it with playwrights. Yeah, but it's something about screenplays that lends itself to collaboration.

Balfour: What gets you inspired?

Payne: For general ideas . . . well, being in the shower, or driving, or hopefully sitting in front of a desk on the computer [laughs slightly]. That's really where you force inspiration to come: sitting down and facing that blank page. And also, I work with a co-writer. We always try to make each other laugh, and it comes from there. Then while directing, I take a nap every day and I get ideas for the afternoon during my naps.

Balfour: You really seem inspired with *Sideways*—this is your most rigorous film.

Payne: I hope to God—if there is one—that I'm learning more about how to make a film. I mean, what the hell is a film? I don't really know, and I consider myself a film student who is just getting paid professionally. I feel like I'm at a professional apprenticeship program—How to Make a Film. So I am so happy that this seems to be my best-made film so far. I have a sure grasp on the craft but I am always aspiring to know better film craft. I mean, the more I know I see, the less I know about film craft. It's just that I know myself better as a person. At forty-three, for Christ-sake, I hope I learned something about experience. That's the most important thing—that it gets channeled.

Balfour: How do you decide what goes in the screenplay from the book and what you change—what's the process?

Payne: That's a really hard question to answer, "How do we do it?" Because we just do it. It's very instinctive. You would do it differently. So it's just what strikes Jim and me as being appropriate that we can encase, within a form—a two-hour movie. So there were wonderful set pieces in the book, for example, like Jack and Miles go boar hunting. They met up, they were singing karaoke one night and they meet up at a bar with a guy and he talks about boars, because there are a lot of wild boars in the area. And it would have been a really great sequence, it's like when they play golf or when they get that wallet back, but that would've been like a twenty-page commitment.

Balfour: You felt so passionate about this film that you wanted so much control over it. Is that what made you guys do this as an independent production?

Payne: Oh, it's wonderful to work alone, without overseers. I just don't understand why when people have an idea, the first thing they think is,

"How can I get paid to write it?" Or later when they're going to be casting a film, "Oh! I can't possibly raise fifteen or twenty thousand dollars to cast it on my own?" People just make my life hell in order to pay for that relatively small amount of money, especially if you're sharing it with someone. So the wisdom was that you don't get a studio involved until the last possible moment. Then you don't have to have go through the name game and "Oh, change the script." *Election* was a job, for example. Jim and I were hired to write, and I was hired to direct that film. But then they can impose changes like, "Oh, we're not going to make it this year, we're going to make it next year." They can say, "No, go approach Tom Cruise first," and who wants to go through all that? Or they'll decide not to make it at all and you can't take it elsewhere, and you've just lost six months of your life. And they'll say, "Well, we paid you" and you'll say, "Well, who cares about that?"

Balfour: You really put attention on casting. . . .
Payne: I won't claim that I'm very talented at any single aspect of filmmaking, but I am talented at casting.

Balfour: You took a risk with some of these actors; you thought that Virginia [Madsen] would always be the person to play that character.
Payne: I'm always very proud of my secondary characters. Like in *Sideways*, I like the guy who plays the bartender at the Hitching Post, Gary [Patrick Gallagher]. And Miles's mother, Mary Louise Burke, she's a stage actress. I cast off-the-street nonprofessionals, and non-actors, even.

Balfour: Since you're married to Sandra Oh, was it difficult directing her, or easier?
Payne: Easy. No, I wouldn't say "easier," but I think she's just generally an easy "directable" actress in general, a real pro.

Balfour: Did you hold back, not be as tough with someone you're married to?
Payne: No, it's pretty much the same because in the moment of directing, I don't see her as my wife. I see her as another one of these pieces of meat I put in front of the camera. [laughs]

Balfour: How were the wine drinking scenes with the actors?
Payne: With the fake wine? Yeah, I'm sure the actors have maybe talked

about it. No, I didn't force it. If the actors had wanted to drink the real wine, they could have it. I didn't care. As long as they can still mumble the dialogue.

Balfour: Did you enhance your own wine collection?
Payne: A little bit, yeah. At least I enhanced my knowledge about wine.

Balfour: Have there ever been times where you think that you'd spend more time writing or editing rather than directing?
Payne: No, Jim and I have done three film script-doctoring jobs. But only because they're two-to-four-week jobs. We're often approached to write scripts for other directors, like from scratch. And we're not interested.

Balfour: You always wanted to direct?
Payne: I've been trained as a director.

Balfour: Then what interested you in producing *The Assassination of Richard Nixon*?
Payne: It was co-written by two guys, my closest friends from film school, and I liked the script very much. Anything I could do to get that made and lend any bit of a momentum to it, I would do. So I'm really not interested in being a film producer at all. I get approached a lot now to produce or executive produce films, but I'm very selective about it. So I usually just do it for friends I believe in.

Balfour: And what attracted you to it?
Payne: It's *Taxi Driver*-ish in a way, and also there's a political side to it which I found interesting. It has dialogue when Nixon tried to run in '68 in a promise on ending the war in Vietnam. He escalated the war. Later he ran in '72 on the very same promise of ending the war, and was reelected. In our country, people are sheep and are easily susceptible to being sold ideas. That's an important message to get out there. It may even be relevant to our times.

Balfour: In terms of control, how different was doing *Sideways* compared to *About Schmidt* and *Election*?
Payne: It gets easier every time, because I'm learning more and my collaborators are learning more, and not just because we're learning more: but our collaboration is sweeter and there is more shorthand.

Balfour: And not having to be under the studio's scrutiny?
Payne: My stuff is not typically commercial and possessed of easily marketable elements in today's cinema. But as more people in Hollywood get more of what I do and what the tone of my films are—and how to read one of my screenplays—then it becomes, I won't say easier, but less hard to get one of my things made. Also, when I'm arguing about something, I'm believed more often now that it could work. Also Fox Searchlight is such a fantastic studio. They're all about doing independent, personal, author-istic, director-driven, or whatever term you want to use. That's the kind of films they're making. And they're doing so very successfully, by trusting the directors, and trust is the best weapon you can wield.

Balfour: Now you've seen the completed movie with an audience. Is the reaction what you expected, or better?
Payne: Better. Oh yeah. And who else? I just hope my friends will like it. We sort of like it; it's okay. But you never know how it's going to get received.

Balfour: Do you feel that you just never know with each film?
Payne: The best definition of film directing is groping in the dark. You hope that it's all instinctive, and you hope other people will like it, but who the hell knows? So that it's getting such early general notices—I mean at the receptions, people laugh a lot. I think they're happy to laugh a lot, and people seem to be responding to the fact that it's just sort of a human movie. And that's kind of rare today in American movies. It seems to be hitting people at the right time, and I have no control over that.

Alexander Payne:
Sideways Glance at America

Kenneth Turan / 2005

Transcript of a Regis Dialogue at the Walker Art Center, Minneapolis, Minnesota, June 3, 2005. Published by permission of the interviewer.

Kenneth Turan: We're at the Walker Art Center for a Regis Dialogue with filmmaker Alexander Payne. We're going to be discussing his artistic vision, his sense of humor, and his love of film. Alexander Payne's films, characterized by his ability to bring emotional reality to drop-dead funny comedies, manage to be achingly true to life while dealing with seriously out-of-control situations. Even the setting of most of them, Payne's quintessentially all-American home town of Omaha, Nebraska, emphasizes the notion that these people could well be anyone's friends and neighbors, maybe even yours.

Well, I wanted to start at the beginning; I wanted to start with Omaha. You are famously born in Omaha. I had kind of a two-part question about that. I wonder, first of all, do you think people make too much of that . . . there's always every article that is written says Omaha, films in Omaha. Do people make too much of it? And on the flip side, what do you get from it; what do you think being born there, coming from there has done to the way you look at the world?

Alexander Payne: It's so funny because you're commenting on the question *and* making too much of it.

KT: It's not easy to do!
AP: You can't have it both ways. I think for my taste people do, I mean I get so sick of the question: the B-side of "Why do you want to shoot there?," because I always say, "You never ask Spike Lee, Martin Scorsese, and Woody Allen that question about New York. It's just, they happen to

be from there. Quentin Tarantino and Paul Thomas Anderson happen to be from L.A. and you don't ask them those questions: "Why L.A.? Why would it occur to you to shoot in L.A.?" But because I'm from Omaha ... you know, and I like to point out that Fellini shot early on in Rimini and even returned later for *Amarcord*, and I just think in many arts early in your career you feel a necessity somehow to connect to that ... and I don't really know how to answer that question, other than it occurred to me to do so. I was, and remain, tired of seeing American films really only set in L.A., which I feel is an anomalous place within this country, and yet it's shown to the world as being typical of the U.S. It's only because the film business is located there and they're lazy and they don't go shoot in other places. And the thing is too, I think we're all (it's kind of my tirade) we're all so anxious to see a version of ourselves mirrored in art and in cinema that I didn't grow up seeing myself—a midwesterner—in film. I mean, you grow up in Omaha and you just see all those people in L.A.

KT: Even though it is trying to have it both ways, where we come from has an impact on who we are. What did coming from Omaha have to do with who you are today as a director?
AP: Well, the real answer to that would I think be more with how did where I come from have to do with me as a person. We could get into that but, I don't know, we have other stuff to cover.

But I'm glad I'm from there for a variety of reasons. I think it's a great place to grow up and, you know, good values and a good rhythm of life, and a certain honesty and frankness and humor with which I grew up. I think Omaha *is* of the Midwest in that way but also specific, in its own way. The other thing, too, just in terms of me personally as a filmmaker, is because I like to get reality in film—like, somehow, you could even, say, have a documentary approach to fiction filmmaking—that I felt I needed to get it right first in Omaha, the place I knew the best, before I could move on. And I think if *Sideways* is successful at all in terms of getting a sense of Santa Barbara County, it's because I went armed with tools I had learned in finally starting to get it right in *About Schmidt* with respect to Omaha.

KT: I read that you had a camera when you were quite young—that your family had gotten a kind of 8mm camera. Is this a true story?
AP: Sort of. My dad owned a restaurant in downtown Omaha, which his grandfather had started, and from Kraft cheese he had received a not

even Super-8 but regular-8 movie projector. In those days, I'm sure many of you remember, you used to buy like three and twelve minute versions of films in regular-8 and Super-8 at the camera store. Castle Films and Blackhawk Films later, so I took to that. At about five or six, when I started developing an interest in movies, my first thing was threading that projector and showing movies. And then later on, when I was about fourteen, I got a Super-8 camera . . . used.

KT: You still have it?
AP: I do.

KT: We hear about filmmakers who got interested young and they immediately go off to film school. I was interested in the fact that you did not. Did you think about being a filmmaker at that age? Did you dismiss it? You almost went to graduate school in journalism. Undergraduate, you went to Stanford and had a classic liberal arts education. I just wondered what was your thinking about being a filmmaker at that stage?
AP: It was a far off dream. It was a dream like: "Oh, wouldn't that be great?" But it was so distant and, you know, you grew up in the Midwest with . . . I'm second generation immigrant, and it's not the mentality to think that that's possible. I'm so jealous meeting people on the coast: "Oh, you know, my parents are in the arts . . . I grew up in the business." Like it's a no-brainer. But for me it was so far away, and so, in a way, I was headed toward it my whole life because I was such a film buff my whole life and, on the other hand, it took me to go through college then actually get to, like, fall quarter senior year to think: "Well, where the hell am I going to apply to grad school?" and resisting my parents' pressure to apply to law school. I ended up taking the LSAT but you know, eh. . . . But then I was a double major in history and literature, with an eye toward either journalism or film. I still had it in the back of my mind. I thought, you know, I gotta apply, unsure whether I had the talent or the interest: an interest that would extend to making films as opposed to just being a film buff. And then I got in and then thought, I have to try this . . . maybe I'll suck at it, but I have to try it.

KT: UCLA is a very particular kind of place. I know other UCLA graduates—film school graduates. Can you talk a little bit about the sensibility of the place?
AP: Well this was the mid-eighties when USC was like the hot-shot, white guy film school to go to, and I got in to USC as well, and went down from

Stanford to L.A. and spent two days in each place. Really what tipped the scales is USC and AFI are much more industry feeder schools—*very* Hollywood oriented. And then you're paying through the nose for tuition, and they retain rights to your negatives of your student films, and you have to compete to make advanced films. Whereas at UCLA, it's a public school and it's one person/one film. You're expected to make a film and it can be anything you want. I think the best film schools in the U.S. continue to be UCLA and NYU because NYU is similar.

KT: The filmmakers who come out of there tend to be more adventurous. They tend to be less kind of cookie-cutter filmmakers. I wonder what films you liked then when you were in film school. Who were the directors that you admired, who you admired also when you were younger?
AP: In film school, in my twenties, it was Kurosawa. The film that really tipped the scales toward my saying, "I have to go to film school," was when I saw *The Seven Samurai*, when it was rereleased in '82 and I saw it at the Castro Theater. I'd never seen it, and I thought, I'll never make a film that good but what nice footsteps to *try* to follow in. It was so cool and it's still basically my favorite film. Then I spent most of my twenties reading everything I could about Kurosawa and I got deeply into Japanese cinema. As a kid growing up, it was a lot of silent comedy and Warner Bros. pictures—the gangster pictures—and Universal horror. I was never that much into MGM movies; it was mostly Warner Bros. and Universal, and silent comedy. Going back to the projector story, the only films you could get were basically silent films.

KT: The public domain.
AP: Yes. In fact, David Shepard, whom I met later, was running Blackhawk Films and I used to use my allowances to send off to Blackhawk Films.

KT: I wonder if you'd talk a little bit about the films of the seventies. That's a crucial period in American filmmaking that a lot of directors today look back on with a real kind of admiration.
AP: Well, it's had a real impact on me, I think, only because, even though in growing up and in my teens I was fairly obsessed with older movies, still the new movies were seventies movies. I was born in 1961 and graduated from high school in '79. My buddies and I were all great movie watchers, and somehow that golden period—you never know it's a golden period while you're living in it—but that period formed my

idea of what a commercial, adult, American film is and it's just never changed. In a way your tastes lock in your late teens: your taste in music and your taste in film.

KT: There is something I was going to ask you later but I want to follow up on it now. Why don't we have more films like that now?
AP: You're a critic; you tell me. I mean, you think about those things more than I do.

KT: I do think about those things: the way the whole industry has changed in terms of what they're doing.
AP: The common answers, which you could explain better than I, are the home-run mentality of *Jaws* and *Star Wars* and all that. I don't know. On the other hand, a deeper answer is that any time in the arts or even in politics or in culture, things happen in bursts, often in ten-year spurts that stem somehow from a historical necessity to have it. And certainly seventies filmmaking, you can, in a way, trace back to Italian neorealism, which came from a very specific historical necessity, both for culture to express itself and redefine itself, and a necessity for cinema—a hunger for cinema. And then how that bled into French New Wave and auteur theory and how that then affected American filmmakers who were dealing with such heavy—can I say "shit" here?—with such heavy shit in the seventies with the war and all. And somehow we needed a cinema which was very close to society: a mirror.

KT: That's an interesting thought.
AP: Well, I'm hoping that now with all the heavy stuff going on, although somehow we haven't really realized how heavy everything is... as a society we're not getting it, we're trying but it bounces off us somehow... but my hope is that now we need it again in a new way. It's a horrible time in general for the world and certainly for this country, but I'm hoping that will translate into a good time for the cinema. You know, the seventies—oh, a wonderful time for the cinema—let's not forget that Nixon was reelected by the biggest landslide ever.

KT: Now 1990 was your student film, *The Passion of Martin*. It was, for a student film, a huge success. What did that mean for you? You had been a student at UCLA, you had been working kind of on your own. This film was shown and what happens?
AP: Did you see that movie, *The Big Picture*, Christopher Guest's first

film? It was like that. And it's what you hope happens. It's also a good thing of going to film school. You don't need to go to film school anymore but if one does, to show your work within a context that can help you get more work is a benefit. And I lucked into it. I made a fifty-minute thesis film loosely based on a very famous Argentine novel, and it hit somehow, again in a way I never could have predicted. It was one of those dream scenarios for a film student in terms of within a month I had an agent and a studio deal.

KT: I interviewed Todd Solondz once. He also had a hit student film. He said agents literally went down on their knees in front of him and begging that he sign with them. And it was very disorienting and ultimately it drove him out of the business. Did you find it disorienting? Were there troubling aspects of it or did it all seem like it was great?

AP: The most disorienting experience I've had has been the success of *Sideways*.

KT: Really?

AP: Actually, far more disorienting because at that level so much has come at me in the last few months—it's a whole new level of having to deal with stuff coming at me.

KT: You mean as a result of *Sideways*?

AP: Yes, a whole level. The thing that filmmakers have to know that I've learned the hard way, and continue to have to learn it is, you know a filmmaker is always concerned about the next film—and not just the idea for the script and can I come up with anything, but the opportunity to make it, obviously, and getting the financing. So there's genuinely a skill about when you finish a film and it has some notoriety, there's a window of opportunity where stuff comes at you and people are interested in you and then they move onto the next thing. Knowing how to capitalize on that window is something that I continue to witness and which I haven't known how to do until more recently. And, just to follow up on the film school thing, everything seemed assured that within a year, I would be directing my first feature, yet it was five years.

KT: Why did it take that long?

AP: Because I didn't know what to do. Not to get too much into the film school thing but when you're in film school, they always say, "When you show your thesis film, make sure you have your feature script right there." But no one ever does, because you're working so hard editing and mixing, and then you're exhausted and then it's time to screen your film and often basically you're running a wet print up to the screening room. [sighs] And actually when I got out of film school, I told you I got a studio deal. I wrote a script, the first draft of what only twelve years later became *About Schmidt*. *About Schmidt* was supposed to be my first feature, not my third.

KT: You went to Universal: what was your studio experience?
AP: It's the velvet coffin. Studio deals are the velvet coffin. It feels good. I made enough money in one year to last me for five years. I made $125,000 in one year of which you keep about half, which was $60,000, which lasted me five years [laughs]. 'Cause I never changed my living situation from that of a graduate student 'til, basically, after *Election*. I never paid more than $800 in rent until the year 2000.

KT: Wow, save your money.
AP: Well, didn't have it. After *Citizen Ruth*, I had to borrow money from my dad to pay my taxes. But, how was the studio deal? It's great but my advice always to younger filmmakers and film students is: never take studio deals, if you want to direct. If you just want to write, then it's fine. But if you're going to pitch an idea and be paid for it, because then they own it. And they can sit on it, or make you go through really hideous casting hurdles. The moment someone else owns your creative work, it's not good.

KT: Yeah, it's a devil's bargain.
AP: *Sideways* was something which no studio had any part of until the very, very possible last moment. That's basically the reason why it was made in the way it was which was with no movie stars.

KT: It's better. One of the things I thought about that you can see in *The Passion of Martin*, and you see it in all your films, is that you see comedy where not everybody would be seeing comedy. I think there's a quote (and I hope these quotes are accurate) where you said, "I like satire and comedy based in painful experience."
AP: Yeah, yeah.

KT: Are you bored with talking about that?
AP: No, I mean, these quotes . . . it's fine.

KT: You sort of said them but you didn't really say them?
AP: Well, it was years ago where you say it 'cause it's convenient or something.
[Turan and audience laugh]

KT: Seeing all your films at once made me really see that people are going through difficult times in these films but we're laughing. And that seems to be kind of a dynamic.
AP: Well, isn't that life, if you have a sense of humor? At this point, I have to include Jim Taylor, because he's a central figure. He's my co-writer. The films that you're talking about are very much an expression of how Jim and I are as friends together, and then how we write together. It really dates back just to how we hang out and say, "Did you read this article?" and, "Look at that guy over there," and, "I had this really painful experience yesterday." You know, talking about the pathetic side of our own lives. At least, what we enjoy is senses of humor. So the films are an extension in a way of how we occur together.

KT: Clearly, you and Jim Taylor spend an inordinate amount of time making sure the writing is exactly the way you want it. Is that true?
AP: We spend a lot of time writing, and when I direct, I pretty much like our dialogue recited exactly as written.

KT: No one's kind of riffing on what you wrote?
AP: No.

KT: You and Jim Taylor did not meet in an ordinary way.
AP: For us, the old days is the mid-eighties. I was in UCLA film school and he was working at what was then Cannon Films. He had gone to Pomona and went to LA to work in the film business. Later, he went to film school in the nineties. But we had a mutual friend and we met socially a couple of times. Around '89, I needed a roommate. I put out word to my friends that I needed a roommate and he showed up. He needed a place to live. And so our collaboration came from the friendship, which came from our living together.

KT: Every writing team has a different system. I wonder, in a technical sense, how you collaborate.
AP: It's hard because he lives in New York and I live in Los Angeles so we have to schedule our time together. But we always work together, in

a room at the same time. Sometimes writing teams divide and conquer. Maybe they outline the whole script and: "You take Page 1 to 60 and you take 60 to the end and we'll bring them together or rewrite each other." We don't do that. We're always together in the same room at the same time, and usually sit around and talk about what might happen next and how it might happen, because we don't outline or anything. And then one or the other of us typically will say, "Alright, let me have a crack at it," and go up and pound out two to five pages and say, "Okay, I'm ready." And then together we rewrite. We have a system which is one monitor with two keyboards. So you don't have to pass the keyboard, because we rewrite together, both there. Sometimes we do it like battleship. That's why we used to have two monitors opposing, so it would be at opposite ends of the table. But now it's one monitor. We're a little more comfortable with each other, so we sit next to each other.

KT: This is a system that works for you. Writing is not easy under any circumstances. Is it easier with another person?
AP: I'd be interested in what you have to say about this, but there's something about screenwriting which lends itself to collaboration. The only other narrative form I can think of is Broadway musicals. But you never see plays that are co-written or certainly novels that are co-written or poems, or anything. But, somehow, screenwriting—and with no detriment to a singular voice—like all the great Italian directors and Kurosawa had between two and six writers on something. Somehow it makes the solitude of the process less hideous, 'cause it's always hideous. And it's more fun, 'cause we like to hang out together. And then, since we make comedies, it's, well, what makes both of us laugh. And also, when you're writing and you think of twenty terrible ideas before you come up with that good one, and sometimes you don't even know what that good one is, so the other helps you identify. Then you get into, "Oh, yeah, yeah, yeah." Like, I'll see you and raise you. "Oh, that's a good idea. And then, what if this . . . ?" Sometimes I can't think of the exact content of what the joke should be, but I know the form of it. I'll say, "Here's the bad version of it," and he'll supply the good version, and back and forth. Somehow, it works out.

KT: As you said, you sense a single sensibility. It feels like a melded mind, in really the best way. I wanted to talk a little bit about *Citizen Ruth*. Was there something about the project that took it a long time to get made?
AP: Who's going to finance an abortion comedy?

KT: I guess not very many people.

AP: No! And it *barely* got made. My career got started with such hideously fine fibers—sinuous, I mean, my whole destiny hung on them. Finally, Harvey Weinstein financed it after he said, "No," four times, and only because of the producer Cary Woods, who had other films going on with him, said, "Please, Harvey, please, please, it's only $2.5 million dollars." "Oh, all right." My whole destiny hung on an, "Oh, all right," screamed over his shoulder out the back of a Lincoln town car in midtown Manhattan. I would have had to have waited how many more years to write something else?

KT: Why did you decide that this was a subject that was right for a funny movie? Or right for any kind of movie?

AP: I've always had the feeling that I don't really choose ideas but that somehow they choose me. Jim and I had found the inspiration for *Citizen Ruth* in an article in the *New York Times* in early '92. It was a case of an American Indian woman over in Fargo who was a recidivist inhalant abuser and had eight kids and then the Lambs of Christ got into a tug of war over her and her fetus with the gals at the local clinic. And money was offered and we just thought, "Oh, that's a comedy."

KT: And it was a comedy.

AP: Yeah, it's being made into a musical right now. We saw a read-through about two months ago in New York, and we were expecting a train wreck. They did one thing which brought it up to date nicely, which is at the end of Act One, they have the pro-lifers singing about the pro-choicers: "They're crazy. They're insane. What's going on with our country? This is terrible. They're crazy!" And then it cuts to the pro-choice people singing the same song about the pro-life people: "They're crazy. They're insane. What's wrong with our country?" And then both sides together, the whole company comes out on stage with Ruth in the middle singing: "They're crazy. They're insane." And I thought, "That's good," because that's what's going on.

KT: I remember quite clearly, the first time I saw it, *Citizen Ruth*, I didn't know anything about it. It was a film and I'm enjoying it and basically one of the pushes of it is to make fun of anti-abortion people. And yet, you're making fun of everybody that's worth making fun of. This idea that everyone is a target—I'd like to hear you talk about that a little bit.

AP: Everyone's a target [laughs]. Even those who represent points of view with which I might agree. I like the moment where they're so proud that they're going to pay for her abortion, and they want her gratitude. She's like: "Whatever." All good deeds just sort of really secretly want gratitude.

KT: I just like the fact that everything is a target—that you don't allow your personal beliefs stand in the way of . . .
AP: But that is a personal belief: that everyone is a target. A lot of critics wanted a specific political point of view expressed in the film, and accused Jim and me as writers and me as a director of being cowardly—or copping out.

KT: Is that right, really?
AP: Oh, yeah. A lot, a lot. And I don't know still what's wrong with the point of view of . . . you know, this is Terry Schiavo or Elian Gonzalez where it's two dogs fighting over a bone. And yes, you can have a point of view about it, as I have in all of those cases, but people get more motivated by their own personal agendas often than by what the thing is actually about. Not always, but often.

KT: Seeing it the second time, I loved even more Laura Dern's performance—the way she throws herself into that.
AP: And also, with respect to that, we talked about freedom of choice but what does choice mean to an animal and, essentially, she plays an animal in that—literally unequipped to choose. So what does that mean? Not that we answer it or anything, but for me, that question is interesting.

KT: Was she hard to cast? Did she get it immediately?
AP: She lobbied hard for that part. Also, there aren't a lot of great, interesting, juicy parts written for women. And one of the reasons that made this somewhat easy to cast with a lot of name people was that the whole cast is basically women and not a lot of parts come along like that—not good parts for women, not since the forties or so.

KT: But I like the way that your characters embrace extremity. They just really are what they are. They go all the way. You're smiling. That's something you really like to see happen on screen.
AP: I like extreme things.

KT: You want to say a little more about that? You don't have to.

AP: We're portraying middle America, you know, normal people. But, for me, I like emotions fairly vividly. My favorite thing is really to see my films dubbed into Italian, because the dubbers get *really* emotional and I kind of like that. I like when film is vivid in some way. And I think that *Election* and *Sideways* were both fairly faithful adaptations of books. There's a lovely thing for me in adapting a book I like; in a book, there's the moderating voice of the narrator, which keeps things within a certain band frequency. Then when you can bring about and have close-ups, and have actors go there, and have montage and music, it's like taffy. You can pull it out and have things stand in relief, which I like.

KT: A lot of your characters are not easy to like, your protagonists. You don't start off *Citizen Ruth* with, "I'm going to love this person." But by the end of the film we kind of get on their side to a certain extent and I'm fascinated by that dynamic.

AP: Well, you don't have to like them as people but you have to like them as movie characters, and, I hope, have compassion for them as people or as movie characters. When I hear that I think, well, no one in my films kills anybody. How to you feel about Alex in *A Clockwork Orange* or Michael Corleone? I don't really approve of what they do, but why do you like the movie? We love them as characters.

KT: You had Tippy Hedren and Burt Reynolds in *Citizen Ruth*. Was that fun for you? I think they're great in the film. What was the impetus to use people like that: people who have a real history?

AP: Well, it's kind of fun. It's also kind of stunt casting. I don't do that so much anymore. It was my first film. I was finding my way and trying to get financing, and every added little bit of star power helped the money keep flowing and all that. And it's cool for a first-time feature director working with people with such history. But stunt casting isn't always the best thing for the film, as a film. You see where I started in *Citizen Ruth* and where I wound up in *Sideways* so far, in my short career. Now, I'm really only about who's exactly right for the part, not about the context.

KT: I want to talk a little bit about *Election*. I wonder if there are any other reasons you like using novels. Is it correct that three of your films have come from novels?

AP: Yes, but *About Schmidt* is a little bit sui generis. It's basically an original.

KT: Aside from what you said about pulling everything out, what else is appealing about working from novels?

AP: To get a movie idea! I'm just always desperate for a movie idea. I don't really know what my next feature is right now. I have an idea but it's going to take some work. I would love for something to drop into my lap and I'd go, "Oh, this is perfect!" The nice thing about a novel is there's basically a milieu, there's an idea, a premise. And then even if Jim and I change a whole bunch of it, at least there's a reaction to something. Don't forget, eleven of thirteen of Stanley Kubrick's features were adaptations of novels. It's nice to have something to have a discourse with, even if you change a lot of it.

KT: Are there any pitfalls with novels—things that you want to make sure you don't do when you're working with a novel?

AP: For example?

KT: Oh, being too faithful to it. . . .

AP: Well, if it deserves to be faithful. The thing is, the better the novel is, the more unfaithful you have to be, in a way, because a good novel succeeds on terms exclusive to literature, and you're turning it into a film, which has to succeed in terms exclusive to film. So, often the way Jim and I work is, we read a novel two, three, four times—however much we read it—and then never look at it again, and write an original, based on our memory of the novel. Now in *Sideways*, because it was very much lived by that writer, Rex Pickett, and his sense of dialogue was so unique, we'd refer to it: "What did Rex do, what did he say that was so good here?" and we'd look and use that. But, basically, it's just what I said: it's writing an original based on our memory of the novel, and we'd never get involved with a novel that's so popular that the readers are expecting . . . and then you come up with some piece of crap (I never saw it), like the first *Harry Potter* film, which, although wildly popular, as a film is like a filmed book on tape, because of the exigencies of the writer, who has it in his or her contract to be involved with it, the expectations of the fan base and the nervousness of the studio. I couldn't work like that.

KT: With *Election*, I think one of the things you like to do is use non-professional and professional actors—you kind of mix them.

AP: And sometimes non-actors, like the Dairy Queen girl in *About Schmidt*. She works at that Dairy Queen.

KT: Why do you enjoy doing that?
AP: Because it's fun.

KT: Are you worried it might backfire?
AP: It doesn't. Every once in a while . . . but it's worth the risk. I just think if you have a day player, someone who's just there for one line or two, and it's a doctor or a Dairy Queen gal or something, why bring in an actor to learn what it's like to make a Blizzard? "How do you do this?" Hire someone who works there! You can do it when you hire people who are playing some version of themselves. Real cops play cops, real doctors play doctors, and you don't need any technical advisors—they're right there. And also, I think in my films, it's nice to have huge movie stars with non-actors because it makes the non-actors look as though they're acting better than they really are and it makes the stars seem realer than they're capable of being.

KT: Do the stars enjoy it? Do the stars feel that it's okay? Do you ever ask them?
AP: I don't ask.

KT: Do they ever complain?
AP: [*long pause*] No. The only one who almost complained was the guy who's screwing Laura Dern at the beginning of *Citizen Ruth* and later yells at her. He really is that guy. . . . I mean not that he really was screwing Laura Dern, but he didn't have his teeth at the time and we found him in a bar and he has this intimate scene. So, fearing some trouble, and Laura Dern was like, "Now who's this guy that you've cast?" I came up to each of them before we shot. I came to the guy and I said, "Look, Laura's really nervous. You're going to have to help me out." And I went up to Laura and said, "Now, Lance is really nervous, so you're really going to have to help me out." So it worked.

KT: It's a great scene. And you discovered Chris Klein in *Election*, who's had a career, who's a wonderful actor. Did you know immediately that he was going to be good?
AP: Not that he would be good but I knew I was interested in him. I toured all high schools in Omaha, looking for the right high school in which to shoot. And I was touring Millard West High School, and the proud principal was showing me around. Chris Klein walked out of a

weight room as we were walking through that wing, and he said, "Oh, look, there's Chris Klein. He was marvelous in *West Side Story*." They'd just done *West Side Story* and he'd played Tony. And I just met this guy and thought, "Wow." Good looking kid, and something about him, and I was living with those characters. And then I went back to L.A. and read about thirty or forty guys and didn't like any of them. I didn't believe they were in high school. Then I went back to Omaha and called up the school office and said, "I'm the guy who's making that film, and I met a guy. The principal introduced me to him." And then she called the Klein household and then Chris Klein called me. I said, "I really am a movie guy. Would you come into the Omaha Film Commission office and audition?" And he did. And the lesbian gal, his sister, I cast off a tape from St. Louis. I hadn't met her before the first day of shooting.

KT: I had read that, originally, *Election* had a different ending that had been changed. Can you talk about that process?
AP: We wrote the ending of the film that was in the book and then as we were testing the film, previewing it, it just wasn't playing well and then even I wasn't happy with it. Basically, the problem is, the book is very melancholy and somewhat funny and then allows for this melancholy ending. The movie came out very funny with a little melancholy and then delivering us to a melancholy ending, and it felt totally inconsistent. And a lot of the humor had actually come from the editing, because *Election* is a highly montage-heavy film. So Jim and I, with the blessing of the studio, went to work on something that we might have written, had it been an original. We came up with that ending and the studio spent an extra six or seven hundred grand to let us do it, and that's it.

KT: So the whole scene in Washington is all yours? It's not from the book?
AP: Yes.

KT: It works great. You'd never know that it wasn't planned that way from the beginning. Speaking of the studio, I think every critic in America was frustrated about *Election* because the studio didn't seem to know what to do with it, didn't seem to know how to sell it. It was, and remains, an extremely funny film and you can feel that the studio was looking at it and saying, what do we do? I'm assuming this is very frustrating for you. Can you talk about that a little bit?
AP: They never got high school movie and MTV Films out of their brain,

as far as what it was when, in fact, I never saw it as a high school movie. I couldn't have been less interested in making a high school movie. I didn't even read the book for about five months because I thought, "Oh, it's set in a high school. I don't care about that." And MTV Films just happened to be the producing entity and, at the time, that was Paramount Studio who was, in those years, like GM. It's like put the star's face on the poster. Just like how GM, you know, it's the new sedan, show it in the desert and call it a day. And it needed marketing more like what Fox Searchlight just did with *Sideways* which is a little bit more like you're marketing the Mini. You're not marketing a Chrysler. And so a little bit more care and find the niche audiences that you want to find. And then maybe allow the director to have some input on the marketing. Maybe.

KT: It's interesting that they think they know so much and they don't.
AP: The two times that they pushed me out of the marketing meetings are the two films which have performed the worst. I'm not saying *post hoc ergo propter hoc*, but I tell marketing departments, "You know, I'm paid a lot of money for my ideas. I'm an idea guy. That's all I do. I'm giving you my ideas for free. Take 'em or leave 'em." And it's really to their benefit. Fox Searchlight was so good that they actually started driving me crazy in terms of consulting with me too much. It was like, "Leave me alone. You guys figure it out."

KT: I guess you just have to shrug. Finally, you can't be driven crazy. Or *can* you be driven crazy about what happened to *Election*? Does it take you a while to get it out of your system?
AP: No. Because I'm not going to fall into that thing of, "My film is so good, and just the marketing screwed it up." I'll think, "Oh, the film must have been bad." I think it's too arrogant to say, "It's their fault." But it was. But it's also where I was in my career at the time. It's fine. I'm just happy I get it made. I'm just happy I get to be a filmmaker and get them made. I'm happy we live in a century when the cinema even exists.

KT: I've read that in various of your films that studios try to foist people on you and make you talk to people like Tom Hanks and people like that.
AP: Not anymore.

KT: Did it happen on *Sideways* or did it not?
AP: No. On *Election* it happened a lot. Again, if there are any film students or potential directors in the audience, don't make studio deals

because then they make you go meet or offer it first to all the big actors, whom you don't want and who never, in a million years, are going to do it. "Oh, but you never know. You've got to find out." All they care about is the most famous possible people at any given time, regardless of the correctness for the part. And it's a big time suck. Months go by. Cumulatively, it takes two, three, four films off your life.

KT: Are there any people you remember specifically that you had to meet for *Election*?
AP: No, because they weren't interested. It's like Tom Cruise, Matthew McConaughey types. Tom Hanks would have been okay. He's good.

KT: Talk about the importance of music in what you do.
AP: It's huge. We were just at the Cannes Film Festival. I was on the jury for *Un Certain Regard*. I can't tell you how many of those movies didn't have music in them. It doesn't make you feel good to watch a movie without music. Even in the silent period, image and music have a magical relationship.

KT: It seems like the critics always focus on the dialogue and the writing, but I started to think we should pay more attention to the music in your films.
AP: Well, as writing-and-dialogue-heavy as my films are, there's a degree to which a part of me is making silent films. I'm really just interested in images and telling a story *without* the use of words. I hope that you could judge my films even without the dialogue, in the way that they used to judge Warner Bros. cartoons, which is: can you turn the sound down and still utterly follow the story? I still try to do that with my films. Not in the way that, if you don't buy the headphones on the airplane, you can tell, only because you've seen that movie one hundred million times before in your life. But in a good way, that you could still tell what's going on.

KT: Rolfe Kent scored almost every one of your films, I think.
AP: Yes, all of my features. I like melody, and I don't find too many current composers have a gift for melody. I'm a big fan of Italian composers from the fifties and sixties: Nino Rota, Ennio Morricone, Piero Umiliani. And the French ones: Georges Delerue and Francis Lai. My favorite opera is *Carmen*. I like things where I can hum melodies later. I don't like just atmospheric tones and sounds and rhythms. I like melody. And Rolfe, I found early on, has a gift for melody, and I always encourage him in that

way. He also has a wit about his music which I also appreciated in the Italians. *Sideways* is a fairly showy jazz score and it's upfront but I recommend the *About Schmidt* score as a CD. It's surprisingly good, I think.

KT: Do you say anything to the composer or do you show him the scene and say, "Just do something"?
AP: Show him the movie. I have some ideas. In *About Schmidt*, when we cut to Kathy Bates and she's eating the pork chop and sucking her fingers, suddenly we hear the erhu, which is the Chinese upright violin. We had conceived of Denver as China, somehow (it's just what you get into, however arcane it is), and she is the dowager queen. So in the film, basically, whenever you see her, you hear erhu.

KT: Directors, when they can, like to use as much of the same team as possible on their films.
AP: Some do.

KT: What are the virtues of that?
AP: Shorthand. Like, I can talk to Jane Stewart, my production designer, whom I go back with not just to *Citizen Ruth* but even to films that we made for the Playboy Channel. I go back the farthest with Jim Taylor, Jane Stewart, and Rolfe, because we did a series for the Playboy Channel in 1991 together. Rolfe and Jane were the staff composer and production designer, respectively, and I met them there and I was just knocked out by them and have worked with them going on fifteen years. It's so nice to say to Jane, "Oh, yeah, remember that thing?" We don't have to break each other in to anything—the sensibility. Actually, you're asking about collaboration, which has become for me the most enjoyable and best part of filmmaking: collaborating with my department heads. It's all due to the quality of questions that you ask each other. I'm not like Zeus and the film is Athena that springs fully formed from my brain. It isn't like that at all. You listen to one another, you and your creative department heads. It's about the quality of questions you ask each other.

KT: I want to talk a little bit about *About Schmidt*. You mentioned the original script you did earlier, called *The Coward*. Can you talk about how the book and *The Coward* came together to become the film?
AP: When I was in film school, I was imagining that my first feature film would take place in Omaha and would be about this Greek guy from Omaha who retires from an insurance company. I was somewhat

influenced by Kurosawa's *Ikiru* and Bergman's *Wild Strawberries*, and even *The Graduate*, in terms of someone who reaches a milestone event, like graduation or retirement. And rather than feeling accomplishment, feels nothing but alienation and loneliness. I always liked that about *The Graduate*. Basically, the first half of *About Schmidt* is what I wrote alone about ten years ago. And the second half of it, I hadn't really figured out. When we were commissioned to adapt the novel *About Schmidt*—it's a very good book but what was connecting me to the theme of retirement was really what I had already written, and Jim agreed. So we solved narrative problems together, which I had not alone solved ten years previously, using some narrative threads from the book. To wit: that he has a daughter who's about to be married, who has an overbearing future stepmother, that she's going to marry a boob, that the wife dies and he's widowed during the course of the film. Even those elements are enough to make a movie out of.

KT: Working with an actor like Jack Nicholson, you have an extremely gifted actor and a large reputation. Is it at all daunting to work with someone like that or can you not even allow yourself to think that way?
AP: By the time we were shooting, I'd already known him for ten months. It was daunting the very first time I went to meet him. As Jane, my production designer, would say, "Just remember: he might be filet but he's still a piece of meat." And he made it easy for me. He is aware that he's Jack Nicholson and he makes efforts to disarm you and be cool and professional. He was great to work with. My experience is the better they are, the bigger they are, the easier they are because they can do it. The hardest thing is when you have someone who freezes or can't remember his dialogue.

KT: Did anything surprise you about working with him that you hadn't expected?
AP: Well, extending from what I just said, how easy it was. We were always very respectful of him. I mean, he's an older gentleman, working with me on my film and he's great at it. But we didn't have a huge budget with which to make the film. His salary was about half the budget. The rest was basically the same budget realm as *Sideways*, which means I can't allow too much experimenting on the set. I have to make all my days and I have to kind of pre-imagine and impose the blocking, to a certain degree. I'm pretty loose with that. But I remember the first couple of days telling Jack Nicholson, "Okay, Mr. Nicholson, you're going to come

in and walk to here, then I'm going to cut, then we'll make a close-up and then we'll reset the camera over here and you'll walk here," laying out the scene. And I said, "Is that okay?" And he said, "Look, anything you come up with, I can find a way to justify it to myself, so what do you need?" The exact opposite of what you hear about in the movies: "My character would never do that . . . and what's my motivation." None of that at all, ever. It was almost like, "Yeah, anything you come up with, I'll find a way to make it work." He's a total pro, and don't forget, he worked for a million years with Roger Corman, so he understands all that and refers to those years more consistently than he does to his more famous films since. Maybe he's just making me feel good.

KT: One of the things that I really love about *About Schmidt* that you use a lot in your films and that sometimes people frown on is a lot of voiceover.
AP: Oh, I love voiceover.

KT: Talk about why you like voiceover.
AP: Oh, I love voiceover. I think, along with music, it's one of the greatest contributions of talking cinema. The novel still has it all over the movies in so many ways. I mean, I love a great movie but, in a way, there's nothing better than a great novel in terms of really capturing the complex fabric of life and thoughts and just the richness of character. A novel can go this way and that but a narrative movie is fairly analog. It has to proceed in a certain way, and anything that goes too far this way or that tends to fall off the edges and tends to simplify character and that's frustrating to me, because I want to get real people. So it's nice to be able to have voiceover as an added element, but it's been much maligned because it's been badly used. Yet, when well used, it's extraordinary, like in Kubrick films and Wilder films and Malick films. Also, since we make comedies, the use of voiceover is often largely ironic, unreliable narrators.

KT: Even though everyone thinks of your films as very verbal, there's this physical comedy element that's very prominent.
AP: It's really all I'm interested in. You learn from Chaplin and from Fred Astaire movies to show comedy full frame, not cut up. Lloyd is much more montage-based. So there's no cutting in *About Schmidt*'s waterbed scene. I wanted it only performance.

KT: Do actors get this?
AP: A lot of it's in the script. In *Election* when Reese Witherspoon's character is hopping, the verb in the script is she "pogo sticks" up and down. It was pre-imagined that she would do that. When she's jumping up and down, there is a piece of voiceover written and recorded for that spot but I so liked just watching her that I got rid of it.

KT: I want to talk about *Sideways*. You saw a lot more potential in that novel than I would have seen. This is a novel that, as we know, had trouble getting published. What did you guys see in it?
AP: I guess we just saw a movie in it that you might not have seen. And I'm happy about that, by the way, because there's competition for the good novels sometimes and I'm happy that I got something that no one saw. I have to say the same thing about *Election*. *Election*, when it reached Jim and me, was similarly unpublished and had made the rounds with filmmakers and no one bit.

KT: Can you put your finger on what you see in these things?
AP: That it corresponds to real life and is relatively free of contrivance, other than the contrivance of the idea of the piece: four characters telling their points of view around a weird high school election, or two old friends go on a road trip through wine country the week before one of them is to be married. It's a premise. I want to distinguish premise from contrivance. And that they're really real and contain sadness and humor: that they're somewhat lifelike.

KT: For an independent film, you had a fairly leisurely shoot on *Sideways*. It was fifty days or something?
AP: Yeah, but all my films are about fifty. Even *Citizen Ruth* was, I think, forty-two days and the last three have all been about fifty days.

KT: What are the benefits of not having to go crazy?
AP: You still have to go crazy. It's still short, but it's about right. You need to have time to play with the actors, and the actors shouldn't have to feel rushed. It's so nice to have time. You need time to write, you need time to edit, you need time to work, so that everything isn't just lighting and then hurriedly cram the performances in and just have them say the words in the right order. Especially since my films are so performance based. It really is the writing and performance. The camera could be a little bit this way or that way, and it wouldn't make that much

difference. But it's writing and performance, because it's all about the tone. The actors have to be appropriate vessels for the tone that Jim and I have conceived.

KT: Was *Sideways* hard to cast?
AP: No, the whole thing was pretty easy—surprisingly so. It became so easy and calamity-free that I even stopped fearing saying so, out of fear of jinxing it. The whole thing: casting, getting it financed, surprisingly, was easy. It was the first time in my career where I could get financing without having to have a star.

KT: Was that all because of the success of the previous three?
AP: Yes. And god bless Fox Searchlight, the studio, that they gambled on me and won.

KT: Nobody tried to make you change the cast?
AP: Other studios did, and we didn't go with them.

KT: Who did they want?
AP: Good actors. I don't want to say these are stupid choices or anything. Like one studio wanted Will Ferrell to play Miles, and I love Will Ferrell. He's great but he's not Paul Giamatti for that part.

KT: Fox let you go with him.
AP: Didn't say "boo." Didn't say anything.

KT: These kind of character movies are so wonderful. Are there other people? Do you feel alone out there sometimes, making these kinds of movies? The ones that are so involved with character—that try and be real, to have that kind of tang of reality. Do you feel alone among directors? It's not like there are a lot of films.
AP: You have to say American films, because European films are still doing it. There are some younger directors who are trying to do it: David Russell, the gang that I get lumped in with. I'm forty-four so there's a bunch of us between thirty-five and forty-five who, like me, were all weaned on seventies films and the idea of personal cinema, as opposed to corporate cinema.

KT: One of my favorite scenes in *Sideways* that most people hate is when he steals money from his mother. I really love that scene because, for me, it says, "This is not a great guy. Don't make any mistakes; don't think this is a movie where he's really a great guy."

AP: He could still be a great guy and still steal money from his mother. He's not killing anybody. Most other movies, they're killing people. Its, "Oh, I like Schwarzenegger in that film, yeah."

KT: But have you taken grief about that money-stealing scene?

AP: Yeah, and I don't get it. All he's doing is stealing a few bills from his mother. What's the big deal? Each of us does things that are reprehensible in some way, at some point or another in our lives. What is it . . . the mote in your neighbor's eye when you have a beam in your own. I mean, c'mon.

KT: One of my favorite film books is Elia Kazan's autobiography, and he talks in it about the "I coulda been a contender" scene from *On the Waterfront*. And Kazan says in his book, "Whenever I'm watching TV and that scene comes on, I say, 'I hate that scene.' I've seen that scene so often, I can't believe they're showing it again." And he watches the scene and when it ends, he says, "You know, that's a really good scene." Do you have those kinds of feelings?

AP: You never know exactly what people are going to like. You never know what's going to be a key scene. Sometimes when you're too precious, directing something like, "Alright, everyone quiet. We're filming the end of the movie now." It doesn't work. You have to keep it really workaday.

KT: It's a spectacular cast. Did you feel that going in?

AP: I was confident with that cast, because I won't claim to have many talents within filmmaking, but I think I'm good at casting. And the old cliché: 90 percent of directing is casting. You just cast right and then you don't have to work as hard. They do it.

KT: One of the things I read is that you were interested in doing a western.

AP: Oh, yeah. I love westerns. We were talking about Anthony Mann backstage, my favorite western director.

KT: Is that still in the back of your mind?

AP: It is. But the story's got to be right. Because in the last twenty-five years, we've really only had one good western, which is *Unforgiven*. So it's a bit moribund. Two things: one is you have to return to primary sources and not make a Xerox of all the other westerns, because no one wants to see that. And the other thing is in what way can it be pertinent to our times. So I think you have to approach a western nowadays like *Little Big Man* or *McCabe and Mrs. Miller*. What would they be now? And like *McCabe and Mrs. Miller*, with a genuine ring of authenticity.

KT: This is a quote, possibly spurious, from you: "I think films have to have a little danger."
AP: Oh, yeah.

KT: There are things in your films where you really use raunchy language. There's a great full frontal male nudity scene in *Sideways*. You seem to like to make audiences sit up a little bit.
AP: You achieve that, I think, only through restraint. My problem with Farrelly brothers films is that's all there is and it loses meaning. But if you have a long time in the film which doesn't have . . . so *Election* starts off twenty minutes in with the line about having sex with Tracy. *Citizen Ruth* climaxes, if you will, with that line where the mother says, "Well, what if I had aborted you," and she responds with a very sordid line. And then guys in *Sideways*.

KT: Which comes out of nowhere.
AP: But then it has impact! Impact comes through restraint. Things have to be in relief.

KT: Will the success of *Sideways* make making your kinds of films easier? Is there all kinds of stuff that gets thrown at you that doesn't interest you?
AP: I still remain very inner-directed. I can't force myself to like something I don't like. I actually want to catch my breath a little bit. The whole *Sideways* tsunami, the success of it, was something I've had to deal with and adjust the way I live a little bit, and I don't want it to interfere with my filmmaking and with what I want to make next. But, the great thing about the success of *Sideways* is I'm going to get the opportunity to make things—or thing—which otherwise would be very difficult to get made, and I'm thinking both in terms of content and form. I think, increasingly, about film form and film language. As much as you can talk about what the content of American films need, content is form and form is content. So you have to talk about film language. The thing about seventies film is there was a constant influx of new film language and we really

need that now. Screenwriting books and corporate filmmaking, which seeks to have movies (I'm quoting myself) as readily consumed as McDonald's hamburgers, seeks only uniformity. It's death in terms of form. Who knows what I'll come up with but this is, at least, what I'm aspiring to tonight.

Alexander Payne Talks *The Descendants*, Clooney, Next Black and White Film, New Trailer

Anne Thompson / 2011

From Indiewire.com, October 18, 2011. Reprinted by permission of the interviewer.

Of all the fall movies, the one that hit me in the solar plexus, made me laugh and cry, and struck me as a likely Oscar contender in multiple categories, was heartfelt low-budget comedy *The Descendants*, Alexander Payne's return to the screen, after winning best original screenplay (with Jim Taylor) for 2004's *Sideways*. "Alexander should make more movies," George Clooney told me at Telluride. Of course he should, but this is the one Payne was able to get made. And it was worth the wait.

In Telluride, I interviewed the laconic writer-director as we walked from one theater to another. He'd rather watch movies than talk about them, and convinced me to check out Serge Bromberg's night of rare silent films, including a wonderful rare Buster Keaton short and George Melies's magically restored *Trip to the Moon*. Payne and I had never talked at any length before; he's a funny, thoughtful, intense writer/observer who is confident yet diffident, clearly comes from Nebraska (he splits his time between Omaha and Los Angeles), yet maneuvers to get movies made as a director/achiever in Hollywood. He doesn't give it up easily.

One thing Payne was willing to admit at *The Descendants* Q & A: "I cast well." Clooney is perfect in the role of the hapless Matt King, a sad sack real estate lawyer and leading member of the landed gentry in Hawaii who is dealing with his comatose wife and his two lively daughters. He considers himself "the back-up parent, the understudy."

Many characters in this story are hiding deep emotion. In one scene, lovely teen Shailene Woodley reacts to news of her mother's worsening condition by silently losing it underwater in a pool, away from her father's gaze. Payne often opts for restraint when others would overplay a big moment by hitting it on the head. I cried frequently in this movie. You care for these people, who get to say great lines like, "Paradise can go fuck itself."

The slapstick moments often come out of left field or at moments of intense feeling, as when King, learning he has been cuckolded, flaps down the street in flats to glean details from a neighbor. "Why do all the women in my life want to destroy themselves?" asks King, who at one point turns to his daughter's callow young boyfriend for advice.

Robert Forster as King's father-in-law is an old prick who still hits us hard with his abiding love for his daughter. The movie recalls James L. Brooks' *Terms of Endearment*, with its hairpin turns from comedy to tragedy. Neither Payne nor Clooney have children, yet this film, adapted by Payne (Nat Faxon and Jim Rash wrote an early draft) from the novel by Kaui Hart Hemmings, rings true, as do the various Hawaii island settings—"all alone, part of some archipelago drifting apart."

Anne Thompson: You wound up adapting a book—when you were writing something else original that was more difficult to get funded.
Alexander Payne: Jim Taylor and I worked for two and a half years on a script, a film which hasn't been made yet. It's kind of a large canvas, science-fiction social satire.

Thompson: Expensive?
Payne: Yeah. Yeah, yeah. We finally finished it around May or June of '09, and it looked like we had grim prospects to get financing for it. Around that same time *The Descendants*, another director was going to do that, and he fell out. So somehow the gods were telling me, "Why don't you do it?" Because my little company had optioned it for the previous two years and I had not expressed interest in doing it because Jim and I were writing this epic masterpiece. So we hired two other writers, who are the two guys credited. But when I decided to do it, I didn't overhaul it—I started from scratch. I did my own. And then of course the way the Writers' Guild works in Hollywood, they adjudicate it and things are often in favor of people who did previous drafts, even if not used, so we all got credit. So I wrote it between July and October of '09.

Thompson: So is it your hope now that you will get this other epic movie, *Downsizing*, made?

Payne: That's still going to be a couple years away. I'm so anxious to just shoot movies now, just regular human old films, I want to do about two more before I enter that time suck of pre-visualization and visual effects and all that kind of stuff. I just want to shoot.

Thompson: Do you know what you're going to do next?
Payne: Yep. Next is a film for Paramount, and it's tentatively called *Nebraska*, but that title may change. It'll be the first thing I direct (it's too obvious), that I have not written. It's written by a guy out of Snohomish, Washington, and it's a father/son road trip from Billings, Montana, to Lincoln, Nebraska, that gets waylaid at a crappy town in central Nebraska where the father grew up, and where he has scores to settle.

Thompson: And modestly budgeted?
Payne: Especially because I want to shoot it in black and white.

Thompson: Have they said OK to that? If you do it for a price, is that their deal with you?
Payne: For a price. But it'll be black and white for theatrical, DVD, and streaming. If they need a color version for their TV output deals, they will have it.

Thompson: That's great. Did you see *The Artist*?
Payne: I did. I couldn't wait to see it! I stayed after my first screening of *The Descendants* to see it. So that's another new film I saw, and enjoyed it immensely.

Thompson: Is writing a painful thing for you? You're awfully good at it.
Payne: Yeah, but it's getting better. Thank you. It's always painful but it's getting a little less so.

Thompson: You've been with Fox Searchlight a long time, they're backing you. This wasn't hard to sell to them?
Payne: Well, they wanted me to do it. When they read it, because they helped my little company option it, they said, "Why doesn't Alexander do it?" Well, because he's busy writing his epic masterpiece. So I'm so lucky, and I'm not just saying that. Because I couldn't care less about needing to say nice words about the studio for some political reason. I really feel I'm so grateful to them for the opportunity to make a film such as this today. And with great support. The whole budget I needed. For George Clooney wanting to be in it.

Thompson: So George. He gives one of the best performances he's ever given in this. He managed to navigate the shoals of deep emotion and slapstick comedy, and sometimes in the same scene. Was there one scene that was more difficult than any other, along those lines?
Payne: It's all easy and it's all hard.

Thompson: I'm a parent; the relationship between the father and kids in *The Descendants* rang true. Do you credit the original source material for that? Or your own observational abilities? It feels authentic.
Payne: Good! Yeah, and everyone involved has lent an eye that it's happening correctly. And the actors. But if I were to credit any real co-writer on this, it would be Kaui, because I was very faithful to the book. I felt, not just because of the parental concerns but the whole Hawaii aspect of the film, it's not my world. I was entering as kind of a documentarian. So I had to rely on her because not just Hawaii in general, but that class, that corner of Hawaii, this kind of largely, but not entirely, white upper-class, who are somehow involved with the branch of the eight or ten families who have kind of controlled Hawaii for 180 years.

Thompson: So when you developed this material, you must have seen different threads that you could play with. But there was also a challenge: you don't fall into the sentimental abyss, and you don't seem to be preaching to some environmental choir. What were those hazards?
Payne: Well, you just said them. You want emotion without sentimentality in your films, and no pamphleteering.

Thompson: But you're timely. You're addressing something that still matters. And we're all dealing with families, estate and inheritance issues. . . .
Payne: Yeah, and these are issues going on every day, so it's not a dated issue. The link between the two stories I saw more as an emotional one for the lead guy. He just witnessed one death, and he doesn't want to be a part of another.

Thompson: And yet with all the deep emotion you found great comedic opportunity with Clooney, who makes you care about him—as he's being a complete schlub. What was your challenge with this character?
Payne: I don't think about it at all! It's what the story is, who the guy is, he's got to be believable.

Thompson: Well, there are moments where you're putting him in flats and he's running around looking like an idiot.
Payne: Yeah, well, that's my weakness for visual humor. It is! I just thought, "Oh that would be funny." In the script it was this: "Matt runs down the street." That's all it was in the script. But I wanted to invent a little comic sequence out of it. I didn't think, "Oh this will make him a schlub and more likable." I just thought, "That's funny."

Thompson: And you said that you were good at casting: where did you find the kid (Nick Krause) who plays Shailene Woodley's boyfriend?
Payne: He lobbed a taped audition to our office from Austin, Texas. His mom is a casting director, she heard it about it, went home and told him, he put himself on tape. We (meaning my casting director and I) follow every single lead that comes to our casting office—we'll watch anything—and we found him and said, "Please." We were doing some casting in New York, his mom flew him to New York, he auditioned, that was it.

Thompson: Some moments are intense and emotional, as when the kid reveals—and you play with our expectations as he evolves as a character—that his own father died. Matt King reacts, says nothing, just silently walks away.
Payne: For me there's more than nothing. For me, he sees what the audience sees. "Alright, there's more to this kid than I thought." He's not going to go put his arm around the kid. But he says, "He wasn't putting me on, and I get it why Alex wanted him," and all that stuff. That's why we saved the close-up on George.

Thompson: That's what they're for. It's not all about talking, is it?
Payne: Cinema avoids dialogue. Theater laps up dialogue like a kitten with warm milk. So even though it's still a talking film, you want pictures, not words, as much as possible.

Thompson: And you want actors' reactions?
Payne: Yeah. An actors' face can say. . . . It's not anything that hasn't been said for decades.

Thompson: Terrence Malick, at the end of every scene, he shoots a silent version. And Gus Van Sant has adopted this as well.
Payne: Oh, I didn't know that.

Thompson: Are there significant differences between the book and the movie—a question of tone or some change you made?
Payne: There's a lot more in the book to do with the younger daughter. And I just wasn't as interested in her. You have to do some selection for an adaptation, and I opted to do a lot more with the older daughter because I was a lot more interested in that story.

Thompson: Woodley was terrific, where did she come from?
Payne: Well, I know it. She auditioned. And she is on *The Secret Life of the American Teenager*, fairly popular with teenage girls. ABC Family TV show. So she has chops but still reads like an actual honest-to-God kid. A lot of people you audition who have chops are too polished. And a lot of people who aren't polished at all don't have the chops. So thank God I found her. And she's the only one—there was no also-ran.

Thompson: And when did you come up with the idea of having her emote under water?
Payne: It's in the screenplay. I don't think I'd ever seen that in a movie before. I wanted to see how that would play.

Thompson: Now, you're often showing us emotions that characters are trying to hide.
Payne: Like her and the father-in-law.

Thompson: Right. He's a tough bastard, a prick, and then he's incredibly loving, and that breaks your heart, that scene when he says goodbye to his daughter. With Forster, you did some unexpected things, like clocking the kid, to shock us out of our seats.
Payne: Yeah, that's in the book. He's definitely the most heartbreaking character for me in the whole film. The prick who's in such pain, that guy. Ex-military guy.

Thompson: How many takes would you go for on any given scene, usually?
Payne: I'm a three-to-six kind of guy.

Thompson: Let's go back to the period where you were putting this follow-up to *Sideways* together. What's making it so hard for people to do the movies they want to do, what are the constraints?
Payne: I had dinner about a year ago with a venerable older director

and his wife. And I told them what sort of film I was making, and they said, "You're so lucky to be making a drama right now." Hollywood is not making dramas. It's a genre which has fallen out of fashion, at least as far as the financiers/studios are considered. So, empirically, I don't know. I'll see what comes out this fall to verify if what they say is really true.

Thompson: So you consider this to be a drama. It is, even if it is funny.
Payne: Yeah, I guess so. On PBS Sunday morning there was a lead story about four months ago—and not just one of the stories buried in the midst of the ninety minutes, but it was the lead story—about the disappearance of the tearjerker, that we used to say, "Oh you should go see this movie and have a good cry," and how much the country enjoyed *Terms of Endearment* and *Kramer vs. Kramer*. And I never saw it, but *Beaches* is apparently something of a tearjerker. And I was just finishing editing when I saw it—we were mixing—and I thought, "Huh, I wonder if this film might somehow satisfy a part of that hunger." For an adult drama this does have a bit of emotionality. Not sentimentality, but emotionality at the end. And so I'm very curious to see if that happens. And if it does satisfy that hunger to some degree, I'll be very happy.

Thompson: That's what happens. And that's why *The Help* is doing so well. There's so little of that kind of filmmaking around, so few movies are feeding the hunger for women's material.
Payne: Or adult material.

Thompson: Or what you're talking about: emotions, real people dealing with trials. We all have parents, we all have to deal with death at some time or another.
Payne: During the year, there are very few modern American films that I go to see. I watch old films. I go to the cinema, but I would say one out of five films I see are old.

Thompson: Which films do you admire that hold up really well? You're watching Netflix?
Payne: Netflix and TCM. Good stories! It's hard for me to pin just one or a director, because there are thousands and thousands of great films.

Thompson: You're watching this stuff because you want to learn something? Or you want to enjoy what's good? Because you have nothing to learn from the bad stuff that's made now?

Payne: I put on a film when my Mom was over. She was recovering from surgery in May and she was living in my apartment in Omaha because there were no stairs. So each day at 4 P.M., we'd watch a movie together. And one day I put on a movie, a modern film which had been nominated recently for an Academy Award for Best Foreign Film. I thought she'd like it. We got ten minutes into it, she turned to me and said, "I don't find this interesting." I said what I often say to myself: "Alright, let's put on a real movie." So we put on Jules Dassin's *Thieves' Highway* and just had a great afternoon.

Thompson: The one I watched recently, just to treat myself, was *Now Voyager*. Incredible. Because they were making movies for adults back then.

Payne: Oh yeah. Fantastic. But I often say to myself, "I'll try to watch something modern," and then I'll say, "Okay, I have to watch a real movie now," and put on some great old Hollywood—like a good film noir from the fifties. I've got to watch a real movie.

Thompson: And you made a real movie. Do you ever test? Do you show it to people?
Payne: Yeah, but not finished. That's done while it's a work in progress.

Thompson: So you do that to see where the laughs are?
Payne: Oh yeah. I love screening. After I have a first cut about fourteen weeks in, I screen constantly. We only had two of the studio-financed, official card preview screenings, but I'm always screening for different groups of friends. It's the only way to be able to get a grip, to take a step back and then go back in with a magnifying glass in the eye.

Alexander Payne on *The Descendants* and Why It's a Minor Work

Eric Kohn / 2011

From Indiewire.com, October 24, 2011. Reprinted by permission of Eric Kohn, head film critic and senior editor, Indiewire, and Dana Harris, editor in chief, Indiewire.

Alexander Payne is in a good mood, or at least a little more chipper than usual. If the consensus means anything, the man behind such noted black comedies as *Election* and *About Schmidt* has yet to break his winning streak. Seven years have passed since his last feature, *Sideways*, and now he's back with another acclaimed work: *The Descendants*, an adaptation of Kaui Hart Hemmings's novel. Star George Clooney joins a roster of A-listers, including Reese Witherspoon and Jack Nicholson, who have been attracted to Payne's caustic and emotionally complex style. No one has been let down yet.

The new movie finds Clooney playing a wealthy Hawaiian landowner coping with his comatose wife's dying moments. He's also committed to gathering evidence about her affair with a mysterious real estate broker (Matthew Lillard). At the same time, he has to keep his feisty adolescent daughter (Amara Miller) at bay and face off with her rebellious older sister (Shailene Woodley).

Sentimental yet twisted, *The Descendants* is vintage Payne. The film has been a major crowd pleaser at the Telluride, Toronto, and New York Film Festivals, setting the stage for Fox Searchlight's release next month. But over the course of a recent conversation with Indiewire in New York, Payne reined in his enthusiasm, talked about some of his favorite movies, his love for *The Wire* and why he's already set the bar higher.

Eric Kohn: You haven't made a feature since *Sideways* in 2004. Is it annoying to get back into the game of promoting your work?

Alexander Payne: Yeah, but it's still pretty early in the process. It's only shown at three festivals. I've been present at fewer than ten screenings. Telluride was the first time I saw it finished with a fresh audience.

Kohn: You're often asked about the challenge of writing pitiable characters. Do you feel like you have to justify the kinds of movies you write?
Payne: I'm completely uninterested in justifying it. The justifications are the films themselves. I'm a practitioner; I just like doing it. Do I like answering the same questions over and over again? Two answers to that: One is, "No," and the other is, "Depends on who's asking." If it's somebody asking a super-standard question that he or she could have found on a hundred online sources, then I may grow quite impatient.

Kohn: At the Toronto International Film Festival premiere, you looked a little flustered when Toronto International Film Festival programming director Cameron Bailey said that none of your movies have heroes.
Payne: Right.

Kohn: But that seemed like a natural question to ask of someone who has made these kinds of dark comedies. Are you saying that if someone can figure that out without your help, it's not worth your time?
Payne: No, it's not that it's not worth my time. I'm always grateful for the interest in my work. I'm super-grateful for having an audience and having that communication with them. I'm not ungrateful on any level. It just depends on who's asking. These are kind of pretentious things to cite, but I remember Antonioni saying, "Don't you know that anything I tell you about the film may limit rather than enhance your experience?" You want the viewer to have his or her own interpretation. Look, I'm a film geek and I like reading interviews with directors. I'm mad that Anthony Mann didn't do more interviews. I think that there's only one interview with Henry Hathaway extant. So you look for clues into their work.

Kohn: Going back to the absence of heroes in your movies . . .
Payne: See, it takes a second for me to catch up to that, because I'm not thinking about those things. I'm just working intuitively.

Kohn: But you realize where that question is coming from.
Payne: Yeah, I just get caught off-guard by it. Actually, that's why I look

to critics and good film writers for clues to how I work, which I hope won't hinder my creative process but might help articulate something I'm doing, or something that I could do better. This thing that Cameron asked, in his lovely way, about flawed protagonists—that nonplussed me, in a way. As a film viewer and a reader, I wonder: What is Oedipus? What is Michael Corleone? What is Alex in *A Clockwork Orange*? What is a protagonist? What is the guy in *Sunset Boulevard*? He pimps himself out! Isn't good narrative about people bumping up against their limitations, flaws, hubris, delusions, discrepancies? They're wanting the wrong thing, or they're wanting the right thing and going about it the wrong way. That's what makes drama.

Kohn: And yet, in the case of *The Descendants*, you have made a much warmer film: There's a stronger feeling of resolution and life-affirmation than, say, *Election* or *About Schmidt*. Even *Sideways* had a more ambiguous finish. The last shot of *The Descendants* wraps things up more decisively.
Payne: Well, I don't think I'm selling out or making a particularly Hollywood film. Also, the term—not to take you too literally—"life-affirming": Is it "life-affirming" or "life-observing" to say that tragic stuff happens and we move on?

Kohn: It's both.
Payne: Well, I also want my films to be charming and entertaining. As for the ending of the film, rhythmically this wouldn't have worked, but if I could've found a way to end the film with that close-up of Clooney on the boat, where he delivers that *Wild Bunch*-style line: "Well, I guess that's it. . . ." [laughs]

Kohn: And cut to black.
Payne: Cut to black! [laughs] I mean, that would've been pretty funny. It's still in there, this almost semi-nihilist line. By the way, a couple people at the studio said, "Do you really need that line?"

Kohn: It sort of mirrors that line Matthew Lillard has much earlier in the story, where he says "Everything just happens."
Payne: Yeah, that's a weird philosophical thing. Thanks for picking up on that; you're the first person to ask me about it. Nothing just happens? Everything just happens. That's just a kind of existentialist thought to fling in there.

Kohn: But it could apply to your entire filmography.
Payne: How so?

Kohn: They all involve the avoidance of specific conclusions and meanings. Nobody gets a definitive answer to his or her problems.
Payne: Well, I guess I feel like that in real life. We're not bad people; we're just doing it all for the first time.

Kohn: You've had a lot of luck with finding existing material and adapting it. The majority of your movies are adaptations of novels.
Payne: The big example here is Kubrick. I think eleven of his thirteen features were adaptations. You get from books the suggestion of a storyline or a world that you yourself never could've thought up in a million years. This Kaui Hart Hemmings book, *The Descendants*, I could never have thought up any of that stuff, but I'm sure glad I that I found it. I'm sorry to use a cliché, but these are more the types of movies we had in the seventies, movies made in a modern cinematic vernacular that are just about life, and seeking to avoid the movie contrivances that so dominate our cinema today.

Kohn: You're very much a story-driven filmmaker, which leads people to discuss your characters and the world they live in, as we have been doing here. And yet you also have a distinctive visual style. *The Descendants* has a number of memorable shots: The repeated motif of George Clooney running somewhere, the underwater shot of Shailene Woodley crying, and the overall serenity of the Hawaiian landscape juxtaposed against the family's grief. These kinds of things are often not noticed in your work.
Payne: I think so, too. As written as my movies are—I've gotten compliments on my dialogue—I'm really just interested in visual storytelling. With all respect to Louis Malle, I never would've taken on *My Dinner with André*. On Saturday at the New York Film Festival, when I shared clips of my favorite movies with [Film Society of Lincoln Center programming director] Richard Peña, I showed the last ten minutes of *La Notte*. I was astonished, yet again, at how [Antonioni] was able to make a lot of yakking work with relatively static visuals, but you're not bored for a second.

I still watch a lot of silent film. I'm very much interested in wordless storytelling. It's just more cinematic. When I watch *The Descendants* and I get to scenes like [Clooney] running on the beach and crossing paths with [Lillard] and then spying on him—no words, no music, just the washing of the waves for about six minutes. That, to me, is more welcome in the proceedings. It creates a foggy mystery to enter the next part of the film. [Clooney] talks to the wife on the beach, played by Judy Greer, and then there's a brief, interstitial montage of darkening clouds and rain appearing, which is saying, "Aha! The plot is thickening." And it's getting weirder, moister.

Kohn: There's a line at the beginning of the movie that you lifted from the book: "Fuck paradise."
Payne: I would say that's pretty much the theme of all human experience, is it not? Fuck paradise? [laughs] Isn't that the theme of Adam and Eve? They're given paradise and they fuck it up.

Kohn: You're taking this movie to Hawaii for a screening there soon. What's your own relationship to that setting?
Payne: My very first trip to Hawaii was in 1990 to show my fifty-minute-long thesis film from UCLA. It was accepted into the Hawaii International Film Festival. I stayed at a friend's house from film school in a far-flung part of Honolulu. So my first experience there was film-related, not as a tourist, feeling a little bit on the inside. So for me it will be a very lovely circle to come back to that same film festival twenty years later with a film about Hawaii.

Kohn: How have your expectations evolved since those early days?
Payne: I'm obviously the same person, but I remember at that time, I had just gotten out of film school and, of course, had high hopes for being able to forge a career in a very difficult métier of filmmaking. I was five years away from my first feature. Now, twenty years later, I'm extremely happy and lucky about being able to have a career in filmmaking. Like you, I desperately love movies. I'm so glad that my love of watching movies as a film geek was able to translate into a career. I'm very mindful of film school friends and other colleagues who have not had some of the same breaks I've had. I've gotten some praise for my first five features, but I hope in my life to now make one really good one.

Kohn: So the existing films are what? Just okay?
Payne: These are all fine, but I personally consider them minor works. That might seem like a statement of humility, but also great ego.

Kohn: Do you have some kind of abstract ideal to which these films pale in comparison?

Payne: Yeah, I watch a lot of great films and think, "Boy, it would be nice to make one good one someday." Look, you can't even get film students to easily watch *Citizen Kane* these days.

Kohn: You directed the pilot for the HBO series *Hung*. Do you think there's similar potential in cable television?

Payne: Well, that's a broad question, but I will say this: TV is doing a lot of stuff that we used to get from features. I'm currently re-watching *The Wire*. I'm up to episode ten of season one. Re-watching it is so much richer than watching it the first time. You have this vague memory of loving *The Wire*, but do you really remember it, character by character? And then you watch it again and go, "Fuckin' A! This is just off the hook." Something like that, so deeply intelligent, I mean, talk about making cinema. I hired the director of photography on *Hung* who shot the first two-and-a-half seasons of *The Wire*, Uta Briesewitz. They used to do those one-hour shows in six or seven days. She ended up marrying the location manager. Nowadays, everybody's like *Breaking Bad* this, *It's Always Sunny in Philadelphia* that. I don't have time to watch everything when I'm trying to watch Jean Renoir and everything else I need to catch up on.

Kohn: You talk about those filmmakers as having legacies. You certainly have made a name for yourself as well. Does being considered an auteur have an effect on getting your movies made?

Payne: The auteur status helps financing because my previous films have made money. But I think about movies in terms of directors and their bodies of work. If I get to enter that group, I'll be very grateful. Bringing this back to Cameron's question about anti-heroes: Some of that comes from a generous urge on the part of the questioner to piece together what might be a body of work, which is still finding its way, and I'm grateful for that.

Director's Chair: Alexander Payne's *The Descendants*

Iain Blair / 2011

From *PostMagazine* (www.postmagazine.com), November 1, 2011. Reprinted by permission of the interviewer and the *PostMagazine* editor, Randi Altman.

Post: Your last film was seven years ago. What took so long?
Alexander Payne: I was pretty busy writing three scripts, one of which I'll make in the future, doing a pilot, I did a short in Paris, I got divorced, had surgery. Those seven years went very quickly.

Post: What sort of film did you set out to make?
Payne: I never have a vision for my films. I just felt this was a good story that hooked me, and I never question it. I never say, I'm making a drama or whatever, until afterwards, and then it turns out to be whatever it is—in this case, it's more dramatic than any other film I've done.

Post: As usual, you assembled a fantastic cast. Any surprises working with Clooney?
Payne: Directors don't hang out together very often, except at awards shows, but we all talk to each other about actors and so on, and everyone had told me how great he is to work with and that you're lucky to have such an actor, and that was really true. He understands everything about filmmaking and he's been on a set most of his adult life. He's more comfortable on a set than he is anywhere else, and he knows how to keep positive energy going and everyone's spirits up. He's a total pro.

Post: He's also a very accomplished director himself. Was it very collaborative?
Payne: The best actors are always the ones who have directed as well,

since they understand all the problems you face. He's just directed his fourth film; he's a great collaborator.

Post: You filmed in locations around Hawaii. How tough was that logistically?
Payne: Fairly tough as it was all location work so you're constantly moving around. We only built one set. But the local crews are great. We got a lot from *Lost*, who then moved on to *Pirates 4* and *Hawaii Five-0*, so they're very experienced. And the new governor is a big movie fan, so he's working hard to increase production and tax incentives, since it's more expensive to shoot there. We shot 35mm, 3-perf, which shaves 25 percent off the film stock cost. On the other hand, when it comes time to doing the full-frame transfer, you don't have as much latitude north and south to re-frame. But then not many people watch full frame anymore. Finally, the era of letter-boxing has prevailed.

Post: Do you like the post process?
Payne: It's my favorite part of the whole film. Writing is necessary but painful, directing is exhilarating but exhausting—and you have all those egos to massage. Post is where cinema really happens, where montages unique to cinema among the arts come alive.

Post: Where did you do the post?
Payne: We just rented offices in Santa Monica as usual. It was about eight months long.

Post: Your editor was Kevin Tent, who edited *Sideways* and *Schmidt* for you. Tell us about the editing process.
Payne: He's edited all of my projects since '95, and it's a great relationship. He doesn't come on location; he stays in LA and I call him every day from the set and ask him, "How's it looking? How are the performances reading?" I trust his taste and judgment totally. After the shoot, I take two weeks off and then we watch all the dailies and start from scratch. I don't watch an assembly—it's too depressing. We cut on Avid, and it's typically about fourteen weeks to the first cut.

Post: Do you ever preview?
Payne: I do, a lot. You have to screen it constantly to get a real sense of what you have.

Post: Is it true you have final cut?
Payne: Yes, and I feel very lucky to have it and wish never to abuse it. As Billy Wilder famously said, "The Ten Commandments of filmmaking are: one through nine, thou shalt not bore; and ten, thou shall have final cut." I gather that very few directors really have final cut, so I treat it very seriously and I've found that it makes me very receptive to comments and suggestions. But I predict it'll become an issue if and when I make a large-budget film. I bet they'll bring it up. I'll resist of course. But I'm very concerned that my films make money. They don't have to be huge hits, but they have to make a profit.

Post: How many visual effects shots were there?
Payne: Not that many. Mark Dornfeld's Custom Film Effects in LA did them all and it's my third film with them and they're really good. Visual effects now are what we used to call opticals and I'm pretty old-fashioned about it, except when it comes to digitally removing a boom mic or cleaning up stuff. It's great for all that, and combining takes. If you're doing "overs," and what I do is better in one take on my back, we can switch that out. We can also speed up and slow down performances, which is another great thing. It's really important editorially, so you can combine different takes and overs.

Post: Tell us about audio and the mix. How important is it in your films?
Payne: It's hugely important, a huge part of any film. In terms of post, I have a really tight team of people I've worked with since the beginning, *Election*, like my sound designer and sound supervisor Frank Gaeta. It's a big advantage, and we're still happy working together. I love doing all the mixing and I'm there for every moment of it.

Post: Did you do a DI [digital intermediate]?
Payne: Yes, and it was my first time. It was great, though to be honest, I think people can go a little crazy with it if you're not careful. You have all these windows and possibilities, and I finally felt I got the hang of it when I just decided to throw away all the tricks you can do and just treat it as though I was still doing it photo-chemically. So I'd go, "That shot should be four points more cyan and a little denser," instead of saying, "Can we make a window there and brighten that one spot?" Because I also wanted to trust what my DP [director of photography], Phedon Papamichael, did and not screw around with it too much. But every once in a while, it's great to be able to change the color or de-saturate

something that came out a little too vibrant or add a little light to an actor's face without brightening the whole shot—that's when the DI really works for me. And, obviously, DI is here to stay. It's hard to do it photochemically anymore.

Post: Did the film turn out the way you hoped?
Payne: My second unit director is a trained philosopher, and he says I have a phenomenological approach to film, meaning that I'm a bit like a documentarian. You go in to see what's there and then shoot that and order it. I don't have some vision I pursue. But I do have my own innate sense of rhythm which you impose on the project—in all phases, from the writing and directing to the speed of performance and number of angles shot so you can then control all that later in post and in the editing. So rhythm is very important, and part of it is being able to find the film's rhythm. There's that great 1956 film, *The Mystery of Picasso*—not to compare myself in any way with him [laughs]—and you see him painting and it goes through so many different stages until he finally says, "Okay, that's it. I'm done." It's kind of like that. He's not like Edward Hopper who's painting one thing very carefully that he's had in mind for months and months—he just figures it out as he goes along, and I work more like that.

Post: You also co-produced. Do you like producing?
Payne: It's the first film of my own I've produced, and it was a good experience—the inmates get to take over the asylum. I've produced quite a lot, but basically for friends and their projects, like *King of California* for Mike Cahill, an old film school buddy. We now have a production company, Ad Hominem, under Fox Searchlight, and we have two projects coming out this year. The first was *Cedar Rapids*, a little comedy with Ed Helms and John C. Reilly, and the second is *The Descendants*. But I intensely dislike producing for other people.

Post: Any interest in doing a 3D film?
Payne: It'd be fun, but here's the truth about 3D—it comes around every eighteen years for three years. So it'll disappear next year and be back again in 2030.

Post: The digital world rules in post. Do you think film is dead?
Payne: I think we'll probably keep shooting film for a long while even as digital cameras replace film cameras. But the moment the film runs

through the camera, it's all digital from then on. Even projection is going digital finally. I was just in Norway and 99 percent of all their cinemas are digital. I still contend that flicker is better than glow. Flicker is more hypnotic and compelling. But at least digital gives local projectionists less chance to fuck up the film and show reels that are wildly different in brightness and color.

Post: Will you shoot digitally?
Payne: Absolutely. My next film will be shot digitally on the Alexa, precisely because I want a filmic look. It's a B&W film, but in order to get the different degrees of contrast and grain structure that I want, we have to shoot digitally because they don't make enough B&W film stock anymore.

So ironically, you have to go digital so you can dial in how much contrast and grain you want. It's a father-son road trip from Billings, Montana, to Lincoln, Nebraska, that gets sidetracked in a crappy town in central Nebraska where the father grew up and where he's got some scores to settle, and I thought it'd be really cool to do it in B&W.

Filmmaker Alexander Payne on *The Descendants*

Edward Douglas / 2011

From ComingSoon.net, November 11, 2011. Reprinted by permission of the interviewer.

Filmmaker Alexander Payne has been out of the limelight for over six years, when his previous movie *Sideways* was nominated for numerous Oscars, winning for Payne's screenplay with regular collaborator Jim Taylor.

Now, Payne has teamed with George Clooney for *The Descendants*, an adaptation of Kaui Hart Hemmings's novel about Hawaii-based real estate lawyer Matt King, whose wife ends up in a coma after a boating accident, which leads to him discovering she had been having an affair behind his back. With only days for his wife to live, Matt decides to find the man she was sleeping with to let him know about her condition. Coming along for the journey that takes him to other points on the islands are his two daughters, seventeen-year-old Alex (Shailene Woodley from *The Secret Life of the American Teenager*) and ten-year-old Scottie (newcomer Amara Miller), as well as Alex's dim but well-meaning boyfriend (Nick Krause).

It's another beautiful mix of humor and drama from Payne, one that takes full advantage of the location and pulls out surprisingly strong performances, not only from Clooney, but also from newcomers and veterans (Robert Forster and Beau Bridges, for instance) alike.

ComingSoon.net spoke with Alexander Payne a few weeks back, the day after the movie premiered at the New York Film Festival to a standing ovation. That in itself was already after many kudos had been heaped on the movie from earlier festivals, which have put Payne's movie as a frontrunner for many awards in the next few months. Payne is a rather laid-back, introspective filmmaker, one who doesn't just field questions but actually will throw a couple back your way, and not in a rude way either, but simply because he really wants to know what others think.

ComingSoon.net: I saw *Sideways* again for the first time in probably about four or five years on television.
Alexander Payne: How'd it hold up?

CS: It held up really well. I literally had to stop what I was doing because I started watching it.
Payne: Good.

CS: I know you've been developing other things since then and producing other filmmakers' movies, so did you end up dropping some of the other things you'd been working on to do this? How did it come about?
Payne: My little company, which is paid for by Fox Searchlight, optioned this book *The Descendants* in probably '06 or '07. I was in the midst of writing a different script with Jim Taylor, something we have yet to produce, but we will. That script took about two years to write. As much as I loved *The Descendants*, I thought, "No, I don't want to make it right now. I don't want to stand in the way of it." Jim Burke, our producing partner, said, "Go ahead and do something with it." We hired a couple of writers to take a pass at it and even trolled around for a director and for a spell, Stephen Frears was flirting with the idea of making it. Anyway, long story short, by mid-'09, Jim and I had finished that script, but we weren't going to be able to get the right financing to get it off the ground. We needed a lot of money, and I was anxious to make a movie. Stephen Frears had dropped out, so I picked up the pen and did *The Descendants*.

CS: Did you actually use anything from that other screenplay or did you literally start from scratch?
Payne: They did about eight different drafts, and I didn't read all of them, but I read most of them, and I saw that, while I respected their work a lot, I had to start from scratch and find my own way into the story, make it personal to me if I could because it's not my world, it's not my story. In a way, my co-writer was the novelist, was Kaui Hemmings because I wound up being pretty darn faithful to the book.

CS: That's what I've heard. I haven't read the book myself, but I hear it's very faithful.

Payne: Pretty darn faithful. You know, you have to exclude a lot, because a book has so much more leeway and isn't trapped by that analog form and trying to keep it under two hours and still let things breathe and develop, so you have to exclude a lot. A lot of what I excluded was high jinks with the younger daughter.

CS: I loved the stuff with the younger daughter, Scottie, because when you introduce her into the movie, or really any of the characters, it adds another dimension to the movie and takes it to a different place. At what point did George get involved?

Payne: Early on. I mean, from the get-go I asked the novelist Kaui Hemmings, "Just out of curiosity, have you ever seen anyone in your mind's eye for the lead? I mean, who would you cast if you could get anyone?" She said, "I like George Clooney and I could believe he would be from Hawaii." I thought for a minute and I said, "Great, let's get him." So he was my first and only choice. I mean, of course I had thought about him too, but it was great to hear it reinforced by the writer. So we went after him and I had dinner with him in September of '09, gave him the script in November of '09 and we were shooting by March of '10.

CS: What's he like as a collaborator? It must be different, because he is a writer, producer, and director and quite successful in his own right on top of being a great actor.

Payne: He's one of the most successful humans who have ever lived, I think. He's great, a total pro, super-gifted actor, nicest guy in the world, a heart of gold. People had told me, "Oh, you're in for a treat working with him." And they were right. I had the same experience with Nicholson, too, but it's always great to direct actors who have themselves directed because they understand the director's problem. They're there to serve and help out.

CS: It's funny you should mention Nicholson because this film feels almost more of a follow-up to *About Schmidt* than it is to *Sideways*, although *About Schmidt* was an original story.

Payne: Mostly, I had a couple of narrative ideas stolen from Louis Begley's book. Yeah, maybe this is sort of in a minor key like *About Schmidt* was. Maybe *Sideways* gets, I guess, dark at times or is a little bit more in a major key.

CS: I'm sure you've heard this, but it's hard when you talk about one of

your movies, because you can't really tell someone "It's a comedy," and yet, as I'm sure you also know, there's always someone trying to market or label a movie to make it easier to sell. This isn't a comedy although there are a lot of funny scenes, and it's not entirely a drama either.
Payne: Of course, I feel flattered by its difficulty to pigeonhole. If it somehow achieves a unique or a thick tone, then well, I'm sort of gratified by that.

CS: It must always be hard to capture that both in writing and in all aspects of the filmmaking process because obviously in *Sideways* there were also some very funny moments even when he hits rock bottom, but this one is tougher in some ways because you have a woman dying, and he has to deal with that, but there's still humor in there.
Payne: This one plays it straight a little bit more than previous films of mine, but it's still got some laughs in it. Even some stupid physical humor like when he's peeking through the bushes at the guy. I have a weakness for just kind of silent comedy at times.

CS: Complete tangent, but have you seen *The Artist* yet?
Payne: Yeah, I loved it. I loved it. I loved it. I was very jealous that he beat me to making a silent film.

CS: I also like that you tend to go for rather unconventional casting. When you did *Election* no one really knew who Reese Witherspoon was except for maybe from *Cruel Intentions*.
Payne: And *Freeway*, she had been good in *Freeway*. You know what I think? I think *Cruel Intentions* shot after I did, but came out before mine.

CS: For this, you have George Clooney, who everyone knows, but then you have a couple of young actors who people may not be familiar with. Maybe Shailene Woodley from her show.
Payne: She's going to be a big star clearly.

CS: Then you also have these legends like Robert Forster and Beau Bridges, which is amazing.
Payne: Yeah, the old lions.

CS: Right, and it's interesting, because you look at this cast and ask, "How are all these people in the same movie?"

Payne: Yeah, plus people off the street. Little Amara, the ten-year-old, she's eleven now, who had never even been in a school play.

CS: So how hard was it casting all those other roles?
Payne: When I picked up the pen to start writing the screenplay in July of '09, I knew we probably wouldn't shoot until the spring, but I told the studio, "I'm going to start writing now, but I want you to start paying immediately for scouting and casting because finding those kids is going to be time consuming." I had some experience in casting young people on *Election*, and I knew that there's a conundrum because often young people who are well-trained and have the chops and they've been doing it for a while and they're reliable don't seem like kids anymore.

CS: Right, they seem like they're acting.
Payne: Yeah, sixteen going on thirty-five. Then if you want someone right off the street, he or she may not have the chops, so I need to find that right balance, and I found it in Reese Witherspoon. Look at *Election*. Reese Witherspoon, a trained actress, been doing it since *Man on the Moon*, since she was twelve. A huge, huge talent, a total pro up against Chris Klein whom I plucked out of a high school in Omaha. So then Amara Miller, this ten-year-old, as I told you, she'd never even been in a school play. What she had was the ability to be comfortable in herself as a young girl. So unleashing her in front of the camera was like unleashing a cat. It only knows how to be itself, but it's a cat who has memorized some dialogue, and then it's just comfortable being there.

CS: I spoke to Judy earlier. She said you didn't even have Scottie cast when you did the first table read.
Payne: Judy played the part of the ten-year-old and she was magnificent!

CS: I know. I was saying, "Why didn't you just use performance capture, 'cause you could have had her play a CG ten-year-old?" But it ended up working out. When you were writing this, did you actually spend time in Hawaii to pull in the atmosphere and vibes?
Payne: Yeah, I went twice, and to spend some time with Kaui, the writer, to get to know her world and start to see it through her eyes. I wanted to serve her voice as much as I could and to begin to scout locations and begin other research, meeting other people who could help me. I needed help from trust lawyers, for example, to get that area of the land sale correct, so that trust lawyers watching the film would say, "Oh, he got that

right." So I went once in August of '09 and I returned in December of '09. By December, it was actually more for local casting.

CS: Do you expect to have a big audience of trust lawyers seeing this?
Payne: Or lawyers who would understand and who have heard the term rule against perpetuities and that kind of stuff—or rather estate lawyers, trust lawyers, yeah.

CS: I want to ask about working with Shailene and the younger actors. Do you have a very different process or approach for working with actors depending on their experience?
Payne: Yeah, I gotta say in general that of course, even with actors with great experience, it's part of the director's job to see what those individual actors need in terms of support or reinforcement or discipline or whatever it is. Then, as a director too, you have to know if you're going to have two actors in the same shot, and you know that one actor is better in takes one or two and the other one is better typically in takes four and five. How do you figure that out? All that stuff is part of the job. But whether the actors are very beginning, if they're complete tyros or if they're very experienced, I really just tell them what I want them to do and tell them the truth. Say, "That one wasn't so great. Just try it a little bit more this way or do it like that." I have an extremely direct style. I just tell them what I think.

CS: I don't know if you consider yourself a visual filmmaker, but sometimes when you have an amazing location like this one and you have an idea of what you want in the background, some directors might storyboard things, while others just go to the location and then try to figure things out on the day. Which one of those are you?
Payne: I've never storyboarded in my life and am very location-based. I don't shoot on stages. Very often locations will tell you how they themselves want to be shot, or if you find a location and you see that it itself is suggesting, "Shoot me here, shoot me here, shoot me through this window. You can get great depth here." It tells you. It informs you, and I really like that. I like locations telling me how they want to be shot.

CS: I love the last shot of the movie, the end credits.
Payne: Thanks a lot. What do you like about it?

CS: There's just something about it. Tony Gilroy did it in *Michael Clayton* and you just have this single shot and suddenly the credits roll and you stay on them. Normally, it would fade out or cut away, but you're just watching these people continue to live their life after going through so much.

Payne: Were you surprised by the moments the credits started? Were you expecting something else?

CS: Yeah, very much so; I think everyone is. I think you have this amazing scene with George and his wife and something about that last scene is sort of uplifting.

Payne: *La vie continue.*

CS: Did that just come out of shooting the last scene and just letting cameras roll?

Payne: No, it's in the screenplay. I wrote that.

CS: What about this stuff you've been working on? *Downsizing* was something which I know you've already gotten going.

Payne: That's comfortably aging in an oak cask, and we're going to get back to it. The Latin poet Horace used to recommend eight years is the perfect time to let a poem lie uncorrected before picking it up to correct it. We won't take eight years, but we'll get back to it. In the meantime, I have my next two movies lined up. April or May I'll start shooting a father-son road trip from Billings, Montana, to Lincoln. I'm hoping to kick that one out pretty quickly. After that, I'm going to do the adaptation of a Daniel Clowes (*Ghost World*) graphic novel, which he himself has adapted called *Wilson*, about a misanthrope up in Oakland.

CS: I'm a fan of Daniel Clowes's work but don't know that one.

Payne: Oh, it came out probably the year before last. Look it up. It's a good one.

CS: So you're working with him on adapting that?

Payne: Yeah, I love the guy. We're exactly the same age, very likeminded, and he's doing his own adaptation. He's a terrific screenwriter. He's as gifted a screenwriter is he is a graphic novelist. He's just very talented, that guy.

CS: It's interesting that you're doing another road trip movie. This, you shot on Hawaii for four months.
Payne: Yeah, and it's kind of a road trip movie.

CS: It is, yeah. *Sideways* was also a road trip in this beautiful Northern California wine country. . . .
Payne: And *About Schmidt*.

CS: So you've found all these beautiful locations and it seems like, "I'm going to make a movie here." Is that just kind of a coincidence that you've ended up doing so many road movies in these gorgeous locations?
Payne: I guess so, though the next one is going to have a much more austere visual sense. It's going to be in black and white and shot in the late spring in Montana, South Dakota, and Nebraska. I want it to have a certain stark visual style.

CS: You're going to shoot it in black and white?
Payne: We'll probably shoot digital, but it'll be released on black and white film.

CS: Are you going to use the same director of photography?
Payne: Yeah, Phedon Papamichael.

CS: Did he shoot George's movie *Ides of March* before or after?
Payne: After. He and George really hit it off well making *The Descendants*, then he hired Phedon for *Ides of March*.

CS: Both movies look amazing, though they have different looks.
Payne: Yeah, very different.

Interview: Alexander Payne

Scott Tobias / 2011

From the *Onion A.V. Club*, November 15, 2011. Reprinted with permission of THE AV CLUB. Copyright © 2011, by ONION, INC. www.avclub.com.

Born in Omaha, Nebraska, director Alexander Payne established himself early as a comic voice for middle America, staying close to home for his first three features: 1996's *Citizen Ruth*, a scathing satire about the unseemliness of abortion politics; 1999's *Election*, another political satire, this time in the cutthroat world of high-school student council elections; and 2002's *About Schmidt*, about the seriocomic adventures of a newly retired Omaha insurance salesman. But for his last two films, Payne left his Midwest comfort zone without losing his keen sense of locale or his talent for observational humor. An Oscar winner for Best Adapted Screenplay, 2004's *Sideways* followed two middle-aged buddies through California wine country. Now, after a seven-year absence from feature directing, Payne has returned with *The Descendants*, a richly textured comedy-drama that captures, among other things, the way everyday Hawaiians live on the island paradise. Based on Kaui Hart Hemmings's novel, the film stars George Clooney as a widower who grapples with the fallout of his wife's catastrophic injury in a boating accident. This means being a better father to his two daughters (the eldest, played by Shailene Woodley, proves especially troubled) and processing the revelation that his wife was having an affair. Meanwhile, as the trustee to a heavenly piece of ancestral land in Kauai, he's under pressure from his extended family to sell it off. Payne recently spoke to the *A.V. Club* about balancing comedy with drama, emulating Chuck Jones, and making most of his films too long.

A.V. Club: Jim Rash and Nat Faxon initially adapted the book. How did the project come to you, and how did it change once it got into your hands?

Alexander Payne: My producing partners and I optioned it in '07, and I was in the middle of writing a script with my writing partner, Jim Taylor. I liked it. I admired it very much, but didn't jump on it immediately. Our other producing partner, Jim Burke, hired Rash and Faxon to adapt it, and they did their own adaptation. And then finally, when I decided to jump in to direct this film myself, I did my own adaptation, starting in July of '09. How did it change? From the book?

AVC: No, from the material you got. You got this script, and you have a writing credit as well.

AP: Both the book and their adaptation had a lot more to do with the younger daughter, with Scottie. I was far less interested in her than I was the man's relationship with the older daughter. Plus, as a director, I know when you work with minors, you only have eight hours per day to work with them, and who needs that?

AVC: What excited you about this book?

AP: I just thought it would make a good movie. I had never seen exactly this story in a movie before, and then the fact that it was told in Hawaii, and not just generally in Hawaii, but amidst that decaying aristocracy, made it very interesting to me. I wasn't so much interested in Hawaii as I was Honolulu. I had never seen Honolulu in a film. So I was eager to see it. As the years go by and I make more films, I am increasingly interested in capturing place as a vivid backdrop for my films.

AVC: One of the compelling things about the film is how you look at Hawaii not as a tourist destination, but as a place where people actually live.

AP: It's not a story about tourists. It's a story about people who live there, so that point of view comes automatically with the story. I wasn't wishing to evoke anything. There's a bit of a joke made at the beginning of the film, "Paradise can go fuck itself." The voiceover and the images tell the viewer right off the bat, "You're going to be seeing a different side of what you consider Hawaii." So yeah, I took care of that right away. After that, it's telling that story.

AVC: Have you spent much time there? Maybe it's different in Honolulu,

but the impression you get as a tourist is that the tenor of life there is not as fraught as other American cities.
AP: You mean not as fast-paced and all that?

AVC: Right, not as tense. Even if you're a resident, there's a different feel.
AP: I would say that's true, even though people from the rest of Hawaii accuse Honolulu of being that fast-paced monstrosity, just as I talk to people—I'm in Omaha now, and you meet people from small towns of Nebraska, "You'll never catch me driving in Omaha! They drive like crazy!" So it's all relative. Out of a state of 1.2 million people, Honolulu has 800,000 to 900,000. It has many of the problems of a big city, but for sure, it's more leisurely paced. And I think the film is more leisurely paced. Not because I wanted to make a slower film, but I think the rhythm one feels out there found its way into the film, and I'm happy about that. I remember when I was showing the film to some filmmaker and he said, "Why, if the wife is dying and there's such an urgency to find her lover, are they stopping to go to the beach, or see this land on Kauai? I don't believe that." Having lived there, I completely believe that. Plus the fact that when you're amid a family crisis, you treasure having times out of war.

AVC: You mention finding the rhythm of the film. Does that take place in the editing process? This is a very tricky tone you're trying to manage in this film.
AP: Right. Are you talking about pace or rhythm?

AVC: Rhythm.
AP: All three parts of filmmaking [writing, shooting, editing] contribute to that. It's a search for economy. You want the script to be a tight as possible, you want the acting to be as efficient as possible on the set, and you have enough coverage to manipulate the rhythm in the editing room, and then in the editing room you want to find the quickest possible version, even if it's a leisurely paced film. I definitely in filmmaking more and more find writing and directing a means to harvest material for editing. It's all about editing.

AVC: *The Descendants* is a film about grief and other difficulties, and yet it's a comedy, too. Was managing the tone a challenge? Was it difficult to know when to go for a laugh and then to pull back?
AP: No, not really. I'm fifty now. I can do whatever the hell I want.

[laughs] I think if you look at my other films, it's just a style that for some reason comes out. I guess I'm complimented when people say "There's a tricky balance between comedy and pathos, how do you do that?" There's no how, it just comes. I would say it especially comes when you have a comedy director like me doing dramatic material. I want material like this to still have a certain charm and nimbleness to it, a certain buoyancy. Some good old laughs.

The other thing I was going to say about tone-mixing is that it's often comedy directors who do that. *Make Way for Tomorrow* has a lot of pathos in it for a comedy director [Leo McCarey]. [Yasujiro] Ozu is known for his melodramas, but he started off as a comedy director. Or even *The Apartment*. I wouldn't say it mixes comedy and pathos, I'd say it mixes comedy and skeeviness.

AVC: You forget the director of *Make Way for Tomorrow* is the same guy who directed *Duck Soup*.
AP: Yeah, and *Big Business*, my favorite Laurel and Hardy short.

AVC: So many of today's comedies are verbally very strong and visually indifferent. But that isn't the case with your work. What were you trying to accomplish visually with *The Descendants*? Were there films you were looking at as a model?
AP: I don't think so much about verbal comedy. I always think about visual comedy. I was raised watching silents, and I'm always thinking about how to make cinema, not good talking—although I want good talking. I'm much more interested in framing, composition, and orchestration of bodies in space, and so forth. My goal is always what Chuck Jones wanted his Warner Bros. cartoons to be, which was if you turn down the sound, you could still tell what's going on. I think if you watch most of my films with the sound off, you could still tell what's going on. As for models, I could tell you some other films, but I didn't have any concrete influences for this one. *Sideways* was very much trying to emulate, in some ways, [cinematographer] Gordon Willis in Hal Ashby's *The Landlord*. Not in all scenes, some scenes. Sometimes I have those visual references, but not in this one. We just winged it.

AVC: You talked about the importance of a tight, economical film, but this film does embrace some *longueurs*, where you hold on shots for longer than expected.
AP: I think you need that. I think it could have been longer in some

ways, too. You need to give people time to think about things during a movie. I know I appreciate that. But you don't want to bore the shit out of them. You have to find the balance. The worst thing for people to say about your movies is, "Yeah, it was pretty good, but it was too damn long." I think *About Schmidt* is too long. I actually think all my movies are too long, except for *Election*. *Election* is probably the only one that's just right.

AVC: Does it become a problem of continuity or finding scenes that you just like too much to get rid of?
AP: No, no, no, no. I don't think it's any of that. My editor and I remain very disciplined. It's just sometimes when you're making a film, you get into the cutting room and you see a scene that's slowing you down in a certain section, but if you remove that scene then, emotionally or story-wise, another scene a half-hour later won't have the same impact. You just get stuck with it. This one's pretty close. It's slightly brisker, but also slightly more languorous in areas, too. But anyway, what the hell?

AVC: Were there any happy accidents in the film, moments that occurred on set that you didn't expect that wound up shaping the film in a different way?
AP: No. [laughs] It's all shot pretty much as scripted. The one thing that's very lovely that I had as a kind of visual spice rack was those interstitial shots of landscape, which my second-unit director curated, and which I feel have made a very significant contribution to the film. I would call it an accident, but when I was shooting A-unit, he was shooting B-unit, really covering the islands and doing a bang-up job. Accidents? Nope, no accidents.

AVC: So you come to the set with things pretty much planned out. You're not like Robert Altman. It's not a controlled chaos situation, right?
AP: No, I think so far, my style has been pretty controlled, which is not to say I don't invite constant input from the actors and the creative people. I absolutely do. I want all the right views. The moment we shoot, we know what we're doing. There's no improvisation.

AVC: But in order to shoot material to harvest once you get to the editing room, do you wind up on set saying, "Well I need to have this done in a lot of different ways?"
AP: Yes, yes. That's exactly right. Earlier when I said that writing and

directing is just a way of harvesting things to edit, that's exactly what you do. There are some things on the set where that seems exactly right, let's not get a variation. But there are other times when you want the actor to do it two or three different ways, because you're not exactly sure how you want to modulate it in the editing room.

AVC: You've used voiceover narration in many of your films. What do you think makes good or bad voiceover and why did you choose to turn to it for *The Descendants*?
AP: The novel is in first person, and I like first-person literature, and I like first-person film. I even like third-person voiceover in a film when it's well done, like *Barry Lyndon*. You think about how first-person is used by Sissy Spacek in *Badlands* or the dead guy in *Sunset Boulevard* or the first-person omniscient narrator in *A Clockwork Orange*. It's just so fucking delicious, so great to see those proceedings through the point of view of your protagonist. It's just delicious. Probably the most creative use of voiceover I've had was the "Dear Ndugu" letters in *About Schmidt*. That was a nice little device for that. Here's one [in *The Descendants*] that served a slightly more exclusively expository purpose than I'd normally like. There's a lot of exposition in the first reel, reel and a half. I tried to do it as delicately as possible. It anchors us in George Clooney's character and how he's viewing the proceedings. I think it invites the viewer to watch the rest of the film through his eyes, and care for him and what he's going through. It's slightly more expository than my taste usually is. However, the viewer had to have all of that information, and to try to get that information into scenes would have been far more time-consuming and uncinematic.

AVC: These are the problems you face when you adapt books, right? Books can do that so easily, and here you're like, "I can't really explain the situation about this piece of land without—"
AP: If you watch the first ten minutes of Kurosawa's *Ran*, it's a bunch of guys sitting around. They don't move, the camera doesn't move, and they're talking. They're getting across all the exposition, which is going to set the whole rest of the film cinematically into motion. There are certain films where the filmmaker and the audience have to take their medicine and then be scot-free.

AVC: Let's talk about your approach to adaptation. Is fidelity important to you?

AP: No. Not at all, not at all. I could never be a part of an adaptation of a film where there's pressure to not disappoint the immense fan base. In those cases, they often wind up with filmed books on tape, quite uncinematic. Having said that, I'd say all the adaptations I've done are quite faithful to the original, with the exception of *About Schmidt*, which is only titularly an adaptation, and is actually an original with some narrative threads borrowed from Mr. Begley's book. All the other adaptations I've done are pretty darn faithful. You have to pick and choose which storylines and plot threads, because you don't have the time to fill in the film as they have in novels. All those pages with detours and plots and different storylines. But films add a lot, and you gotta keep it moving. I am happy to change names from what the author had originally. I like having the dialogue come from the material, but I've chosen that dialogue because I like the book a lot, and want to make it into a film.

AVC: Are there awkward conversations with the authors of these books about this process?
AP: No, no. Never had an awkward conversation. On *Election*, I had never even met Tom Perrotta until the film's première, I think. This one, though, is the adaptation that most involved the author, because I'm not from Hawaii—that's not my world, that's not my state, that's not my class. I really relied upon her, not so much for the adaptation, because that was all in the book, but more so when I went to direct the film to get tips on how faithfully to portray that work. She was very involved, and I'm super-grateful to her.

AVC: You dabbled in television a couple of years ago by directing the pilot for *Hung*. Do you see yourself returning? Are there opportunities in television now that might not be there for film?
AP: Interesting question, because as sucky as a lot of American cinema is today, we've been living in a golden age of television for a few years now. My directing the pilot for *Hung* was just as a hired hand. I was in the midst of writing this other screenplay, I hadn't made a feature in a couple years, and I was eager to just go roll some film and beat up some actors. So I agreed to do a pilot. There are a couple of TV-show ideas I do have, and we're going to be exploring, probably sometime in the next couple years, with Jim Taylor, my co-writer.

AVC: What's the status of your adaptation of the Daniel Clowes book *Wilson*?

AP: Oh man, thanks for asking! I'm really excited about that. I'm doing that two films from now. Dan Clowes turns out to be a very fine screenwriter, and he adapted his own book. And damn if he didn't come within striking distance on the first draft.

Payne Find His Way to *The Descendants*

Marshall Fine / 2011

From HollywoodandFine.com, November 16, 2011. Reprinted by permission of the interviewer.

The last time out as a writer-director, Alexander Payne received an Oscar nomination as best director and shared the Oscar itself with partner Jim Taylor for best adapted screenplay.

Of course, that was seven years ago, with 2004's *Sideways*. You'd think that, with encouragement like that, the next one would be easy. Not so, says Payne, who returns to theaters this week with his new film, *The Descendants*.

"I don't want to take so long between films," Payne, fifty, says with a shrug, sitting in a hotel suite during a recent press day. "It just happened."

So what took so long?

"I was with *Sideways* until the spring of '05," he says. "Then I started working on a new script with Jim Taylor (*Downsizing*) that took a lot longer than I thought. We were working on that until 2008. But that script would have needed a lot of dough because we included a lot of special effects and were working on a broader canvas."

In the intervening years, Payne and Taylor did some script-doctoring (including the Adam Sandler film, *I Now Pronounce You Chuck & Larry*). They also served as producers for other filmmakers (including *The Savages* by Tamara Jenkins—who is Mrs. Taylor—and Miguel Arteta's *Cedar Rapids*). Payne directed a short segment of the compilation film *Paris je t'aime*, and also worked as executive producer (and directed one episode) of the HBO series *Hung*.

The Descendants—in the form of galleys of Kaui Hart Hemmings's novel—reached Payne through Taylor and the two of them began working on it in 2009. The film is already being touted as an Oscar contender, based on several film festival screenings in the fall.

"When I read it, I thought it was a good solid human story with little contrivance," Payne says. "That upper-class of Hawaii is a milieu I never in a million years would have thought of. I've been to Hawaii a number of times and, having visited friends there, I got a sense of the complex social climate. And then my interest was piqued by the book. I had a desire to get a temporary passport to enter that society and that contributed to my desire to make the film. When I saw my other project was doomed because of the length of finding financing, I was so anxious to shoot something that I put the other one on hold to do this."

The film stars George Clooney as a member of a wealthy Hawaiian family, which owns a large, valuable piece of undeveloped land that it must sell. Clooney's character, an attorney, is in charge of the sale—but as the deadline approaches, he also finds himself at the center of a family tragedy, when his wife is left comatose by a boating accident. As he tries to deal with his daughters, he also discovers that, in fact, his wife had a secret life he knew nothing about.

Like Payne's earlier films—including *Election* and *About Schmidt*—*The Descendants* blends absurdly human comedy with tragic and touching situations. Achieving exactly the right tone from scene to scene challenged Payne as he finalized the film.

"This film is more serious than the other ones I've done," Payne says. "But it's still directed by a comedy director. I write a certain way and, to me, this all seems like part of the tone of life. Life mixes tones all the time.

"Really, that calibration of the tone comes a lot in the editing. That's why this film had a nine-month post-production. We screened it a lot; calibrating the tone is like calibrating rhythm. I'm glad the film is somewhat polychromatic."

Part of achieving that complexity included shooting large chunks of the film in sequence.

"We shot as much as possible in sequence," Payne says. "But shooting out of sequence is just part of filmmaking. It's my job to remind the actors where they are emotionally. Jack Nicholson (who starred in Payne's *About Schmidt*) does an interesting thing when he shoots. Every Sunday, he rereads the entire script to remind himself where everything is so he can remain oriented for the long week's work."

The toughest casting challenge was finding a tween-age actress who could be as natural as the rest of the cast. After seeing hundreds of girls, with the start of production looming, Payne found young Amara Miller, who had never acted before, through a video sent by a friend of a friend of a friend.

"One minute into it, I knew that she was the one," Payne says. "She seemed very comfortable being herself. She had no acting chops. The way she read the dialogue seemed naturally sassy, which seemed appropriate for the character. She was comfortable in her own skin. It was like putting a cat in front of a camera, a creature just comfortable being herself. It's only the second time I've cast someone without meeting her first."

The biggest film challenge? A shot of Clooney and the two daughters in an outrigger canoe, filmed half a mile or so from shore in the Pacific Ocean.

"I'd grown weary of shooting in automobiles, but George, who appeared in *The Perfect Storm*, told me, 'If you don't like car work, boat work is like car work on steroids.'

"Most of filmmaking is hauling around a bunch of heavy equipment. So we had to coordinate lugging all the heavy equipment onto the water. We had a big boat with equipment, another boat with the camera and then the actors in a little boat. Plus we had guys in the water under the little boat to keep it from capsizing. Well, it's a process that tends to destroy the intimacy of the moment. In fact, it turned out to be a lovely scene—but getting there was arduous. I have new respect for Roman Polanski for *Knife in the Water*."

Payne is quick to note that he won't take another eight years to make his next film after *The Descendants*. He's set to shoot *Nebraska* next year and has a second film in the works as well, along with a TV pilot that he and Taylor are writing.

"I want to move more quickly to make films," he says.

And that special-effects-laden script that took him off-track for so many years? Quips Payne, "It's now aging in an oak cask."

An Interview with Alexander Payne

Glenn Kenny / 2011

From *Some Came Running*, November 16, 2011. Reprinted by permission of the interviewer.

The writer and director Alexander Payne has a quietly elegant presence that's a comfortable match for his penetrating intelligence, an intelligence that's a sparkling feature of his conversation and, of course, a crucial component of his films. With producer and frequent co-writer Jim Taylor, Payne has made five feature films (and one notable short, in the omnibus picture *Paris, je t'aime*) that are searching and sometimes sardonic studies of unique but nevertheless representative American characters in unique American settings. The social-activism satire *Citizen Ruth*, the high-school-as-metaphor-for-cursed-life comedy *Election*, the dying-of-the-light road picture *About Schmidt*, and the wine-dark story of love for possible losers, *Sideways*, have all made their mark in both the critical and commercial realms. And now Payne delivers his most accomplished, and moving, film yet, *The Descendants*. Based on a novel by Kaui Hart Hemmings, *The Descendants* begins with a lyrical image of a woman enjoying some power boat time in the blue, blue Hawaiian waters. But all is not well for long. The moment we see is directly before a disaster that puts the woman, Elizabeth, into a coma, and sends her husband, affluent lawyer Matt King, into a frenzy of emotional turmoil as he tries to deal with his two young, troubled daughters; the sale of a large parcel of land owned by his family, and the various pressures concerning that sale that his less-prosperous kin are bringing to bear on him; and finally, the knowledge that his wife had been conducting an affair. Funny, wise, deeply sad, and deeply compassionate, *The Descendants* may just be the film of the year. I talked to Payne about its themes and creation as the film was premiering at the New York Film Festival in early October.

Glenn Kenny: I have a couple of questions to start with, to which the short answers would invariably be, "It's called acting, stupid." But I'm hoping you'll indulge me with longer answers. To begin with, I'm just blown away by the way that George Clooney and Shailene Woodley and Amara Miller, who play his daughters, achieved this dynamic that is so seemingly natural and so present. Despite, say, that Clooney himself is not a dad, and so on. So I'm wondering how you were able to lead the performers through the creation of that particular dynamic.

Alexander Payne: Part of the answer is, "It's what I do," and part of the answer is, "It's what I observe." My other experience in doing this sort of thing was in *Sideways*, when I had to have those two guys, Paul Giamatti and Thomas Haden Church, appear as though they had been friends for years, even though they had only met two weeks before shooting. Because in that case, if you didn't believe their friendship, there was no film. So I had them come out to Santa Barbara County two or three weeks before shooting, not just to have rehearsals with me but so they could spend time together and go play golf and see movies. They were as eager to forge a relationship as I was, because they wanted the movie to be good. So the same thing applied for this film. I brought all those players out about two weeks before shooting and we got together at the house I was staying at in Hawaii, and on locations. It's always important to take actors to locations before you shoot. And we just hung out. And then *they* just hung out. And then it started to show up on screen. The process of making a film is so long that each day is a bit of rehearsal for the whole rest of the shoot. And the only compliment I really pay myself in filmmaking is that I cast well. And I think that, a) they were well-selected, and b) I thank the film gods that those particular actors reached me because for *none* of those three parts—Clooney, Shailene, or Amara—was there an also-ran for the role. It was really them, those three specifically. It's as if, for example, well, who else is going to play *you*? And then, of course, there's film's remarkable capacity to lie. [laughs]

GK: I think Clooney goes as deep as he's ever gone. In part it's because of the themes. Did you discuss this beforehand, or did you just keep it specifically related to the character and the narrative?
Payne: The latter.

GK: Because he's a smart guy. He doesn't need you to lay that stuff out.
. . .
Payne: No, he gets it. He knows what's going on. Then it's just a matter

of what you get day by day on the set and take by take. Little surgical instructions I might want him to find helpful, like what I tell him between takes. And then decent editing.

GK: I wanted to ask you about the editing.
Payne: Thank you. I'm real proud of the editing in this one.

GK: I wanted to talk about how long it took, because you have this narrative through-line that's incredibly strong and never feels over-determined. You've got the engagement of the audience at all times without ever over-emphasizing any one thing. How'd the process go for you and your editor, Kevin Tent?
Payne: Kevin and I typically edit for a long time. *Election* we edited over a year. I still think it's my only film that's not too long. *Sideways* and *The Descendants* were each about thirty-six, thirty-seven weeks total. It's not all just picture cutting, it's also sound and sound effects, music and stuff. But start to finish, it was about thirty-seven weeks, so just over nine months, ten months. And we screened a lot. Actually, we had a couple of those Hollywood screenings. I forget what they call them—you know, recruited, focus group–type screenings—we had two of those. But I screen constantly for friends and people who come into the cutting room, or rent a small screening room, watch it, because that's really the only time when you know what you have or how it's functioning. And then we just go on, continuing to calibrate tone. And it takes a while.

GK: There's a real looseness—
Payne: I just think many films today are under-edited.

GK: Well, you get the emotions to resonate without hammering them.
Payne: Thank God. I can't stand being hammered in a movie. I get it. I'm there. I want the viewers to bring their part, their component, to the film-watching experience.

GK: Right. You lead them through it and it feels loose, but I think there's also a real meticulousness to it and a real consciousness of the way you're using the devices and you have—this film has the confidence where it can start off with this voiceover narration and then just dispose of it.
Payne: Correct.

GK: Nobody is going to ask, "Where did the narration go?" But that's the sort of thing that somebody else might worry and say, well no, we need to bring that back at the end, to close the parenthesis or what have you. Or we need to bring it back in the middle. But you—

Payne: You know, I thought of all that. But I'm fifty now, and I think I'm at a stage where I can use whatever film techniques I need at whatever time for whatever efficacy. There's only one wipe in the film. Typically you'd say, well, no, if you're going to have a wipe, you need to have more than one wipe. But I didn't need more than one wipe. The wipe worked well there, the one place I needed it. And you're right about voiceover. It worked well to get us into the story and then I jettisoned it. I didn't need it anymore. The film just uses what it needs.

GK: So you begin with Matt in voiceover giving you a bit of a reality check as to what life in Hawaii is like. It's paradise but it's not paradise. And then, it's not as if you're not aware of the landscape, but there's that one shot where the characters look at the land they own, and it's beautiful.

Payne: You cannot deny that there are jaw-dropping vistas out there. I think the land in that shot is, like, the land owned by Matt and his family, actually in a trust, that will elapse at some point. It's on Kauai, I forget the name of the family who owns it; a huge, huge ranch. They make money at that ranch by allowing ATV tours. These old estates have to resort to a lot of commercial tricks like that to keep afloat.

I did do a lot of research about Hawaii history cause inasmuch as a history is even implied in the title of the film, but he's from one of those fancy old families in Hawaii. I needed to know what I was dealing with. And then get a larger sense of that complex and sometimes intimidating social fabric.

The book on which the film is based, a novel by Kaui Hart Hemmings, reached us, and by us I mean my producing partners, Jim Burke and Jim Taylor, about four, five years ago. And Jim Taylor and I were in the midst of writing something else, which I haven't shot yet. And so I eschewed it for the moment, even as I recognized its merits. And so Jim Burke went ahead and he hired a couple other writers to just get the thing up on its feet. And then they lured another director who was involved for a while, Stephen Frears, who was very interested in doing it. And the writers did a couple drafts for him. But anyway, finally, in '09 I decided to do it after Stephen Frears dropped out. He had a conflict with something else. So then I did my own adaptation. And there we were.

GK: Did you like the idea of going to Hawaii?

Payne: Absolutely. I think more and more my filmmaking, not that I've made that many films, but each one takes a lot of effort and time. And I find myself now auditioning place as well as much of the story there. So yeah, recently—for example, recently, I've been flirting with a book that would half take place in Dublin. I had never been to Dublin, so I flew over to Dublin a few weeks ago, just to sniff around. And it was lovely, but I didn't find it particularly inspiring to me on a superficial visit. So I don't think I'm going to do it. But Hawaii was a place I had loved already. I've been there many times and had a sense of that complex cultural fabric. And not just Hawaii, the island itself. I was interested in seeing Honolulu, which is a real city. I had never seen Honolulu in a film.

GK: And you do get this really engaging sense of place, not unlike the sense of place you brought to bear on *Sideways*.

Payne: Which is a skill set I finally began to get a handle on in *About Schmidt*. And the short I did for the omnibus film *Paris, je t'aime* was a kind of a reinforcing exercise for me about humans in foreground, place in background. Even when I did a pilot for *Hung*, I didn't go quite as deeply, but even that, I think, has a genuine redolence of Detroit, where it's set and was shot.

GK: People are going to ask why has it taken so long between this and *Sideways*. And obviously you do other things. But for a filmmaker who does the kind of films that you do, is it just more difficult to get things going?

Payne: No, I think it's just . . . it's always about material. Everything is always about material. The fact that it was essentially four years between when I was able to put *Sideways* to bed and picked up the pen on *The Descendants*—that was about, well, most of that time was spent writing. Writing the script that Jim and I have yet to see shot. And for dough we script-doctored a couple of other things. And I did the *Hung* pilot. Time just went by fast. But I rue that, because I am in this to make features. I like it! Fun.

GK: In terms of the casting, how much were you aware of playing a little bit with iconography relative to George Clooney's celebrity status and having him cuckolded?

Payne: Every once in a while I'd hear, and even maybe now you might—before someone's seen the movie—"Well, who's going to cheat on George?" Well, everybody cheats on everybody.

GK: Matthew Lillard, who plays the character with whom the wife had had an affair; it's interesting because Matthew's so often played a goof, and there's a scene where he has to deliver one of the film's more profound moments, when his character steps back and admits, in so many words, "I didn't do it for this reason, it happened."
Payne: Yeah.

GK: It's a beautiful moment, painful and true.
Payne: He does a good job, that guy Lillard! See, though, I hadn't seen him in anything else. I saw *Scream* a million years ago, but I didn't remember it. I've never seen him. He just auditioned really well.

GK: Patricia Hastie, who plays Elizabeth, the comatose wife—what was she like?
Payne: Thank you for asking about her. I am so proud of her work. She was a local hire in Hawaii. She was really, technically, a "featured extra," because she was a local hire with no dialogue. But I ended up bumping her up to giving her front-end credit and full scale, or however much she was paid. That woman took it very seriously. She lost a bunch of weight. She would stay up all night, come in to work the next day, go through hair and makeup, climb into bed, get hooked up to the IV's, take a melatonin and say, "Don't wake me even for lunch." She was out a lot of the time. And we'd have to re-adjust her body, because they'll get bed sores. She really showed up for work. There's an old Latin phrase, *Dum tacet clamat*. "Although silent, she speaks."

Interview: Alexander Payne

Dave Davies / 2011

Transcript from *Fresh Air* radio show, November 17, 2011. Published by permission of WHYY, Inc. *Fresh Air* is produced by WHYY, Inc. and distributed by NPR.

Terry Gross: This is *Fresh Air*. I'm Terry Gross. Though he's directed only five feature films, our guest Alexander Payne has managed to build a reputation as one of Hollywood's most respected filmmakers. His movies find comedy in the crises of his flawed protagonists, among them Matthew Broderick as a high school teacher in the 1999 film *Election*, Jack Nicholson as a widower in *About Schmidt,* and Paul Giamatti as a struggling author and wine snob in the 2004 film *Sideways*, for which Payne shared an Oscar for Best Adapted Screenplay. Payne's latest film is *The Descendants*, which is set in Hawaii. George Clooney plays a lawyer whose life turns upside down when his wife falls into a coma after a boating accident. Alexander Payne spoke with *Fresh Air* contributor Dave Davies.

Dave Davies: Alexander Payne, welcome back to *Fresh Air*. This film stars George Clooney, and I know that you have had films in which you've done big stars like Jack Nicholson, others with less recognizable actors, and I know that casting is really important to you. How do you approach that, whether you want to get a big name or not?
Alexander Payne: Well, I think first who is right for the part, be the actor famous or not so famous. And it just so happens that Jack Nicholson was very right for *About Schmidt* and George Clooney is very right for *The Descendants*. But *Sideways*, for example, I thought no one kind of superfamous was quite right for those two parts.

Davies: Right. And I heard that George Clooney was interested in the part that Thomas Haden Church got. Why was Clooney right for *The Descendants* and maybe not quite the right fit for *Sideways*?

Payne: Yeah. Well, the part in *Sideways* called for a guy who's a failed TV actor and the fact that George Clooney is this handsome, extremely successful television and film actor, I thought that if he were playing that part, that that would've been one of the jokes of the film and I didn't want that to be a joke of the film. I wanted the film to have its own jokes.

And he's right for *The Descendants* because he's the right age. He's the right look and coloring for someone, one of those handsome rich guys out in Hawaii, and also emotionally for the part, the fact that maybe we film viewers have detected in George Clooney's work a certain charming detachment from emotions or how he looks at the proceedings going on around him, with a certain twinkle in his eye but slightly detached.

I thought that that would be accurate for the character of someone who's detached from the emotions of his own life and has, over the course of the film, to kind of grow into being more connected and in touch and aware, more in touch with his own feelings. So I thought that would be interesting.

Davies: In this film the lead character Matt King has two daughters, a teenager who's a handful and a younger kid, played by Amara Miller and Shailene Woodley. If these young actresses don't pull it off, this movie's just not going to quite work. You want to tell us a little bit about finding those two actresses and casting them?

Payne: Yeah, finding young actors is, so far in my career, the hardest thing to do. Well, not necessarily hard but very, very, very time consuming. I had had some experience doing it on *Election*, finding all of those young people, and then going into *The Descendants* I told the studio, yes, I want to—I'm beginning work on the screenplay, but even as I'm writing the screenplay I want my casting director at work.

Because it's going to take a long time to find those two girls. And why? Because the young actors who have acting experience and a lot of acting chops often don't seem the age that they really are. You know, it's like seventeen going on thirty. And they seem like actors, they don't seem like real people.

And if you try to cast someone off the street or a non-professional actor, they may not have the acting chops to memorize a lot of dialogue and remain focused with all of that movie-making machinery around them, and having to do it take after take after take. I saw at least two hundred girls for the older part and at least three hundred for the younger part.

Maybe I didn't see them all personally, but between the casting director and myself those were about the numbers we saw. And Shailene is someone who has the chops. She's been acting professionally since she was under ten, yet has maintained a freshness and an innocence that, you know, I believed that she was seventeen, which is what the character is. She was eighteen when we shot. And Amara Miller, the ten-year-old, boy, that was a tough one.

Because by the time the girls would come in to read for me, you know, it's a call back for the director, they come in and they're so drilled and rehearsed by their mothers or fathers that any talent in them has been cloaked by lifelessness, of aping what their mothers or what their parents wanted them to do. But Amara had never even been in a school play. She'd never been in anything.

And I found her only three weeks before shooting by the flimsiest of threads of destiny. I happened to tell the wife of my second unit cinematographer that I was still—just casually in conversation—that I was looking for a girl who would be like this or that. Unknown to me, she told a friend in her apartment building who told another friend who has a sister in Monterrey, California, who has a daughter who maybe is kind of a ham and wants to act.

And three days later, I woke up and in my email inbox was an audition from this little girl, Amara Miller, and a minute into the audition I said, "Oh, there she is. That's she." And that's someone who, as I said, has no acting chops but she's very, very comfortable simply in being herself. And has—that's someone you cast more for the essence that she brings. So I was very, very fortunate to find those two. And I had no also-rans for either part.

Davies: Wow. If that's the case—that you take, in the case of Amara Miller for the new film, *The Descendants*, you simply can tell by your gut or whatever that this is the right person.
Payne: Correct.

Davies: How do you think you get that ability?
Payne: Well, you do have to have some tests to determine if the actors are going to be bulletproof or not, if they're going to get freaked out by the camera and the lights. So you have to do a little bit of research there, but basically it's, you know, it's kind of whom do we respond to as people? Oh, well, I like that person's essence. I like that person's face. It's a whacky choice for this film. It's more like life.

I mean, I'm trying to make films in general, on many levels—on the script level, visually, production design, rhythmically, which are like life. And the casting is the most important of all components of cinema. It's the first among equals. The cast is the primary possessor and expresser of tone. And, you know, De Sica used to say, talking about leads, he'd say, each individual human face tells its own story. And you're telling me that—at the time—three billion faces on Earth, I can only choose from twenty-five? I agree with that. I want to see many different faces in front of the camera.

Davies: Twenty-five, meaning established actors?

Payne: Correct. You know, any time you cast a movie where you need someone famous in the lead, lead part or in the top two or three parts, you're a prisoner of whoever happens to be famous or hot in the six-month window in which you're trying to get a film financed. So I lament that many times a director has to compromise about who those lead actors must be simply in order to get the film financed. When in fact that's the single most important element of the film that should be never compromised.

Davies: Well, with your kind of success I guess you can kind of do what you want now, right, or hopefully . . .

Payne: As long as I keep my prices low. As long as I keep the budgets of my films low, I'm granted more freedom. Absolutely. But it's totally related to budget.

Davies: One of the memorable moments in your film *About Schmidt*, your earlier film, is when Warren, the Jack Nicholson character, realizes that his deceased wife had an affair with a friend. And in *The Descendants* we find that the lead character, Matt King, played by George Clooney, his wife is in a coma. He discovers that in fact his wife was cheating on him. This is a fascinating situation where the people learn of an affair, try to grapple with the most important relationship in their lives at a time when it's too late to do anything about it. Now, I don't know how much of the story we want to give away here, I mean but this character Matt King does find that his wife, who's now in a coma, has been having an affair. And one of the things that happens is that he and his daughter set off to find this man who was having an affair with his wife. And I don't know if we want to reveal too much here, but it's interesting that there's a dramatic confrontation brewing and there are a lot of ways you could resolve it, some of which, you know, you might have him punch out the guy or have an angry argument. And the way it is resolved seems to me that kind of improvised thing that happens in real life, and I'm just wondering how you approach that.

Payne: This is a very faithful adaptation of the novel. And what I liked about it, one of the things I liked about the novel was that when he does learn of the infidelity and he does feel murderous, greater than that he feels a responsibility to his wife to say, you know, I want to kill the mug but I should let him know that the wife is dying and that—and give him a chance to go to the hospital to say goodbye. And I just gave away some of the plot, but that act of love, when it's difficult, was something that I thought was very beautiful and was one of the main reasons I wanted to make the film. And so when you talk about the confrontation between the two at the end, I mean I play it for some comedy as well, for some kind of supercharged drama/comedy.

But more than wanting to kill the guy, I see George Clooney's character in the film as simply someone who wants to know the truth. He finds the guy and says, "Did you love her? Did she love you? Like, what, how did you meet?" Those things. Just wanting to know the truth. And that has roots, of course, in Greek tragedy, where you want to know the truth but of course the truth may hurt you more than you realize. And I don't know, I just think that's interesting.

Davies: Yeah. And in some way he's sort of trying to figure out some things about his own life which he hadn't bothered paying much attention to.

Payne: Yeah. He's taking responsibility for his own complicity in a failed marriage. You bet.

Davies: Now, your films have a real sense of place. This is set in Hawaii. It's based on a novel by Kaui Hart Hemmings. Do I have the name right?

Payne: Yes.

Davies: And I'm kind of curious about what was distinctive about Hawaiian life or culture that you wanted to bring into this film and how you got there.

Payne: I had visited Hawaii many times over the last twenty years, starting in 1990 when I took my thesis film from UCLA to play it at the Hawaii International Film Festival. So my first trip to Hawaii was not as a tourist, but rather as a friend of someone who grew up there and in fact went to Punahou High School, that elite school where indeed even our president attended. And from that point on I always got a sense of the complex social fabric and cultural fabric, ethnically. It's very sui generis. It's very unique out there.

Davies: Why put as much effort as you do in some of these films to make them rooted in a place? And that really struck me in *Sideways*, that we saw a lot of the Santa Barbara wine country. And we see a lot of Hawaii in *The Descendants*.

Payne: Well, I think that for some reason, and it wasn't conscious—now I recognize it in retrospect and now I'm conscious of it, but capturing that sense of place has become very important to me. Maybe because the first three features I did were set in Omaha, my hometown, and I was trying to grasp something about Omaha—something elusive about one's own sense of place. And in making those first three films, and certainly by *About Schmidt* I began to acquire a certain skill set about how to do that, and I think that skill set was refined a bit more in capturing Santa Barbara County in *Sideways*. By the time I got to doing *The Descendants*, and really wanted to show almost with the eye and sensibility of a documentarian, a right feeling—physically and rhythmically—of Hawaii, then it's sort of become something I'm very, very interested in, to the point where now when I consider future movies, I audition mentally not just the story, the emotional story, but also where is it going to take place. Does the setting interest me as much as the story?

Davies: I want to talk about *Election*, the film you made in 1999.
Payne: And still the film I get the most compliments for.

Davies: Really?
Payne: Yeah.

Davies: Well, it's a terrific film. It's based on a novel by Tom Perrotta. And I thought we would begin by listening to a clip. This is the story of a high school class election where Reese Witherspoon plays Tracy Flick, who's this ambitious overachieving kid who is running for class president. She has a conflict with a teacher, who's played by Matthew Broderick, who develops a real dislike for her, and he convinces a football star named Paul Metzler to run for class president. He's a really sweet naive kid. He's played by Chris Klein.
[soundbite from *Election*]

Boy, memorable character here. You know, Reese Witherspoon, I guess she was maybe twenty-one, twenty-two when she played this role, and it struck me, she's playing a younger person, a high school kid, but a kid who is worldly-wise and cynical beyond her years. Want to talk a little bit about getting that performance from her?
Payne: Well, she's a smart actress. She knew what the heck to do. I think the only thing I really helped her out with was the accent. It was slightly, slightly Fargo-ish, and I tried to keep her kind of, you know, on this side of going too far with the accent, and then encouraging her to do some of the more physical humor. But, man, she can do anything.

Davies: The other thing that I noticed about this film and also about *About Schmidt* was the use of voiceovers to kind of give the inner dialogue, the inner voice of the characters. You don't do that on *Sideways* or *The Descendants*. I'm wondering when that . . .
Payne: Yeah, there is—sorry to correct you . . . but *The Descendants* has quite a bit of voiceover, in the first half hour, forty minutes or so.

Davies: So seamlessly included that I didn't notice.
Payne: I'm so happy you didn't notice. But I like voiceover a lot. And one of the main reasons I wanted to make *Election*, in fact, was the challenge of having multiple voiceover.

Davies: Right.
Payne: I had never seen that before. Both *Goodfellas* and *Casino* have a little bit of multiple voiceover but I thought, what if you do a movie, you know, slightly *Rashomon*-like, you know, it's different people's perspectives around a single event. The book *Election* had, I think, seven or eight people's first-person accounts of these proceedings, and then for purposes of the screenplay Jim Taylor and I limited it to four. And this kind of narrative passing the baton—how to do that was the main reason I wanted to make that film.

Davies: Yeah. And there's a wonderful moment when—it's probably the night before the big election when each of them lie down and say their prayers and we can hear them. And it's just this kind of wonderful exposition of their own perspectives of life.
Payne: Yeah. Thanks. I liked that too. I think the reason I still get the most compliments on this film over any of my other films, I saw the film a couple of years ago and to my eye it succeeds on two levels; one, it's not

too long. I think it's the only film I've made so far which isn't somehow too long. It's kind of exactly right. And it succeeds rhythmically. It has a very good internal metronome that just clicks along and just rhythmically it's very good. And second, I think the cynical bite of the film is giving it some staying power. I think cynicism ages much better than sentimentality.

Davies: So why are your other films too long?

Payne: Well, they're not very much too long. But, when working with a feature, it's just sometimes, I don't know, it's hard to get movies to cut finally so they're exactly right and feel exactly the right rhythm and that they end exactly when they should. And usually there's some scene or sections of scenes that drag the film down a little bit—and I'm aware of that while making the film, and then the editor and I have to make the judgment, well, you know, we could cut that scene but if we did cut that scene, then the scene forty minutes later wouldn't pay off and those sorts of questions come up constantly. But *Election* somehow came out just right.

Davies: *Sideways* is a story of two guys on a road trip, Miles, who is played by Paul Giamatti, is this slightly depressed, divorced schoolteacher and aspiring author who hopes to get his book published and a big wine buff. And he is there with his old friend Jack, who is played by Thomas Haden Church, who's sort of a not-terribly-successful actor who's about to get married. This is going to be their little bachelor's trip away to the Santa Barbara wine country. And Miles is all about the wine and Jack is on the make, wants to have a wild time before he gets hitched.

This movie was based on the novel by Rex Pickett, unpublished I think when you read it, right?

Payne: As was *Election*. *Election* was unpublished when I read it.

Davies: Right. You really pull these little known-works. What convinced you this would make a good movie, *Sideways*?

Payne: I knew it immediately. I started reading that manuscript, I was on airplane, and at about twenty pages in I just started rooting for it—please stay good. Please don't disappoint me. Please don't suddenly come up with some stupid contrivance. Please keep it human and idiosyncratic and weird. And thank God it did straight to the finish. And I got off that plane ride and went to a pay phone and called the producer who had sent it to me and I said I want to do this. And that was before *About Schmidt*. So I was sitting on it while making *About Schmidt* and then finally when I finished *About Schmidt*, did *Sideways*.

Davies: Again, you know, casting is really important to you. Tell us why Paul Giamatti was right for this role?
Payne: Well, he's one of our most magnificent actors. And I remember thinking when he auditioned for the part, I thought, man, this is a guy who can make even bad dialogue work. And that's kind of what I look for in actors and leads: those who can, no matter what the dialogue is, make it work.

Davies: Right. And what about Thomas Haden Church, what did he bring?
Payne: Well, he's just such a unique personage, Mr. Church. He had auditioned for me for both *Election* and *About Schmidt* and he always makes a big impact when you meet him. And I had him come in and audition for *Sideways* two or three times because I wanted to be exactly sure, but he's just such a wild guy and there's a really unpredictable comic streak in him. He's one of the funniest individuals I've ever met. And I just thought mentally, I kind of mentally put together Paul Giamatti and Thomas Haden Church and I thought, well, I would like to see that movie. I mean, I didn't, they didn't meet before two or three weeks before we started shooting. I just imagined that they would be good together.

Davies: Did you have them spend time together, tooling around the wine country to get acquainted?
Payne: Oh, yeah. That's why I had them come out to Santa Barbara County two or three weeks before we started shooting, supposedly to do rehearsal but not so much with me but rather so that they could spend time together and play golf together and go taste wine and hang out and go to a movie together, because if their friendship was not believable on-screen then it wasn't going to be much of a movie because they're such different individuals.

Davies: What makes it unique is the wine stuff, the fact that Paul Giamatti is this struggling novelist, I mean, the particular contrast in these characters.
Payne: Yes. Well, I'd seen versions of the film in a way, the male friendship between an extrovert and an introvert or one who is kind of a

centralist and one who is more internal. You see it in *Zorba the Greek*. You see it in *The Easy Life*, an Italian film from the early sixties. You see it to a degree in *Withnail and I*. So that combination has been done before. It's kind of two sides of a single man's soul. But, again, one thing is the emotional story of a film and the other thing is where and under what circumstances? And the fact that it was during a wine tasting trip the week before one of them was to be married and in Santa Barbara County, it just made it unique. I had never seen that film before.

Davies: And there's that memorable moment in the film where the Paul Giamatti character says, "I'm not drinking Merlot."
Payne: Yes.

Davies: Did this movie kill Merlot?
Payne: I'm told it did. It didn't—you can't kill Merlot but I'm told that it had an impact on Merlot wine sales and a positive impact on Pinot Noir wine sales. And that joke, I'm not drinking any, you know, Merlot, I thought was just a nice little joke. I never in a million years could have predicted that it would enter, to some degree, popular culture.

Davies: And before we go, I wanted to ask you just a bit about *Paris, je t'aime*: The film that you made a short for, starring Margo Martindale, which she described in an interview on *Fresh Air* recently and just in the most touching way. Just tell us a little bit about that piece.
Payne: Thank you for bringing it up. I would say that's the only one of my films I would recommend, probably because it's only six minutes long. But I'm proud of it. It kind of, in a way, does everything I'm doing in my feature films and does it in only six minutes. And I wrote it specifically for Margo Martindale. I had wanted to work with her for years since I saw her in *Lorenzo's Oil*, years ago. I was watching the movie and enjoyed it but then this one actress came up and I kept saying, "Who is she? Who is she?" You know, in the way she distinguished herself as Hilary Swank's mother in *Million Dollar Baby* and she's done a ton of other stuff and she's always just terrific and I wanted to work with her, so I wrote that part specifically for her.

Davies: Right. And she is a Denver postal carrier, right, who is describing her trip to Paris in French.
Payne: Yes. In really bad French.

Davies: Bad French with a heavy American accent. Did you direct her that way?

Payne: Yes. Well, when I talked to her on the phone, asking her if she wanted to come do the film, I asked her whether she spoke French or not and she said no. And I said, have you ever even had one class in it? She said no. I said perfect because you'll be speaking only French. And it was quite a process to get that voice performance out of her. She spoke the dialogue for that six-minute film, and it took us about eight hours to get it out of her and then another couple of days of editing, voiceover editing. But, in doing so, I think the film makes fun of both the French and the Americans.

Davies: It's sort of her and her week in Paris walking in various places and describing things she sees in somewhat comical ways at times. But there's this last scene where she's seated on a bench. You want to just talk a little bit about that scene, what's going on there?

Payne: Well, I was trying to capture that feeling I have and I'm sure many other people have of when you're—for me it's like when I'm alone in the middle of a workday and I happen to go to a museum and I'm just all by myself and I walk around the galleries and look at stuff on the wall and think my own little thoughts and maybe I have thoughts that I write down and I feel just sort of connected to the world around me and to myself. And it's one of those feelings you have alone when you're traveling—with a museum example I just used—and that's a feeling. The genesis of that film was wanting to convey that feeling, and it's nice to have the medium of a short film to convey just small feelings like that and not try to have to get them into a feature film. But in that, you asked about the final scene. She's had a bit of a very lonely time walking around Paris by herself, even though she keeps telling herself that she's having a great time but we see visually that she's not, that she's really quite lonely. And then she just has a moment like that sitting on a park bench. And I think she acted it quite beautifully.

Alexander Payne Talks *The Descendants* and His Next Two Projects, *Nebraska* and *Wilson*

Christina Radish / 2011

From Collider.com, November 17, 2011. Reprinted by permission of the interviewer.

In *The Descendants*, director Alexander Payne (creator of the Oscar-winning *Sideways*) follows the unpredictable journey of an American family at a crossroads. Set in picturesque Hawaii, Matt King (George Clooney), husband and father of two girls, is forced to re-examine his life when his wife is incapacitated in a boating accident. While attempting to repair his relationship with his seventeen-year-old daughter Alexandra (Shailene Woodley) and ten-year-old Scottie (Amara Miller), he learns things about his wife and his family that he was never even aware of, but that send him down the path toward rebuilding his life.

At the film's press day, Alexander Payne talked about wanting to bring such a human story to life, how happy he was to get to work with George Clooney on this film after deciding that he wasn't right for *Sideways*, what led him to cast Shailene Woodley, and what draws him to atypical love stories. He also talked about having his next two projects lined up—a film about a father-son road trip from Montana to Nebraska, tentatively called *Nebraska* (scheduled to shoot in May 2012) and an adaptation of a Daniel Clowes graphic novel, called *Wilson* (scheduled to shoot in late 2012 or early 2013).

Christina Radish: How did you find this book? Were you looking for a project to do and someone recommended it, or did you come across it yourself?
Alexander Payne: My flag is always flying. My shingle is always out.

I'm always looking for movie ideas. The hardest part of this whole moviemaking endeavor is finding ideas. That's the real goal. We—and by "we," I mean my producing partners and I—optioned this book in 2007.

Radish: You probably read hundreds of books. What was it about this book that made you think, "I could do a great adaptation. This would be a great movie."?

Payne: It was just a nice, human story in an exotic locale.

Radish: Did you just really want to go to Hawaii?

Payne: Well, that was a bonus, and not just for the obvious reasons. I thought, "I've never really seen Hawaii, or specifically Honolulu, portrayed in a film before," and I like Hawaii a lot. I just thought it would be fun and interesting. It's really weird out there, and it's interesting. I lament that, in big cities, we don't have what we have in small cities, which is just spontaneously going to someone's house and sitting down and talking, for a long time. It's really tough in this city, as you know.

Radish: This film has an incredible balance between the visual and the story. You're in this beautiful location, and yet you're so absorbed by the characters and story that you almost become oblivious to the beauty of Hawaii itself. How did you achieve that?

Payne: I think a lot about how to make movies, where you have a keen eye on the characters in the foreground, but always, in the background, something is happening. You may note that I don't use long lenses very much. I tend to veer more toward wide lenses, where you see the characters in the foreground, but there's always something happening in the background. Among directors whom I admire, who do the same thing, I would cite Anthony Mann, who made a lot of Westerns in the fifties with James Stewart. In my mind, he was a great master at keeping the foreground story, but always having the shifting landscape in the background, which is somehow commenting subliminally on the story.

Radish: Your films tend to have middle-aged men in crisis. Why are you interested in those types of stories?

Payne: I don't know. We can even throw in the Matthew Broderick character in *Election*, as being yet another of these protagonists who says, "Oh, I'm happy in life. I've done what everyone tells me to do. I'm a good citizen. I should be reaping the rewards." And, in fact, they run into a certain crisis, which forces them to strip away all of those material concerns, and somehow confront their essence. But, I don't think about that, at the time. That's only in retrospect. In the moment of making a film, I just think, "Oh, this would be funny. This would be a good comedy."

Radish: George Clooney seems to joke a lot about how he wanted to be in *Sideways*, but you didn't cast him in that film.
Payne: Yeah, I never bring that up myself.

Radish: Why did you think he was right for this film?
Payne: Because he's perfect. First of all, even before I had met him for *Sideways*, I thought that he and I would work well together. I was sad that I didn't think he was right for *Sideways*, and that I'd missed that opportunity to work with him. But, when I began work on this film, he was my first and only choice. He's the right age and he's the right look. In as much as sometimes, in his films, we audience members feel that he's maybe a little emotionally detached, I thought that would work well for this character, who has this emotional awakening from someone who's been asleep or unaware or detached, or whatever word you'd like to use.

Radish: What did Shailene Woodley bring to this role, and why did you decide to cast her?
Payne: Boy, she's the cat's pajamas. She has this seemingly fake enthusiasm and positiveness, but it's for real, and it's creepy. No. She's a positive human, and boy, what a good actress. Between my casting director and I, we probably looked at well over a couple hundred gals for that part. I wanted someone who had equal parts fire and vulnerability. My mental model had been a seventeen-year-old Debra Winger. That's whom I would have cast, in that part.

Radish: Did she have to do a test screening with George Clooney?
Payne: No, I've never done that in my life. I've just had good luck. Those two guys in *Sideways*—[Thomas Haden] Church and [Paul] Giamatti— had never met until about two weeks before we started shooting. I figure, as long as I'm picking them all, it's going through a certain sifter and it will be okay. Thank Christ, I haven't been wrong yet. Also, consider that the cinema has a remarkable capacity to lie. You say, "Here's a father and daughter," and audiences say, "Oh, okay," even if they don't have all the chemistry. But, you certainly can tell in movies where there's no chemistry between the actors. This is a bit of an arcane example, but I

never believed the chemistry between Maximillian Schell and Melina Mercouri in *Topkapi*. I loved the film. It's a super-fun film. But, they're supposed to be lovers, and there's zero chemistry between them. Maybe because her husband, Jules Dassin, was directing it.

Radish: Had you seen Shailene Woodley in her TV show, *The Secret Life of the American Teenager*?
Payne: I'd never seen her in anything. I just saw her in her audition. I cast off of auditions. I always do.

Radish: Which scene did she audition with?
Payne: I make actors jump in head first, so it was the "Mom was cheating on you" scene. And then, she was so good in the audition that I said, "Just to confirm, do you mind reading another scene cold?" I forget what that one was.

Radish: What brings you to these unusual love stories?
Payne: I don't know. We have plenty of those other kinds of stories, and I do like strange love stories. *Midnight Cowboy* is such a beautiful love story. *The Last Detail* is a beautiful three-way love story. *Driving Miss Daisy* is a very beautiful love story. When love crosses gender, age, class, and social conventions, it's very beautiful. *The Last Detail* is a love story between two prison keepers, and their prisoner. None of them want to be there, and they find a way to love through that. It's nice.

Radish: But, rarely do you see a love story between a man and a comatose woman.
Payne: Yeah. A buddy of mine from film school, who watched an early cut, remarked that he had a shifting relationship with the comatose wife, during the whole film. He said, "At the beginning, I had one feeling. In the middle, I hated her. And then, by the end, I just found that I suddenly loved her." That had never struck me before. In a way, she's the one writing the script of the whole film, that the rest of them are just acting out. Although silent, she speaks.

Radish: How closely did you work with the author on this?
Payne: I did my own adaptation, but I would say that it's by far the most faithful adaptation I've ever done. I relied upon her advice, to make sure I was getting the twists and turns of phrase in the script right, and then I also relied upon her a lot to open some doors for me, in that upper-class

world in Honolulu. That's not my world. Always, when you make a film in a sub-culture, like with the Armenians in *Sideways*, you need a guide.

Radish: What do you have coming up next?
Payne: I have the next two films lined up, and I can't wait to start shooting, actually. The next one is tentatively called *Nebraska*, and it's a father-son road trip, from Montana to Nebraska. After that is the adaptation of a Daniel Clowes graphic novel, called *Wilson*. With any measure of good luck, I'll start shooting *Nebraska* in May. And then, I'd like to start shooting *Wilson*, possibly as early as November, but I bet in January of 2013. I want to start moving quickly.

Radish: Is *Nebraska* an original script?
Payne: *Nebraska* is an original, by some guy out of Snohomish, Washington.

Radish: What do you enjoy about taking existing work and making it into a film?
Payne: A book suggests a whole world and story that I could have never thought of, in a million years. I could have never thought of *Sideways*. I could have never thought of this guy whose wife has been stepping out on him, and the aristocracy of Honolulu. Who the hell would ever think of that? Rex Pickett with *Sideways*, and Kaui Hemmings with this one, wrote autobiographically, or at least about a world that they know. I'm then able to get something really specific, and hopefully make it into something universal. It allows me to then travel to a place that I never could have thought of, but still be able to put my personal stamp on it. Of course, it's a highfalutin example, but eleven of Kubrick's thirteen films were adaptations, and yet they're all Kubrick films, from *Barry Lyndon* to *2001* to *A Clockwork Orange*. They are widely disparate films, but with such a strong through-line.

Interview with Alexander Payne

Charlie Rose / 2011

From *Charlie Rose* television show, November 28, 2011. Transcript published by permission of Charlie Rose, Inc.

Charlie Rose: Alexander Payne is here. He is a director and screenwriter. His movies have been praised for their humor and their pathos. *Film Comment* magazine calls Payne, "One of an endangered species." His new movie, *The Descendants*, it is his first feature film in seven years. Welcome. It's good to have you here.
Alexander Payne: Thanks, thanks for having me.

Rose: So tell me how this got started because you were going to make another movie and then you didn't make that movie. And then all of a sudden somebody comes up with the idea of *The Descendants* and you sort of looked at that and you said—
Payne: "I haven't done anything in seven years."
Rose: —so maybe I should.
Payne: Sort of. It's true I was anxious to direct. I was very anxious to direct a feature and after *Sideways* I never would have predicted that seven years would elapse before the next one. So that is true.
Rose: Right.
Payne: But it's kind of been harped on a lot recently as I've been making the rounds of interviews—which is why I understand it but—
Rose: You're absolutely right.
Payne: I mean, I was busy.
Rose: Yes.
Payne: So no you're right. My usual co-writer Jim Taylor and I spent over two years, two and a half years writing something—a very ambitious sort of science fiction social satire.

Rose: *Downsizing*?
Payne: Correct, you are well-informed, yes.

Rose: And so why didn't it get made?
Payne: Well, it was a very difficult screenplay and we finally finished it in about May or June of '09 when the economy crashed and I thought correctly that it was going to be hard to get financing for it and we—by we, my two producing partners Jim Taylor being one and Jim Burke being another—had optioned this book *The Descendants* in '07 and I was urged to do it. I said no, "I'm too busy writing this other thing with Jim," and my mind couldn't really allow another film to enter my consideration. So anyway, I was very anxious to direct and when we finished *Downsizing* I thought it was going to be tough to get made. That's when I dived into *The Descendants* and that was in July of '09.

Rose: And how much of an appeal was making a film in Hawaii?
Payne: Very appealing. Very appealing and not for just the obvious of the sun and the surf and the nature which is all present and fantastic. But I had been to Hawaii many times and I was aware of that very unique and complex social and cultural structure and fabric out there. And I thought making this film would allow me to wear a bit of a documentarian's hat as well.

Rose: You also have been praised for your casting insights.
Payne: The only compliment I would really give myself in filmmaking is I think I cast well. That's true.

Rose: And you didn't cast Clooney in *Sideways*.
Payne: Correct.
Rose: Because?
Payne: I didn't think he was right for the part.
Rose: Because?
Payne: I was flattered that he—this was for the part that Thomas Haden Church—

Rose: Right, right that he did well.
Payne: The role called for a really washed-up TV actor. I mean that was the part. And I thought—
Rose: That's a leap of faith for George.
Payne: Well, I don't normally care about a star or an actor's context

outside of the film but in this case I had to consider it because to have George Clooney, one of the most famous and handsome and successful movie and TV stars playing this guy, I thought that would be too much of a joke.

Rose: Well, how about having him as a character named Matt whose wife is having an affair?
Payne: He's well cast for that.
Rose: How so, sir?
Payne: Well, in this case he was my first and only choice for this. I mean you know that man.
Rose: Even though—yes I do, well.
Payne: And you know he's a delightful fellow and I wanted to work with him since meeting him for *Sideways* and bumping into him a couple times over the years. And I just thought he'd be terrific at this. He's at the right age, the right look; and also the character calls for someone who's a bit emotionally detached having a bit of an awakening. And I thought well, Mr. Clooney is often sort of cool in his parts, not all of them, but in many and to see him wake up to a more emotional state I thought it would be interesting.

Rose: I wonder if he's easier to direct because he's also a director.
Payne: That's exactly right. I've had the experience with both Jack Nicholson and George Clooney who have both directed and directing actors who have themselves directed is much easier. They understand the director's problems and they wish to serve.

Rose: Have you ever wanted to act?
Payne: Yes. A little bit. But I—
Rose: Why don't you put yourself in your own movie?
Payne: I'm shy. I'm shy. I know that I would—because I never think I'm right for any parts in my films.
Rose: Well create a part for God's sake. This is your movie.
Payne: Yes, yes. Thank you for that. Thank you for that, but if someone else casts me and could direct me well then I would do it.
Rose: They have to prove that they can direct you well before you would do it?
Payne: No, as a director I would know how to make their life easy.

Rose: All right, so this movie is about family?

Payne: My own way into it was more from the point of view of the protagonist, dealing with his family like—we can say it's about family and that's fantastic I won't argue but—
Rose: This is about George dealing with his wife who's dying, his daughter who's wonderful in this film, by the way.
Payne: Yes, she is. Yes.

Rose: But tell me more, your entry into the film was?
Payne: Through him. The book is first person—through seeing all the proceedings through his eyes and I was interested in that and I carried over certain first person sense of that narrative into the movie as well. It has voiceover and it's very locked into Clooney's character, you know, through the course of the film.

Rose: What do you say to those directors who say "I'd rather develop new material than somebody else's material"?
Payne: I say that's wonderful. A movie can be anything.
Rose: Yes.
Payne: But I personally love doing adaptations from time to time because a book can suggest a whole world I never could have thought of.
Rose: Yes.
Payne: I never could have thought of a story like this.

Rose: Are you glad that you went to film school rather than whatever else you were going to do? You were thinking about going to journalism school. Columbia, was it?
Payne: Yes, when I was a senior in college I applied to five film schools and to Columbia Journalism School.
Rose: Yes.
Payne: And I would have been very happy also—
Rose: And why did you choose one over the other?
Payne: I had been a film buff my whole life but didn't receive a whole lot of sort of encouragement from my family, let's say. Once I got into film they were very encouraging but I was encouraged to go to law school or do something more straight. So going to film school was more of a distant dream.
Rose: Right, right.
Payne: But I knew when I got the acceptance letters to film school that I had to try it.

Rose: Because you didn't know whether you had a gift or whether you liked it, or both?
Payne: I had to find out whether my love of watching films would translate into loving making them and also to find out if I had any talent at it.

Rose: Is there anything not to like about making films?
Payne: There's a lot not to like.
Rose: Like what?
Payne: There is a lot of despair involved between films.
Rose: Despair.
Payne: Between films. Yes, yes.
Rose: Between films but not within films? I mean, despair might be waiting for the next film to come along or struggling to get it—
Payne: Correct, or if you make a turkey and it's hard to get your next one off the ground or even if you make a successful film like *The Descendants* and still years can go by and what's my next film going to be? There's always a lot of despair—am I going to get the budget I need: all those sorts of things.

Rose: Did *Sideways* deliver everything that you wanted it to do in terms of giving you the opportunity to do other things?
Payne: It actually did more than I thought it would do. I never expected it to achieve that degree of success that it did. I thought it was a nice little comedy, even kind of slight. I mean I had no idea—
Rose: It's a lovely story.
Payne: Thank you. And Rex Picket who wrote the book—it's to his credit.

Rose: About wine?
Payne: Yes.
Rose: And relationships.
Payne: Yes.
Rose: You can't go wrong there, wine and relationships.
Payne: I didn't know. I just thought it was a nice little movie.

Rose: Now your former wife is in the film.
Payne: Correct, Sandra Oh, that's right.
Rose: A great actress.
Payne: Yes.

Rose: And how is it to direct someone that's that close to you?
Payne: Let me see, it's been a few years ago. It was fine. She's a terrific actress.

Rose: Do you know what you're going to do next? Are you going to go back to *Downsizing*?
Payne: I do. No not quite yet I will in a couple years but I'm anxious just now to shoot and shoot—
Rose: To jump right into something.
Payne: Yes. So for the first time in my career I have my next two—not just projects lined up but the scripts are actually written, so I can swing from one to one.
Rose: Your scripts or someone else's scripts?
Payne: They are both written (this is another first in my career) by others.

Rose: Are you scared of that?
Payne: No.

Rose: Do you like the scripts?
Payne: I've written only out of desperation.

Rose: Can you tell us about what these films are?
Payne: Yes, the next is a father/son road trip from Billings, Montana, to Lincoln, Nebraska, that gets waylaid at a town in central Nebraska.

Rose: Aren't you from Omaha?
Payne: I'm from Omaha.
Rose: Right.
Payne: Yes. So that's the basic story there.
Rose: Right.

Payne: And then following that is the adaptation of a graphic novel by a fellow named Daniel Clowes out of Oakland, California.
Rose: Yes.
Payne: Who ten years or so ago wrote *Ghost World* if you recall that film. So he's adapted his own graphic novel for me.

Rose: Now if you look at the kinds of things that you have done is there some link? Is there some common denominator? Are there are certain

kinds of characters that we find in all of these films? A certain kind of male psyche or whatever it might be? And I'm staying away from the word that you hate, which is loser, which I agree with you.
Payne: Yes, there are just—
Rose: Because Matt is not a loser.
Payne: —if they are losers then we are all losers. They're just people.

Rose: Yes, exactly. Yes. But would you like to make an espionage thriller?
Payne: Oh, yes. I would like to. I want to make a Western for sure.
Rose: Yes.
Payne: And I would like to dive into all sorts of different genres but for this first part of my career it's been these nice little comedies.

Rose: If you look at a film like *The Descendants* is there a tone there that some people look for? How would you describe the tone of that film?
Payne: I guess the last few films I've made are essentially sad stories or dramas in a way but told like comedies. I mean, I basically consider myself, to date, a comedy director. But I consider comedy a very serious form.

Rose: What is it about film that that you love? Is it telling stories?
Payne: No, it's a very interesting question because, like so many people, I've been madly in love with film as long as I can remember. I think a lot of it is—if you love film, you love life.
Rose: Yes.
Payne: It's the most verisimilar mirror we have. If we look to art in general to be a mirror of our lives and to give us context and just give us something to reflect off of, we've been waiting millennia for film. This completely verisimilar mirror—I don't know another way to say it, it really is us and it also captures time. It defeats death in a way because you can see people who have long since died. You can capture moments in life, just like you know core samples of someone's life. Now, if you're a film actor like George Clooney or Jack Nicholson who's been in films basically their entire lives, to have your entire life recorded for posterity.

Rose: How about sitting at this table for your entire life?
Payne: Yes, yes. And also I like the plasticity of it. I like the jigsaw puzzle of making a film, of corralling all of these forces and elements into basically a two-hour analog form. I like the feature film form.

Rose: Is an hour and a half or an hour and forty-five minutes; is two hours and fifteen minutes sort of the ideal time?
Payne: Yes, yes, plus or minus two hours. It has been for years. You know that.
Rose: Yes, why is that? Audience's attention?
Payne: I don't know, that's a good question. I wonder if it goes back to theater. Or if it's about how long—
Rose: Those theater pieces are two hours?
Payne: Maybe it has to do with the bladder.
Rose: You think?
Payne: Maybe.

Rose: If you were making *The Descendants* over, having been in the editing room, would you change it at all now that you can look back and now that you've had the experience of talking about it with people?
Payne: That's a rough question.
Rose: Yes, but let me ask you the same question.
Payne: Yes, no that's a rough question because I just finished it and my collaborators and I put our all into it.
Rose: Yes.
Payne: And at the moment, there are a few cuts I'd like to adjust. I mean, when I've seen it at screenings lately, I think, "Oh a few more frames there, sort of little tinkering." But no, it's a good snapshot of where my collaborators and I were at the time we were making that film.

Rose: And is the joy—some directors say to me the thing that they love is shooting. And for you it is—
Payne: Editing. Editing is the natural state of man. It's a really beautiful place to be. You're sitting atop of the pain of writing and the physical exhaustion, although exhilaration, of directing and then, that's really where you put the film together and where you'd have this access to a language exclusive to cinema, which is montage. And that goes back to an earlier question of yours, why do I like movies so much?
Rose: Right.
Payne: Because I really like editing. And my editor and I spend a long time editing, at least by today's standards. This was nine months from start to finish.

Rose: And do you edit a rough cut that's—what?—two and a half hours, three hours.

Payne: Yes, sure. You always start long, you include everything which is in the screenplay and then begin whittling down.

Rose: Good luck to you.
Payne: Thanks, thanks for having me. A pleasure.

Alexander Payne Prefers Actors Who Can Communicate

Jennelle Riley / 2011

From *Backstage*, December 14, 2011. Reprinted by permission of *Backstage*

Alexander Payne is the kind of filmmaker his peers can't help envying. All five of his feature films have been successful, commercially and critically. More important, they were made on his terms, products of an offbeat and uncompromising vision. He can find the heart in any situation, be it controversial (think of the glue-sniffing pregnant woman unwittingly caught in an abortion debate in *Citizen Ruth*) or ordinary (the meandering road trip of *About Schmidt*). And he has a way of making audiences invest in the average, such as the life of the failed author–wine connoisseur of his Oscar-winning *Sideways*. He does so with pathos, humor, and an eye for everyday absurdities; it's not uncommon to find two people who have seen the same film by Payne and to learn one laughed, while the other cried, throughout.

His latest film, *The Descendants*, tells the story of Matt King (George Clooney), a land baron in Hawaii who also is a distant descendant of King Kamehameha. Matt finds himself tasked with raising his two daughters (Shailene Woodley and Amara Miller) after his wife has a boating accident that places her in an irreversible coma. The film is full of complex and fascinating people, from his wife's angry father (Robert Forster) to her secret lover (Matthew Lillard) to his kind but clueless wife (Judy Greer). Even characters with only a few lines create fully realized individuals, thanks to the writing by Payne, Jim Rash, and Nat Faxon. And somehow Payne, a nice midwestern boy from Omaha, Nebraska, understands the culture and lifestyle of Hawaii well enough to make the state its own character onscreen.

There's a reason actors line up to work with Payne, who has gotten career-making performances from greats such as Reese Witherspoon (*Election*) and Paul Giamatti (*Sideways*). As Lillard told *Backstage*, "To speak to the talent of Alexander Payne real quick: This is a movie about a guy, his wife is dying, he's left with two kids, and [he's dealing with] indigenous land rights in Hawaii. There's not a studio in the world that would make that, except for Fox Searchlight. And Alexander Payne made it so that it's funny and touching."

Backstage: All your films have been such critical successes; do you feel the pressure to continue that winning streak?
Alexander Payne: The pressure I have is internal, to make what I think is a good film. The person whose opinion I'm most interested in is my own, in a way. I'm at once humble enough and pretentious enough to say that I'm looking forward to making something really good in the future. These are fine little films that I feel I'm still cutting my teeth on and learning how to make a film and what a film is. I'm fifty now, and I hope this decade I can try and make one really good one.

Backstage: How do you alleviate that pressure for yourself?
Payne: I'm always going to have that pressure in my life, because I want all my films to be good. But I want to work with the freedom that I could also be making a failure, as well. I used to be friends with an old Czech film director, and when I said goodbye to him as I was going off to make *Citizen Ruth*, he said, "Oh, and one more thing." And I turned at the door, and he said, "Make a failure." Which means: Be free. Be free to just make what comes out; don't think about if it's good or bad; just go.

Backstage: Were there different stakes on this film, coming off an Oscar-winning picture?
Payne: Actually, the pressure I felt in this one was about making a film in Hawaii—which is a very unique, complex, sometimes intimidating culture that has a very strong sense of "This is our culture, you're from outside, who is this mainlander coming out here to tell our story." All those traps you can fall into out there, I was very aware of that. And I knew that I wasn't telling a story about Hawaii but about this one little corner, this self-styled aristocracy. Still, whatever's happening in Hawaii in the background had to be right. The rhythms had to be right; it's not just the right locations and costumes. I'm reading some of these reviews now, and they say, "Oh, Payne has a certain languorous rhythm." I would say it's not me. That's Hawaii, coming through the film. Things just kind of

slide this way and that, a little bit. This is all a long-winded way of saying I did feel internal pressure, within me, to get it right.

Backstage: Obviously you had the Kaui Hart Hemmings book as a source, but how did you get to know the culture so well?

Payne: I read a lot of history, talked to a lot of people—I was the frequent victim of the coconut wireless. On the other hand, I became friends with Gavan Daws, who wrote that book *Shoal of Time*, which is still the best single-volume historical survey of Hawaii. He's an Aussie who's been there since '58. He knows more about the history of Hawaii than any other single living human. And even he said, "I've been there for fifty years, and it's more of a mystery than ever to me." So I can't purport to have mastered anything; I just had to get enough right so that the film rang true. Another thing I was proud of was the music in the film. I made the decision to use 100 percent preexisting Hawaiian music.

Backstage: You originally met with George Clooney when you were casting *Sideways*—he was interested in the role that ultimately went to Thomas Haden Church. Is that where you first started thinking of him for *The Descendants*?

Payne: In retrospect, yes. But when I was making *Sideways*, I had no idea that *The Descendants* was coming my way. But it did spark in me an interest to work with Clooney. I really dig him as an actor and a star—he's so appealing and so interesting in what he does. Look at the range he's got, from *O Brother, Where Art Thou?*—which is an extreme comic part—to his deadly sobriety in *Michael Clayton*, and his compelling charm in the *Oceans* movies. He's always good; you always look at him. People tell me, "A half an hour into the film, I'm able to forget it's Clooney. He seems so Everymanish." But still, you look at him, as opposed to other people in the frame.

Backstage: Did you have him in mind when you were writing the script?
Payne: Yeah, I did.

Backstage: I've been told that's dangerous to do, but I guess there aren't many actors you can't get. Does anyone say no to you?
Payne: Early on, on *Citizen Ruth*, I had some noes. I don't think I've had a no since then.

Backstage: It seems every actor wants to work with you—
Payne: Oh good, that means they can take less money and I can keep my budgets low, which I need to do. [laughs]

Backstage: You've said that you like actors who can act "fast"; can you elaborate on that?
Payne: A movie needs to be zippy. Kurosawa used to say of Mifune: "He can express in three gestures what it takes other actors seven." Film is a constant search for economy, so you want actors to act quickly.

Backstage: So you don't necessarily mean talking fast, just communicating things in a short amount of time?
Payne: Yes. I am impressed by how quickly and effectively they can communicate what needs to be communicated.

Backstage: Matthew Lillard said that when he went into his audition, he was surrounded by muscular pretty boys. Were you originally looking for a different type for his role?
Payne: I didn't know what I was looking for. Come one, come all.

Backstage: So you really are open to anything in some instances?
Payne: Absolutely. That's the best. It's very limiting if a director has something in mind super specific for a part; that could be great, but it could also be that the director is the one who is going to suffer the most from the burden of that limited vision. Not always, but it can be so. You have to have your eyes open to what the gods bring you that you never in a million years could have imagined. That's what's beautiful about filmmaking: these beautiful, weird things that the gods bring you.

Backstage: Do you make your decisions pretty quickly? A lot of your cast of *The Descendants* only had one audition.
Payne: Yes. I believe Judy only had one audition. Lillard had only one audition. Shailene went on tape and sent it in; then I met her. I only need once. I get it. I know what the hell it is.

Backstage: Have you ever been wrong?
Payne: Rarely. Sometimes they're one-line parts. I've screwed up a couple one-line day players—one, in particular, on *About Schmidt*. But no, I'm pretty right, and I have a great casting director [John Jackson]. I give myself few compliments in filmmaking, but I cast well. Because that's

your movie. I'm just trying to find the movie that I myself would want to see. That's my job. Even on the set when the actors are doing it and I have my camera, watching their performance, I'm watching them, but it's like it's going in and it's being projected on a movie screen in my brain. So I'm the only one on set actually sitting in the theater, watching the movie. And everybody else has their own little niche—the actors, the photographers, the gaffers, the dolly grip—but I'm the only one who's just there sitting in the movie theater, popcorn in hand, watching the movie. Saying, "Oh, it should be a little bit more to the left. No, that's a little slow; it should be a little faster." That's all it is. It's easy. Anybody could do it.

Backstage: Judy has praised her role in the film as being one of the most fully written characters she's played, even in just three scenes. Do you write with as much attention to detail for every role, not just the leads?
Payne: You have to. And for actors, it's tough for bit players or smaller character parts. They have it hardest on a film, because they have to suggest an entire human being in one or two or three scenes. It's easier on leads, because they have the landscape of the whole film to build and suggest that character. But I learned that from Giamatti. He said, "It's much easier to play a lead than a character part."

Backstage: You've said you have to cast the right actor for the part; are you in the fortunate position that money doesn't enter the equation? There's no pressure to cast a name?
Payne: I mean, if I cast stars in parts, I get more money to make the movie with, typically. But at least I have enough of a reputation that it seems if I keep my budget on the low side, which I always have to date, then I have much greater leeway in casting. *Sideways* was the first movie, my fourth feature, where I didn't have to have a star to get any financing at all. I finally had enough reputation on my own to cast who I wanted.

Backstage: Is there anything you want actors to know if they're fortunate enough to audition for you?
Payne: Take it easy, there are no mistakes, and I don't expect a performance at all. It's really a glorified meeting. But what are we going to talk about? We might as well read the words from the script. And it gives me a vague idea of how sounds sound coming out of your head. Another analogy I've used: It's a pencil sketch on a cocktail napkin for what later

is going to be a great oil painting. And we might even throw that sketch away. I don't care. Give me some credit as a director to see through the artificiality of an audition. It's really no big deal.

The Lei of the Land: A Few Moments with Alexander Payne

Christy Grosz / 2012

From *Variety*, January 4, 2012. Published by permission of *Variety*. Copyright © 2012 Reed Business Information, a division of Reed Elsevier.

Alexander Payne recently spoke with *Variety*'s Christy Grosz about *The Descendants*, the difficulties in finding naturalistic child actors, star power, and why he abhors shooting scenes that take place inside a car:

Christy Grosz: Do you spend time rehearsing before shooting?
Alexander Payne: Not too much. I like to accompany the actors to the locations. It's not fair to begin shooting a man in his house [when] he only went to that house the day of shooting. The actor should ideally visit the locations well in advance, even rehearse on site. Rehearsing is sort of casual. You read through lines, you talk about it, but I'm not a hardcore rehearsal director like Sidney Lumet was or Kurosawa was or Coppola is. I think it came from the fact that I never had the budget to bring actors to the location, to pay their hotel room per diem for very long before we started shooting.

CG: You famously rejected George Clooney for a role in *Sideways*, even though he really wanted to be in the film. What made him the right choice this time around?
AP: Well, he's the right age, and second, his dark coloring leads me to believe that he could be one-sixteenth Hawaiian and maybe have a little Portuguese blood in there somewhere. But ever since I met him on *Sideways*, I thought he and I would work well together, and I really like him as an American star and actor. I think we—meaning we film viewers

and film practitioners—are lucky to have him in our midst. He's a good, disciplined, professional, generous actor, and he's got that star quality where women wish to be with him in one way and heterosexual men wish to be friends with him. And plus, he's just a good human being.

CG: How many younger actresses did you end up auditioning before you found Amara Miller and Shailene Woodley?
AP: Amara was cast three weeks before shooting, maybe even two weeks before shooting. Shailene I had about three months before shooting. I auditioned her in December of '09; we started shooting in March. Between John Jackson, the casting director, and me, I'm sure we saw over two hundred girls for Shailene's part and certainly over three hundred for Amara's part.

CG: Is it a matter of finding a more naturalistic actress?
AP: I feel like actors, the ones who are seventeen are seventeen going on thirty, and the ten-year-olds can just be irritating in how precocious and cutesy they are when they come in. The main problem with the ten-year-olds was that by the time they auditioned for me, they would be so overly rehearsed by the stage parents that their performance for me was lifeless. In the audition, I asked them to try it a little bit this way or a little bit that way, and they are unable. My advice to parents: Make sure your child knows the dialogue, but do not rehearse the child.

CG: Your last few films have had locations that almost have served as ancillary characters in the plot. Do the characters inform the locations during the script process or is it the other way around?
AP: Both. We knew that Matt King needed to have one of those rambling old plantation-style houses that people inhabit in Hawaii, but actually picking the house is the result of tons and tons of searching and discussion between the production designer and myself. *Sideways* and *The Descendants* have one thing in common, which is that I wanted to use real locations mentioned in the novel. Here's a very good example of what you're asking about. I wanted to cast Robert Forster as the angry father-in-law. Well, Robert Forster speaks with a very strong Rochester, New York, accent, so then [casting director] John Jackson and I think, "How does this man fit in this world we're showing?" Clearly he's ex-military because there's a lot of ex-military in Hawaii. So then that has a ripple effect on location scouting and production design to suggest

where an ex-military man might live in Honolulu. We found a neighborhood where they live, and of course it has a ripple effect on costume. That all came from choosing the right actor.

CG: You found a creative solution to a problem.

AP: But they're not problems. To use another overused word, in fact, they're opportunities, and that's what film is. "Who is he? Oh, he's this." It's a wonderful new color to put into the film. Making a film is not executing everything that has been predetermined. It's discovering what the film is, discovering who these people are. Through the act of making the film, you find elements which you yourself never could have thought of and which enrich the film.

CG: Where does your next project, *Nebraska*, stand in terms of shooting?

AP: I started casting but have made no offers or decisions. I cast for about six or eight weeks over the summer, and then we put a pause in the process because we hadn't quite figured out the black-and-white question. I'm making the film in black and white. It's just as well, anyway, because I had a lot of promotion stuff and lovely festivals to attend for *The Descendants*. I actually say that without irony. I'm going to start to gear up to shoot in May. After the first of the year, we will begin in earnest in pre-production.

CG: The story sounds like it has one of those middle-aged, damaged characters that seem to pervade your work.

AP: What I think it has more in common with previous stuff I've done is a road-trip aspect, which puzzles me because I can't stand road-trip films, and I can't stand shooting in cars, yet all I seem to do is make them.

CG: What's so horrible about shooting in cars?

AP: The hardest thing in the world is to shoot people eating dinner around a table. Similarly, people driving in cars. There are no new angles. They've all been done a thousand times, plus the mechanics of doing it are hideous. The camera car, the walkie-talkie, trying to keep it realistic looking, the police motorcade that must accompany you—all of those things conspire to mar the intimacy of what you're shooting. I think they had it right in old Hollywood where they would do it in the studio with rear-screen projection.

CG: Earlier in your career, some critics accused you of mocking your characters, but that argument doesn't seem to come up anymore. Have you changed or do you think critics have come around to your way of thinking?

AP: I have no idea. I reserve the right to mock anyone at any point. But I will say this, and this might sound slightly defensive, but sometimes, and I'll mention *About Schmidt,* I accused some of the critics who accused me of condescension. I thought they were themselves the snobbiest and most condescending critics. The same charge has sometimes been leveled against *Fargo.* "Oh, they're mocking those Minnesota people." Well, the Coen brothers are from Minnesota, and Minnesota people were peeing in their pants at that film it was so funny. The thing is, I don't think [writing partner] Jim Taylor and I put ourselves above the characters. If we make fun of them, we include ourselves on some level. It's never with a feeling of superiority. [Pauses, deadpan] Except sometimes.

Director of *The Descendants*, Alexander Payne, Talks Bristling Egos and Putting Life on Film

Alanna J. Lawson / 2012

From *Yahoo!7 Entertainment: The Hype*, May 22, 2012. Reproduced with the permission of Yahoo!7 Pty Limited © 2013 by Yahoo!7 Pty Limited.

Q: What did you like most about the story of *The Descendants*?
A: What I liked most about the story were two acts of love—or what I thought were two acts of love—in the book and then I'd have them in the movie. One is when [Matt King's character] decides to tell the lover that the woman is dying, and that if he wants to he can have a chance to say goodbye to her at the hospital. I liked that. And I liked that not he—because he's too cowardly—but his wife shows up at the hospital and says, "My husband wouldn't come and that didn't seem right, I thought someone from my family should come." I liked that too.

Q: Speaking of that scene, I often found myself laughing one moment and then crying the next when I was watching the film. How did you find the balance between the humor and grief while making those transitions feel natural?
A: You know it's a funny thing when I was doing a lot of interviews about the film and it was "how do you have those hairpin turns and tone" and I gotta tell you, I just don't know. It's just what occurs to me as being lifelike.

It kind of happens in life, where you have a huge laugh at a funeral—you know that's kind of a cheap example—but it's true. And I just think I want to see that more in film. A thicker tone, or a thicker band-width of tone in a film like I see in life every day. Also, don't forget, I come from making comedy, so in as much as this is the most dramatic film I've made, it's still made by someone with a certain sense of absurdity and with a weakness for comedy. It's a good combination.

Q: I read that you once said you choose to work with actors within who you can detect a full, true person capable of all forms of human emotion. How do you determine these qualities when you meet an actor?
A: Ideally, but that's one reason I don't like a lot of modern American movie-stars, is that I don't see in them full people. I mean my model for a great film actor is always a Marcello Mastroianni, he just hit all of the buttons.

I don't like it when I see actors as a bristling nerve mass of ambition, because that shows up for me onscreen. And in as much as George Clooney is one of those big movie stars, and has done a lot of slick performances, still he's a real guy with a lot of depth. That's what I wanted to see. Because I'm trying to represent life up there. Still, within a kind of narrative commercial vernacular let's say, but there's lifelike as I can get it given my parameters, and the country into which I parachuted at birth [laughs].

Q: Speaking of George Clooney, what surprised you most about working with him?
A: How much he jokes around between takes!

Q: Ah, so he really lives up to his reputation as a practical joker, does he?
A: Well no, not a practical joker, yes but he's a comedian. He just laughs constantly. It's just how he functions.

Q: You seem to have discovered a real talent in Shailene Woodley; what was it about her that convinced you to have her in the film?
A: Her audition. She was extremely good. And I believed physically that she could be the midpoint between George Clooney and some wife yet to be determined. I believed she could be Clooney's daughter. My model had been a seventeen-year-old Debra Winger, in a way, someone who would have "vulnerability and fieriness," great strength and great vulnerability and I think she has it. She's a really great gal, a talented gal.

Q: Speaking of the character of Matt King's wife in the film. She is obviously a central character in the film around which most of the drama unravels, but we never really see her properly or gain insight into her feelings. Were you ever tempted to develop her character, through flashbacks or memories?

A: No, I wasn't interested. I'm much more interested in other people, and in the changing relationships that all the other characters have with her, and shifting attitudes toward her as she's just lying there. And in a way she's writing the screenplay that all the rest of these characters are acting out like puppets.

Q: Which one scene were you most proud of?

A: I think the scene where the father and daughter arrive on the porch of the lover and the lover's wife on vacation; the first confrontation. And through Clooney's interrogation of the guy, I thought that was a very effective scene. That whole sequence, even from when the father and the daughter are walking around the side of the house and they spot the wife, they approach and exchange pleasantries and then finally the father is able to confront the lover in the house, that was pretty good. Pretty well acted, very simply shot—but effectively shot—and I'm proud of that little sequence. And everything that's happening is very sincere, yet also kind of funny on some level.

Q: What I liked most about these characters was that even though some of them don't have much screen time, they are all very distinctive and quite complex in a way, Judy Greer and Nick Krause's characters for example. Was it a challenge to keep the momentum of the movie while paying justice to the depth of the characters in the book?

A: No, that's what a movie is, for me it's what separates the wheat from the chaff. With any movie it's how much attention is lavished on secondary and tertiary characters, or extras. You have to put a lot of time into that and cast well, and then you need actors who are capable of suggesting an entire life and entire person, even in a short scene. There's a great onus placed on secondary and tertiary actors. As a director I give them a lot of attention.

Q: How much of an influence did the writer of *The Descendants*, Kaui Hart Hemmings, have on the film itself?

A: Well it's her vision, you know I really felt that I was serving her, but in the filmmaking; none. But I'm there serving her story and I involved her a lot—more than I have any previous adaptation I've done—in asking her what she thought of the screenplay, and asking her to open doors for me in Hawaii so I could meet the right people and get a sense of the right locations. So she was very involved, but of course she left the final decisions up to me, but I was very invested in serving my version of her vision.

Q: Was she there on location with you?
A: Sometimes. She's even in the movie, she plays George Clooney's secretary.

Q: Oh wow, that's interesting to know.
A: Yeah that short gal!

Q: What was the greatest challenge of filming on location in Hawaii?
A: The biggest challenge in this film was shooting on boats I think. I'd never done that before so a very simple, plaintive scene of the family on the water in the boat toward the end of the film spreading the ashes, that just drove me crazy!

Omaha and the Perfect Ending: The Alexander Payne Interview

Erich van Dussen / 2013

From MPNnow.com, Messenger Post Media, February 28, 2013. Published by permission of the interviewer.

Erich van Dussen: I'll start off easy: Where are you today? What are you up to?
Alexander Payne: I'm in an editing suite, supervising the editing on my latest motion-picture extravaganza.

EVD: That's *Nebraska*, right? I heard you were making another film in Omaha. How did that come about?
AP: Well, I have to correct you—I did not shoot a frame of film in Omaha. I was in rural Nebraska. I spent a couple of days shooting in Lincoln, a city I knew, but I also shot in a bunch of towns that I'd never even heard of before. I always like to say that we Omahans are to Nebraska what New Yorkers are to the rest of the U.S. We're this metropolis on the East Coast, and we're a little ignorant of, and snooty about, the people to our west. But small towns, in their own way, are as exotic to me as Hawaii was when I was making *The Descendants*. It was a lovely education to hang out among my fellow Nebraskans.

EVD: Still, you shot and set three films in Omaha (*Citizen Ruth, Election,* and *About Schmidt*). What's great about making movies in your hometown?
AP: Well, my stock, semi-sarcastic answer is, you don't ask Woody Allen or Spike Lee or Martin Scorsese, "Why do you like to shoot in New York?" But people often like to shoot where they're from, where they have early connections and they're comfortable expressing and exploring things

deep inside them. Plus, nobody else is making Omaha movies—I have a complete corner on that market.

EVD: You're active in film preservation in your region and sit on the board of an independent not-for-profit movie theatre in Omaha. There's so much film in your life—do you have any other interests?
AP: You mean besides watching Turner Classic Movies? [laughs] Well . . . outside of movies? It sounds like a singles ad, but I like the outdoors. [laughs] I like cooking, if you can believe it. Hiking, travel, language, spending time with friends, unicorns, rainbows, sunsets, all that crap. I wondered how long it would take before we got to unicorns and rainbows.

EVD: Yeah, I should have led with that. Seven years passed between the release of *Sideways* and *The Descendants*. Was there anything keeping you from writing and directing a feature during that time?
AP: Well, I was writing most of that time—I took two and a half years writing something with Jim Taylor, the co-writer of my first four films. That script has yet to be made, but we put a lot of work into that, kind of a big-budget science-fiction satire.

EVD: Was that *Downsizing* [a publicized but never-produced project that was rumored to star Paul Giamatti and Reese Witherspoon]? I wondered what happened to that.
AP: Correct. So I never stopped working; we just got caught in a kind of a script Vietnam. And to tell you the truth, when you say "seven years" you're talking about releases, but from my perspective I was working on *Sideways* until March of '05, which is when the awards and promotion ended, and then in summer of '09 I started work on *The Descendants*. So from my point of view, I wasn't directing for four years, not seven. Not to quibble, but I quibble.

EVD: That's an interesting point. It's not thought about much, but your role in making films goes on for a lot longer than the time spent producing the film itself—pre-production and the business end up front, and then post-production and publicity after it's made. There must come a point when you just want to go back to making a new movie instead of talking about the last one.
AP: Absolutely. It's a double-edged sword: You don't want to look a gift horse in the mouth, but if you happen to make a film which reaches the

public and critics, and then you're lucky enough to get nominated for awards, it's a wonderful honor, but also a big time-suck. Those periods rob [the time needed to make] a film from your life. I'm definitely going to truncate the time I spend with that on my next film. I'm over fifty now, so I need to be careful about how I spend my time.

EVD: You've done a little bit of writing on films that you haven't directed. I'm wondering if you'd ever be interested in directing a film that you didn't have a hand in writing yourself.
AP: Well, I would probably always be involved in rewriting, kind of dabble around the edges of a script to match my perverse tastes. But the film I'm editing now, I will not take any writing credit on. It's written by a guy out of Seattle whose parents are from Nebraska. And I did some re-writing on it, but he deserves the credit. I'm delighted to find a script that someone else has written; I just never do. I always write out of desperation.

EVD: I wanted to ask you about the way you end your movies. It seems like there's a kind of signature there, in the way you end your films almost in the middle of a scene.
AP: Really? Can you give an example?

EVD: Well, take *Sideways*, and closing on Paul Giamatti knocking on Virginia Madsen's door. Or George Clooney just watching TV with his daughters in *The Descendants*. Or Jack Nicholson tearing up after reading the letter from his pen pal in *About Schmidt*. It's as if the ends of these films are more about taking a break from the characters rather than really ending their stories—giving the characters permission to live on after the film is ended. Is there a philosophy at work here?
AP: Interesting! There are two things at work there. First, hopefully the final frame where the editor and I decide to end the picture has emotional impact. In that way I think a feature film is more related to a short story than to a novel; in the short story, every word is weighted, and everything that happens in the short story is carefully chosen to direct the reader to a singular effect at the end. Someone once said, "The novel wins by decision, the short story wins by knockout." I think films have to win by knockout. In those pictures you mentioned, the knockout is sort of the dewdrop suspended on the end of a leaf—and just as it drops, you cut.

The other thing is, since my films aren't traditional goal-oriented stories—stop the bank robbery, save the girl, get back together with the lover, that kind of thing—they're much more like the fabric of life, I hope; and an ending has to bring this particular period of these characters' lives to an end, and yet imply that life goes on. Also, usually there's some circularity in those endings that refers to the beginning. In the ending of *Election*, a new little girl is raising her hand just as Reese Witherspoon raised hers in the beginning. In *Sideways*, the film begins with a knock and ends with a knock. In *The Descendants* you begin with a family in crisis, and at the end you wind up with a family with some degree of resolution as they sit there watching television—and even the mother is present, symbolically, in terms of the yellow quilt which had covered her while she lay dying.

By the way, the best ever movie ending—and I think one of the greatest achievements in all of the arts, if I may be so pretentious—is the ending of Chaplin's *City Lights*. That's the greatest movie ending.

Film Director Alexander Payne: Greece "Energizes My DNA!"

Demetrios Rhompotis / 2013

From *NEO Magazine* (neomagazine.com), a Greek American monthly, March 6, 2013. Reprinted by permission of the interviewer.

Demetrios Rhompotis: Your project in the making is called *Nebraska*. What is it about? How was it shooting in your hometown?
Alexander Payne: This film will be my first in black and white and I'm a big film buff. I would say 95 percent of the movies I watch are black and white and I always wanted to make one. It's a very simple story, a father and son road trip from Montana to Nebraska. It's a very modest little comedy, but I didn't actually shoot it in my hometown of Omaha, rather in the rural areas of my state of Nebraska. I have no idea if it's any good or not, but it will be out this fall.

DR: You've been many times to Greece, including as guest of honor in movie festivals, but you haven't shot a movie there. Is there something in the offing?
AP: It's a little bit dangerous for me to mention this because I have no concrete plans, but I have growing within me the urge to move to Greece, not permanently but for a while, learn Greek well, finally, and use my movie camera as a way to tell a Greek story and in doing so find out more about myself.

DR: Are you planning to visit the country anytime soon?
AP: As soon as I finish this film I'm going to Greece, probably in June.

DR: What part of Greece did your family come from?

AP: My family is from three different areas: the island of Syros, from Livadia and also, with whom I'm most in touch, from Aegio.

DR: For the last three years Greece has endured an onslaught of negative publicity. Whether she deserved it or not, isn't that enough of a reason to want to make a movie there?
AP: Look, I am a Greek American, but I'm an American. However, this crisis affecting Greece I feel is energizing my DNA. When I hear things about Greece, I feel, "I can say that, you can't say that! I can say bad things about Greece if I want, but you shut up!" It doesn't necessarily help or cure anything but it helps somewhere. I just think it's the right time for artists including those Greek artists of the Diaspora to make beautiful things and do so somehow with the consciousness of being Greek and helping Greece in mind. Now that sounds kind of vague. I don't know exactly what that means, even though I'm saying it, but I stick by it!

DR: At the [Leadership 100] conference, Jim Gianopulos, President of 20th Century Fox, said that you are somehow the new John Cassavetes.
AP: If he means that I'm merely the newest, the latest known Greek American director, or if he means that there exists a thematic or humanistic similarity, well, I am proud of the fact that the two Greek American directors who preceded me, Elia Kazan and John Cassavetes, both were great humanists and interested in the intricacies of the human heart as I aspire to be.

DR: Which one of your movies is your favorite?
AP: I don't have a favorite among my films but I would tell you that the film I received the most compliments on is *Election*. I think, and I like that film in this aspect, I think it's the only film I made which isn't too long. The other films are good, but are a little bit too long and even as I was making them I was thinking, oh it's a little too long, but there is nothing else I could cut at this point. *Election* has very good rhythm, it moves along like a shark and it ends at just the right point.

DR: In your opinion, what's the state of the American cinema today?
AP: I can only give a subjective answer about the type of movies that I want to see. In general, the intelligent comedy has been lost and the intelligent drama has been lost. They all are making Roger Corman films now: cops, car chases, guns, science fiction. They don't want to spend

$15 million on a small human movie. They'd rather spend $115 million on a big one and get a big turn. I'm fine with that! Look, a movie can be anything. I want someone alone in his tiny apartment making a film about his cat and I want the big film about outer space. But not at the expense of that middle section that made many of us want to become filmmakers in the first place, which is literate dramas and comedies. However, this year has been a good year, an excellent year! That we have *Silver Linings Playbook*, *Argo*, *Zero Dark Thirty* and a bunch of others, it's a pretty good year for films. And also internationally it's been a good year. And I forgot to mention for younger people to see the film *Amour*. That's a masterpiece! It's very beautiful to see a masterpiece created in our time.

DR: As someone who creates spectacle through your camera, your characters, without many technological tricks, how do you think your genre, the classic filmmaking that you do, will evolve, because I think it hasn't much?

AP: The BBC made a series fifteen years ago with a very ugly English nun explaining art. And she became a hit. Her name was Sister Wendy and her program on the BBC and later in America was called *Sister Wendy Explains Art to You*. They would fly her around the world and she would stand in front of different sculptures, paintings and explain them with profound, prodigious intelligent insight. She began the series in southern France, standing in front of those cave paintings of the guys hunting, which are beautiful, and she said, we will see art like this from now to our own contemporary times. Unlike science where each generation stands on the shoulders of the generation before to have progress, art does not have progress. Art simply shifts given the time in which it's created. Because the human heart does not progress, it merely shifts, given the time in which it is born. That's how I feel about your question. In the thirties honest film looks and feels on the surface different from what it was in the seventies, eighties, even now. But underneath its form, it's the exact same humanism and compassion and exploration of the human heart.

DR: Would you go to unexplored waters, by doing a 3D movie, more CGI?
AP: If the story is good. The form doesn't matter, it's the story and who are the people.

DR: What did your mother tell you after you dedicated to her your latest Oscar and in Greek!

AP: You know, my mother is funny! On the one hand she is a little unsentimental; on the other hand, when I received the [first] Oscar, seven years previous, she had said "You didn't mention me. You should have dedicated it to me just like Javier Bardem did with his mother!" So, in a way the fact that I did it was, okay good, now we can move on.

DR: You made your first movie when you were thirty. Did you ever consider the idea of stopping and doing something else, like your parents suggested?
AP: No, I never thought about stopping, I love movies too much.

DR: What kind of other jobs did you do until success came?
AP: I graduated from the UCLA Film School with a hit student film and within a month of graduation I was offered a writing/directing deal at Universal Studios, where I could write anything I wanted and if they want it I would direct it. I was paid for that $125,000 of which because of taxes, agent, and lawyer, you keep about half. So, that was about $60,000 which I lived on for five years because I never changed my lifestyle from that of a student. And then I did a couple of film jobs and also, during film school, I worked as a catering waiter.

DR: If you hadn't become a director, what profession would you have chosen?
AP: When I was a senior in university and applying to graduate film school, I was also applying to journalism school. I would have been also very happy, maybe not as happy, but who knows, as a foreign correspondent.

Whittling Birch Bark:
A Conversation with Alexander Payne

Julie Levinson / 2013

June 6, 2013. Printed by permission of the interviewer.

This interview was conducted the week after *Nebraska* debuted at the 66th Cannes Film Festival, where it was one of twenty films selected for the main competition. Payne was continuing to edit the film in preparation for its theatrical release later in the year.

Julie Levinson: I want to have a sort of meta-conversation by asking about some of the things you've said in past interviews and by taking an overview of your films. There's a great line from Jean Renoir: "A director makes only one movie in his life. Then he breaks it apart and makes it again." As I've read your past interviews and thought about your work as a whole, I've seen a lot of commonalities among your films in terms of your motifs, visual style, world view, and attitude toward your characters. I don't imagine many film directors, as they are making individual movies, think about them as part of a body of work.
Alexander Payne: Tarantino does, I think.

JL: But, generally, that's the job of the historian or the critic.
AP: Yes, right. I agree.

JL: One ongoing motif in your films has to do with men at midlife.
AP: And *Paris je t'aime* is a woman at midlife.

JL: In your last several films (and, from what I've read, in *Nebraska* as well), there are a lot of unmoored characters. From young midlife in *Election* toward the end of midlife in *About Schmidt*, your movies focus on

lost souls. They present men who are adrift and are reassessing their lives because what they thought was mooring them to an identity no longer is. As you look back over your films, does that resonate with you?
AP: I guess, but I never think of it that way. I think if that *is* true, it's because that's the comic figure that Jim Taylor and I settled upon, like Chaplin's tramp or Harold Lloyd's American eager beaver or Buster Keaton's stone face character at odds with the physicality of the world. Ours is somehow that middle-aged fellow. I don't want to write it off or discount whatever thematic resonance it might have, close to my heart and Jim Taylor's of course. But on a workaday level that's just our comic figure. We just derive delight from that character and try to derive meaningful comedy from that discrepancy between our dreams and our reality.

JL: There's a film scholar who coined the phrase "melodramas of beset manhood." I think of most of your films as tales of beset manhood. These men are performing roles that they think they're supposed to be performing and, as often happens in comedy, they have to be stripped of that baggage and those costumes.
AP: Religion, psychology, meditation—all of those things invite us to shed our roles and somehow touch our essence, and I think that's interesting. On the one hand, I guess I have a world view, even if I have no idea what it is. It just comes out through selection of story and treatment of story. On the other hand, I would like to think I'm a professional director who just services whatever story I'm doing.

JL: As I read through your prior interviews, there was something that rightly irritated you: when people pointed out that your main characters are so flawed. That seems reductive to me. In spite of your characters' foibles and insecurities, you have terrific affection for them.
AP: I don't know what it means when people point out that my characters are flawed. If I had affection only for flawless humans, I would love no one.

JL: Still, it must be a delicate balance between making characters the butt of the joke and simultaneously maintaining their humanness. When you write and direct, do you ever have to catch yourself from going over to the snarky side?
AP: I never think of that. I want things to be comic without being caricature. There's a little bit of caricature, perhaps, in *Citizen Ruth*. But things

could be much more comic and much more exaggerated. Even my collaborators—the production designer, or the editor, or even the actor—sometimes will say, "Oh, it would be funnier to do it this way." I always try to keep things actually a bit more serious and a bit more real.

JL: So you sacrifice laughs for the sake of character?
AP: Oh, absolutely. My line to my collaborators is always, "Let's stay on this side of the joke."

JL: I want to ask about your films' endings. Classic comic endings usually aren't believable but they're desirable. Characters become their better selves and the repressive social world, which has insisted that duty takes precedence over desire, also often accedes to the characters' happiness. Your films' endings are definitely not classic comic endings. They're much more in the satirical mode where things end *in medias res* or they end ambiguously.
AP: Well, *Sideways* I wouldn't put in the category of tragic or comic ending. There it's sort of a sweet, human ending. He's at the woman's door but a Hmong family now lives there; she's moved away. It doesn't even mean they'll get together again but he's open to the possibility of loving again. I can't believe certain audience members who think that any good movie can't have an ending that smells of being happy, or else the movie is a Hollywood sell-out and I am becoming a Hollywood sell-out.

JL: Did you get that for *The Descendants*?
AP: Oh, yes. Even for *About Schmidt* a little bit, where he cries. Are we in China, where all endings have to be sad? Part of me just wants to be a director making movies and each story is separate and each ending, whether a little bit this way or a little bit that way, must feel earned and borne out by the story. Each of the endings doesn't really have a closure. The ending of *The Descendants* is a moment of peace and life will go on. I don't know what happens the next day. The movie I'm making now, *Nebraska*, has kind of a happy ending but after kind of a downer movie. But it's also sweet. Hopefully, the endings are earned.

JL: In one interview, you said about *Nebraska*: "It's just a little comedy: nothing fancy, nothing ambitious. It's just a nice little comedy." But film comedy has a long tradition of bait-and-switch; people think they're coming just for laughs and then, in many comedies, there is all sorts of social critique and satirical commentary and character exploration. Do you feel that comedy is a lesser form?

AP: No. I think comedy is a very serious form, and people tell me it's a difficult form. I don't think it's difficult because it's what I do. I just think movies are difficult. We want films to give us a certain distance from the reality being portrayed so we look at it anew and I think comedy does that. Plus, it's delightful. I think films need to be charming and delightful and entertaining. Kurosawa used to say that: film should, above all, be entertaining. You can have serious themes but still make an entertaining film: one that doesn't bore the shit out of the audience.

JL: In a few interviews, you said you don't like your films that much.

AP: I say that kind of tongue-in-cheek. Don't take too seriously anything I say in any of those interviews. But *Nebraska* really is just a nice little comedy. I have some friends who say some of my best work is in it. Some of the reviews from Cannes just now said it's minor and inessential. I have no idea. Maybe it's a transition film. Maybe every film is a transition film to the next one.

JL: You're often referred to as an anomaly in contemporary Hollywood because you've managed to maintain your artistic independence and you continue to make these humanist, low-concept films that can't be summed up in one sentence.

AP: I think they're pretty high concept but, as you say, they can't be summed up in a few words.

JL: How have you gotten to that point of autonomy? Is it simply because your films have done well enough so producers say, "Just go do your Alexander Payne thing?"

AP: I keep my costs low and my films make money, so I can keep doing it. I don't need hits. I need my films to make back their negative costs, their advertising costs, and one dollar. Then I can keep making movies. It's all about being able to keep making movies. When you have a stinker or one that costs too much and there's too much pressure to recoup it, that's when trouble starts.

JL: Do you get a huge amount of pressure these days to cast certain actors? The producers must have been delighted when you cast Clooney in *The Descendants*.

AP: Yeah, well, he was appropriate and it's fun to cast movie stars once in a while because it just makes everybody feel better. If you're on the fence between two actors, in the event of a tie, the movie star wins. It makes everybody feel better. But I will readily sacrifice the budget of the film to have the right cast. Of all cinematic components, two are first among equals: screenplay and casting. I know that because those are the two things that give you the most problems in the editing room: if you have to cut around something flawed in the screenplay or some diseased piece of casting because someone's not right for the part.

JL: As you're writing, are you casting in your head?
AP: Concretely casting? No. It depends. I thought Clooney might be good for *The Descendants* when I was writing but I did not write it for him. I sometimes cast unavailable actors. I wrote *Citizen Ruth* for Giulietta Masina. I wrote *About Schmidt* for William Holden or John Randolph. William Holden also would have been very good in *The Descendants*. This one, *Nebraska*, is really Henry Fonda in *On Golden Pond* or Warren Oates or Walter Brennan. He was a wonderful actor. Or if you could get a serious performance out of Percy Kilbride [Pa Kettle].

JL: I was trying to think of earlier directors whose work is somewhat analogous to yours, and I kept coming back to Billy Wilder.
AP: That's a lovely compliment. Thank you.

JL: Supposedly, Wilder was once asked why his films were so cynical and he replied that he considered cynicism a good defense against a world that never fails to fail you.
AP: That's very beautiful.

JL: I thought of that in terms of your films. They're equal-opportunity satires, so everybody is fair game.
AP: Yeah, of course. Some criticism of my films will say, "He makes fun of his characters . . . and he's gone soft." Both at once! Pierre Rissient, man of cinema, who probably knows more about film than anyone alive, has compared me to Leo McCarey, with a comedy background but doing pathos. I always think, too, that's Chaplin and de Sica—and Chekhov. People who can do comedy can also do pathos. That's a tradition that I think is lovely to admire. Look at where Frank Capra, George Stevens, and Leo McCarey wound up. They all keep it from dipping into bathos. They can have a dramatic story with sentiment and emotion but

still keep it light on its feet. It comes from having a comedy background and also hiring actors who have comic timing. That's important. Even Ozu was very adept at comedy early on in his silents. His movies are very funny. The more you watch Ozu, the more hilarious he is.

JL: Much has been written about how many of your movies are set in your hometown of Omaha, but whether the films are set in Omaha or California or Hawaii or Paris or on the road, you have a vivid sense of place. Your characters are very much defined by their landscape and there is even sometimes a sense of geographical determinism.
AP: Yes, absolutely. When I decide to do a film, I think as much about the setting as I do about the story. I kind of mentally audition both.

JL: You've done three road movies: *About Schmidt, Nebraska, Sideways.*
AP: Even *The Descendants* a little bit.

JL: The road as an enduring piece of American iconography usually represents self-discovery and freedom and leaving one's history behind, but I don't think it functions that way in your films. At the end of the road, your characters may be sadder but I'm not sure they're wiser. At best, they may have a sense that something significant happened out there but there isn't that classic road movie revelation or arrival at some new geographical and spiritual destination.
AP: True, right. But I want to get away from those kinds of movies because I hate shooting in cars.

JL: I know you think highly of Clint Eastwood's film *Unforgiven* and you once said you wanted to do a western.
AP: Yeah. I watched *Ride the High Country* again last night; that one always makes me cry. Beautiful! And Anthony Mann is one of my favorite directors. I'm an immense Anthony Mann fan. I study his films for keeping story and character in the foreground but always with a beautiful sense of landscape or setting in the background. He's tremendous at that.

JL: Are there other genres besides westerns that you'd like to tackle?
AP: It would be fun to make a thriller or a horror film. I really got turned on by the idea of making one in black-and-white. One can't imagine *Psycho* or *The Innocents* in color being as effective. They really need chiaroscuro. A western would be good. I don't think so much about a

musical. A historical epic of some sort would be fun because I like history. Wouldn't it be fun to use technology to do a nice little comedy in, say, eighth-century B.C. Greece? Like an Eric Rohmer film set in Greece. Not a big epic but just an intimate story. And I'd like to work outside the U.S. to make films in other countries and in other languages. I'd like to make a Greek film since I'm Greek American. Who knows? Right now, I'm in a position where I have no idea what my next film is.

JL: What about the rumors that you'll make a film based on the graphic novel *Wilson*?
AP: Not doing it. You know why? Middle-aged sad sack trying desperately to find connection: I don't want to do it again. I've already done it. So I don't know what I'm going to do next.

JL: Will *Downsizing* ever get made?
AP: Yes, it will. I'm just not sure whether it will be next or not.

JL: Is it liberating not to know what comes next or does that feel like free-fall?
AP: Totally liberating. Even though I've made only six features, it's constant work. I'm just a little slower at it than I'd like to be. But I'm always working. Even with the gap between *Sideways* and *The Descendants*, I never stopped working—writing *Downsizing*, and I did the pilot for *Hung* and the short for *Paris je t'aime*. I kind of want to catch my breath a little now: just read and read and think and see art.

JL: In *Paris je t'aime* and in your feature films, I think of you as a quick-sketch artist in terms of character exposition because you so succinctly capture your characters in a vivid and economical way. In *Election*, you efficiently introduce multiple characters with a combination of voiceover and evocative images. *About Schmidt* begins with a lengthy silent sequence in which the audience gets the character right away. When you write your scripts, how do you draw your characters so your audience can grasp their essence in the first few minutes?
AP: It's all about people. We're interested in movies because we're interested in people and stories and gossip. I just think that as long as I know who this person is—and it may not be as clear in the first draft but by the time I have a shooting script, I know this person. Voiceover has helped me a lot. In *The Descendants*, when the Clooney character says, "Paradise

can go fuck itself," I think that's a nice sharp line for a movie and it also plants a flag in him and in what the tone of the movie might be.

JL: Was that in the novel?
AP: A version of it was but I moved that up to give it a little teeth, a little traction into the character and into his predicament.

JL: I want to ask about the process of adaptation from novels. *Downsizing* is not based on a book.
AP: That's an original, as is *Citizen Ruth*, and *About Schmidt* is mostly an original.

JL: What has it been like for you working on scripts that totally come out of your—and Jim's—head?
AP: It's fine. It's all the same, whether you're starting with an idea or starting from a book. The script takes about the same amount of time to write.

JL: When you're reading for pleasure, in the back of your head are you—
AP: I'm cursed! I'm cursed because I'm always thinking, "Could this be a good movie?"

JL: When you direct, how much leash do you give your actors? How much direction do you give them before the first take?
AP: It all depends. When we start in the morning and I show the actors the blocking of the scene, or together we figure out the blocking, I say nothing. They go away while we're lighting it and then they come back in and do one take, two takes, three takes, and I'm observing. Then I start making suggestions: encouraging or putting the kibosh on or sculpting. A lot of it is just sculpting. "This line . . . put a pause in here." "Say this part faster." "You're saying these two phrases as though they're different thoughts. Make them one thought." Or "Here, I must act it out for you." I'll do anything. The only way Chaplin knew how to direct was to act it out. It's all about rhythm. Film, increasingly, is about rhythm: rhythm of dialogue, metronome of the film, different speeds, like a symphony. Kurosawa used to liken it to the different rhythms and different acts of Noh drama.

JL: As a writer-director, do you feel your script is set in stone once you're on the set?

AP: Pretty much. Maybe in rehearsal, reading something through, it doesn't sound quite right or scan quite right. In general, I discourage improvisation and try to make the script work as written. By the time I'm on the set with the script, I've worked it over a lot.

JL: Do you do a lot of takes to give you more flexibility in the editing room or are you pretty efficient on the set and have the finished film in your mind's eye?

AP: I try to be as efficient as possible but because I use that afore-mentioned process of letting the actors show me first what they wish to do, I can impose a certain rhythmic landscape on the shot or the scene or the take. I would say I'm, on average, a four to seven takes kind of guy. Sometimes one, sometimes twenty-two. Usually the ones that are twenty-two are because you have not just the actors doing something tricky but the dolly grip and the assistant cameraman as well. So you have all those things.

JL: Something that comes through strongly in your interviews is your prodigious knowledge of film history. In conversation, few directors evoke other movies as a reference point as consistently as you do in your interviews. You've said that you sometimes screen old movies as you prepare to shoot your own films. When your movies are coming together in your head, do you deliberately look back at certain films?

AP: A little bit. I usually watch *Seven Samurai* before making a movie, just for Kurosawa's sense of cinema and coverage. That's the best movie ever. Each time it's different. For *Election*, I was very much under the spell of *Casino*: kind of fast visuals with multiple voiceovers. For the script of *About Schmidt*, I was thinking about *Wild Strawberries* and *Ikiru*. I saw *Kotch* and *Harry and Tonto* and *Rocket Gibraltar* and other old guy films. I'd probably seen *Make Way for Tomorrow*: that's just the greatest film. But enjoying movies and knowing film history doesn't necessarily make me a better director. D. W. Griffith was not a film buff. They were just discovering film then. How many films did Chaplin see? I just love movies. I'm a film buff first and foremost, and a filmmaker second.

JL: Are there contemporary directors that you admire?

AP: I keep abreast of [Pedro] Almodóvar. I like the Thai guy who did *Blissfully Yours* [Apichatpong Weerasethakul].

JL: Any American directors?

AP: I like David O. Russell's stuff. I have great admiration for [Steven] Soderbergh and [David] Fincher. They really know what they're doing. I always have the impression that they forge their films out of tempered steel while I whittle mine out of birch bark.

Director Alexander Payne on *Nebraska*

Damian Houx / 2013

From ScreenCrave.com, November 18, 2013. Reprinted by permission of ScreenCrave.com.

Damian Houx: Your cast has a lovely, sometimes dysfunctional rapport. How do you go about creating that? Do you have lots of rehearsals or is it spontaneous?
Alexander Payne: It's somewhere in between. I don't have the tradition of rehearsing very much and most movies don't. Some directors really rehearse the hell out of things but I don't come from that background necessarily. Also I've never had the budgets to bring actors to location for their hotel and per diem much in advance of shooting. But the good thing in movies is you only have about two pages a day to do. They only have to get it some version of right once in every set up and we edit it. I think casting it's hard to say really; a really obvious answer but casting, casting, casting. The oldest cliché is the truest: Ninety percent of directing is casting. For this one where we, and by "we" I mean the casting director and I, were wishing to paint very accurately a version of the part of the world where we are from. My casting director is also from that same area. We spent over a year casting, making sure that the people we were shipping in from New York and Los Angeles would be believable there and also making sure that the locals we were hiring, either nonprofessional actors like people from community theater and then non-actors—maybe over a third, maybe half of the actors in this film are right off the street or off the farm—making sure that they would be believable to deliver reliably, once the cameras were rolling, a vivid version of themselves. And my job as a director is to make sure they're all in the same movie. I pay myself few compliments but on this particular film, I'm proud of the fact that the non-actors and the seasoned professionals are all in the same movie: that they don't stick out. In any given scene,

there's a big mix of people off the street and highly seasoned professionals and I hope you can't really tell.

Houx: Working with black and white, it sort of creates a different sense of time. Did you think of removing any modern signifiers?
Payne: It doesn't have to necessarily but it can lend a period air to a contemporary film. *Frances Ha* doesn't. *Manhattan* doesn't necessarily. Maybe Jim Jarmusch's early film does to some degree. No, we didn't think about that too much, maybe it's just because of where we were shooting. I was in Cannes and an Israeli journalist said "Oh, your film, it's like all those people have been kicked out of time. They've been kicked out of history. They live outside of history." And I'm not sure what I think of that observation but it stuck with me.

Houx: When you wrote the script, did you instantly think this should be a black and white film?
Payne: I can't tell you exactly why. The only way I can tell you why the film should be in black and white is that you should see the film and the film will tell you why. I mean, my mother was asking me, "Why are you making a film in black and white?" And my brother was saying, "Keep it in color so you make more money and more people see it." Then my mother saw it at the New York Film Festival and she goes, "Now I understand. It would have been stupid in color, this one." There's just something about it. It's true that as a filmmaker, as a film buff, I always wanted to make a black and white film. Black and white is king. It's so beautiful. But somehow in this story, it came to me that it should be in black and white and that I knew it would be cheap enough. I couldn't do it with an expensive movie in America. But with a cheap one, I thought I could do it. So it all worked out. But I wish I could give you a more substantive answer about why black and white, but just because.

Houx: There's something about CinemaScope, black and white too. Because black and white was coming to an end just as CinemaScope was coming in, those movies that were in CinemaScope and black and white, it's just like "Ahhh!"
Payne: That's one of the reasons we love late Kurosawa films from '57 to '65, black and white, 'Scope—unbelievable. All those Japanese films, late fifties, early sixties, black and white 'Scope. Then they started to disappear. *Hud* is maybe the last great one.

Houx: Was *Hud* an influence?

Payne: *Hud*'s a little bit more lit. James Wong Howe's work from *Sweet Smell of Success* through *Hud* we looked at. Mr. Howe was doing great work. *Hud*'s a little more lit than we were looking for. I mean, it's devastatingly beautiful but it's still kind of more of a studio picture.

Houx: I was wondering, this film was rated R for language; there's two "F" words and...

Payne: ... A "cocksucker" which you can barely hear. I appealed it. I went to the MPAA. I said, "Really?! Really?! I know your rules but this movie is like an Andy Griffith show. The rest of the world is going to laugh at you." You can't make everybody happy. But it says on there "For some language." The MPAA said, "Well, we specify why." "There's no sexuality or violence—just some language. So why don't you put PG-13 for some language?" "No, no, no. We can't do that." And then of course you have these arguments like, "*Eat Pray Love* has two 'fucks' and that got a PG-13 on appeal," and they go, "Yeah, and we heard about it." They got complaints about that one.

Houx: You had Bruce [Dern] in mind on this for a number of years from what I understand and yet, it's not the kind of role Bruce made his bones doing. What did you see in him early on when you say he's gonna be the right guy for this guy?

Payne: It just came to me. That's my job. Oh, he can be interesting. Not just because I knew his daughter—I had worked with his daughter. Plus you meet the guy. I cast him if nothing else for his hair. You meet him in real life, and he's still handsome, but without too much trouble, he looks like an old prairie dog. So for his looks and just that he has that quality of being ... because I knew him personally a little bit, not well, through his daughter I had met him. That he could be ornery and sarcastic but even if it's crusted over, you can sense a tenderness underneath. I wanted that quality.

Houx: Was it also like that with Will [Forte]?

Payne: No. With great respect to Will, there were, depending on ... the casting director and I were meeting a bunch of people for every part. But Woody was the hardest part finally to make the decision on so we were thinking to have a couple, a few different Davids. It came down to two or three or four. But depending on whom we would finally cast as Woody. So if I had cast someone who looked very different from how Mr. Dern looks, I might have gone a different direction. We want not just the best actor—there's no such thing as the best actor. It's like painting—which shade of red do we wish to make this? Yeah, there were two or three others. But I like what Will uniquely brought to the part. And he was among my favorites and I just met him in an audition.

Houx: And June Squibb?
Payne: That lady was also a hard part to cast. It didn't even occur to me for June to do it. I was looking at auditions and I thought, What if we ask June Squibb to audition? So I didn't just call her up and say, "Would you please audition? I want to see what you might do with it." And I loved what she did. I said, "Oh. June Squibb."

Houx: She's great!
Payne: She's great. And I'm so glad to have discovered someone so late in his or her career at least for movies. She's been active in theater for many years but I'm glad she's having this discovery. And the lady in the film who plays the ex-girlfriend in the newspaper office. That's somebody who's been languishing in student films—in short films. She hasn't been . . . you haven't seen her before. I've never seen her before and her resume is short. Like Loyola Marymount undergraduate student films as a granny or something. But she's wonderful.

Houx: That last shot of her with Bruce driving by . . .
Payne: Bruce Dern says that hers is the most honest performance in the film. That's interesting to observe.

Houx: In your films, you've really delivered a sense of place that isn't always easy to communicate. This one was a place you knew from your own personal history. How was that different from the ones you've done before? How were your own feelings about the Midwest as you started?
Payne: Well, it's a skill set. I actually think it is—training one's eye is a skill set of trying to get place. You don't see it so much in *Citizen Ruth* but it begins with *Election*. Trying to say this is a specific place with specific places and if you go there, it's literally what you would see. *Sideways* is literal to that book, which is literal to that area. Even my little Paris short for *Paris je t'aime*, you really see the 14th Arrondissement in it even though there are other intimate stories in the foreground. And also I studied Anthony Mann films. His films have a tremendous sense of place. By that I mean the background is always in focus and is grand

like in his westerns but never at the expense of the intimate story, the emotional story going on in the foreground. You can take that one step higher, which I had never done, but he did, which is to have the landscape and the background reflective—visually—of the shifting of the emotional landscape of the protagonist.

Houx: So you must love *The Naked Spur*.
Payne: It's one of my favorite films, plus Robert Ryan. Robert Ryan's on TCM all today. My prayer for today is not that my premiere goes well, but that my DVR doesn't run out of space.

Houx: How did you connect that technique that you developed to your feelings about that place? And did your feelings about the Midwest change with the film?
Payne: Now you're getting into the truly instinctive area that's hard to comment on other than that it's there. Part of it is feeling about the place, the other is finding a delightful humor in the melancholy. One thing is to say "Why black and white? Why CinemaScope?" But, also, why did I insist on shooting in the fall with leafless trees and stubbly cornfields? It's just more evocative. I never want to romanticize a version of things. Often, in American film you have to fight that. The mere act of photographing it can be romanticizing it. Like, how often we accuse violent movies. They say "Actually it's an anti-violent film." Yeah, but somehow the fact that you see it as romanticizing it and film in color and the warmth of color Kodak stock, you have to light things differently to make it feel colder. Somehow, that's a part of what for me is dramatic and humorous and somehow poetic.

Houx: Do you have a favorite scene in this film?
Payne: I like the laughs that the stealing compressor part gets. I like the scene where they visit the house where Woody grew up—the abandoned farm house. We spent a lot of time finding that location and also, when I watch the film now, I like when there's no talking. I like the silences of the film.

Additional Resources

In addition to the many reviews of Alexander Payne's work and the other uncollected interviews that have been published in newspapers and online, the following sources may be of interest to readers of this book:

Biga, Leo Adam. *Alexander Payne: His Journey in Film: A Reporter's Perspective, 1998–2012.* Omaha, NE: Inside Stories LLC, 2012.
Biskind, Peter. "Inside Indiewood." *The Nation* 270, no. 13 (April 3, 2000): 12–17.
Hochman, David. "The Scorsese of Omaha." *Esquire* 139, no. 1 (January 2003): 20.
Legaspi, Michael C. "Payne's Books of Job." *First Things* 223 (May 2012): 19–20.
Nystrom, Derek. "Fear of Falling Sideways: Alexander Payne's Rhetoric of Class." *Postmodern Culture* 16, no. 1 (September 2005) http://muse.jhu.edu/content/crossref/journals/postmodern_culture/v016/16.1nystrom.html.
Payne, Alexander, and Jim Taylor. *Sideways: The Shooting Script.* New York: Newmarket Press, 2004.
Payne, Alexander, and Jim Taylor. *The Sideways Guide to Wine and Life.* New York: Newmarket Press, 2005.
Payne, Alexander. "Alexander Payne." *Artforum International,* supplement *Bookforum* 14, no. 2 (June–August 2007): 39:3.

The following online videos are informative and enjoyable:

"On Cinema" conversation between Alexander Payne and New York Film Festival Program Director Richard Peña: http://www.filmlinc.com/nyff2012/blog/nyff-video-alexander-payne-on-cinema.
Cinefamily discussion with directors Alexander Payne and David O. Russell: http://vimeo.com/19917265.

Index

3D film, 132, 204
8½, 46
2001, 174

Abbott and Costello, 52
abortion debate, 4, 12, 22, 23, 99
About Schmidt, 47–52, 55–56, 60, 64, 72, 75, 91, 96, 101, 102, 107–9, 136, 141, 146, 147, 148, 157, 162, 165, 187, 212; characters and characterization, 49–51, 72, 193, 210; ending of, 200, 208; music in, 107; writing of, 47–48, 107–8
Academy Awards, 47, 48, 50, 83, 85
Ace in the Hole, 8
actors, 45, 139, 154; chemistry between, 172–73; non-actors, 102–3, 216; young actors, 138, 160. *See also* casting
adaptation, 30, 33, 54, 63, 65, 79, 86, 101–2, 116, 120, 126, 140, 143, 147–48, 174, 178; faithfulness of, 101, 135–36, 147–48, 163, 173
Ad Hominem, 132
All About Eve, 28
Allen, Woody, 43, 68, 77, 90, 198
Almodóvar, Pedro, 214
Altman, Robert, 74, 146
Amadeus, 57
Amarcord, 91
American Graffiti, 29
American Splendor, 62

Amour, 204
Anderson, Paul Thomas, 68, 91
Anderson, Wes, 68
Annie Hall, 76
Antonioni, Michelangelo, 124, 126
Apartment, The, 145
Argo, 204
Arteta, Miguel, 150
Artist, The, 117, 137
Ashby, Hal, 145
Aspen Shortsfest, 55
Assassination of Richard Nixon, The, 88
Astaire, Fred, 109
audience, 61
auditions, 188–89, 191
auteurist cinema, 67, 68, 94, 128
Avery, Tex, 26

Badlands, 147
Bailey, Cameron, 124, 125, 128
Bambi Meets Godzilla, 77
Bananas, 77
Bardem, Javier, 205
Barry Lyndon, 147, 174
Bates, Kathy, 47, 50–51
Beaches, 121
Begley, Louis, 47, 136, 148
Bergman, Ingmar, 108
Besman, Michael, 48
Big Business, 145
Big Picture, The, 94
Black, Shane, 9

black and white film, 83, 117, 133, 141, 192, 202, 217, 220
Blackhawk Films, 52, 92
Blissfully Yours, 214
Breaking Bad, 128
Brennan, Walter, 210
Bridges, Beau, 134, 137
Briesewitz, Uta, 128
Broderick, Matthew, 36, 39, 41, 164, 171
Bromberg, Serge, 115
Brooks, James, 68, 116
Brooks, Mel, 43
Brownell, Herbert, 81
Buñuel, Luis, 8, 9
Burke, Jim, 135, 143, 156, 176
Burke, Mary Louise, 87
Butch Cassidy and the Sundance Kid, 77

Cahill, Mike, 132
Cannes Film Festival, 106, 206, 209
Capra, Frank, 210
Carmen, 106
Casino, 165, 214
Cassavetes, John, 203
casting, 38–39, 62, 66, 87, 101, 103, 111, 112, 115, 129, 137–38, 151–52, 153, 157, 159–62, 167, 176, 187–88, 209–10, 216; as most important component, 162; unconventional, 137
Castle Films, 52, 92
Castro, Fidel, 67
Cedar Rapids, 132, 150
Chaplin, Charlie, 77, 109, 201, 207, 210, 213, 214
characters and characterization, 5–6, 17, 27, 37, 49, 50, 52, 57, 73, 115, 120, 195–96, 212; condescension to, 72, 193; female, 63; flawed protagonists, 124–25, 159, 207; judgment of, 6; likeable, 5, 44, 101; in novels, 109; and obstacles, 8, 71; stereotypical, 6; uncomfortable with the world, 56; unmoored, 206; vulnerable, 75
Chekhov, Anton, 31, 210
Chinatown, 76
Chinese films, 31
Church, Thomas Haden, 60, 62, 64, 71, 85, 154, 160, 167, 172, 176
CinemaScope, 217, 220
Citizen Kane, 76, 128
Citizen Ruth, 3–21, 22–23, 26, 28, 29, 43, 44, 64, 75, 98–100, 101, 113, 207; casting of, 66, 100, 103, 186, 210; ending of, 19, 31; financing of, 98–99; and political agenda, 33–34; title of, 20
City Lights, 201
Clockwork Orange, A, 5, 101, 125, 147, 174
Clooney, George, 115, 116, 117–18, 119, 123, 125, 129, 134, 141, 142, 151, 152, 154, 159–60, 170, 181, 195, 196, 212; casting of, 136, 157–58, 172, 176–77, 186, 190, 209, 210
Clowes, Daniel, 140, 148–49, 170, 174, 180
Clueless, 29
Coen brothers, 193
Columbus, Chris, 65, 84
comedy, 8, 12, 43, 70, 72, 96, 144–45, 172, 195, 207, 208–9; physical, 109; as serious form, 43–44, 52–53, 70, 181, 209; silent, 51, 77, 93, 137; and tragedy, 151; visual, 145. *See also* humor; satire
Coming Home, 76
consumerism, 73

Cool Hand Luke, 77
Coppola, Francis Ford, 58, 190
Coppola, Sofia, 68, 84
Corman, Roger, 109, 203
Coward, The, 47, 48, 107
Cowdin, Dan, 76
critics and criticism, 56, 72, 100, 124, 193, 210
Cruel Intentions, 137
Cuarón, Alfonso, 65, 68
Custom Film Effects, 131
cynicism, 166, 210

Dargis, Manohla, 25
Dassin, Jules, 122, 173
Daws, Gavan, 186
de Broca, Philippe, 77
Delerue, Georges, 106
Denby, David, 25, 26
depression, 49–50
Dern, Bruce, 218, 219
Dern, Laura, 12, 15, 16, 19, 22, 44, 55, 64, 100, 103
Descendants, The, 115–20, 123, 125–27, 129–30, 134, 135–40, 142–47, 150–52, 159–64, 170–73, 175–78, 184–87, 190–91, 194–97, 212; casting of, 119, 151–52, 153–57, 159–61, 172, 186–87, 210; characterization in, 194–96; editing of, 182; ending of, 125, 139–40, 200, 201, 208
De Sica, Vittorio, 162, 210
dialogue, 57, 97, 119, 126, 148
digital intermediate (DI), 131–32
Diller, Barry, 58
Distinguished Nebraskan Award, 81
documentaries, 68
Dornfeld, Mark, 131
Downsizing, 116, 140, 150, 176, 180, 199, 212, 213

Driving Miss Daisy, 173
Dr. Strangelove, 23
Duck Soup, 145

Eastwood, Clint, 211
Easy Life, The, 168
Eat Pray Love, 218
editing, 13–14, 15, 17–18, 40, 104, 131, 144, 146–47, 151, 155, 182–83, 210; final cut, 131
Election, 24, 25–39, 41–45, 61, 64, 75, 87, 101, 102, 105–6, 110, 113, 164–65, 166, 171, 203, 212, 219; casting of, 38–39, 44, 103, 138, 146, 160; ending of, 30–31, 104, 200; theme of garbage, 34–35
El Túnel, 56, 80
emotion, in films, 115, 118, 119, 120, 121, 151, 155, 160, 172, 177, 195, 200, 210
existentialism, 56, 125
Exorcist, The, 77

Fargo, 193
Fast Times at Ridgemont High, 29
Faulkner, William, 79
Faxon, Nat, 116, 143, 184
Fellini, Federico, 46, 91
Ferrell, Will, 111
Ferris Bueller's Day Off, 36
Fields, Sid, 46
Film Comment, 20, 175
film language, 113
film school, 53, 79, 92–93, 95–96, 178
film v. digital, 132–33
financing and budget, 67, 84, 95, 111, 209, 210
Fincher, David, 215
Firesign Theater, 25
Fitzgerald, F. Scott, 79

Five Easy Pieces, 77
Fonda, Henry, 210
foreground and background, 171
Forster, Robert, 116, 120, 134, 137, 191
Forte, Will, 218
Fox Searchlight, 89, 105, 111, 117, 123, 132, 135, 185
Foxx, Redd, 34
Frances Ha, 217
Frank, Joe, 10
Frankenstein Meets the Wolf Man, 52
Frears, Stephen, 135, 156
Freeway, 137
French New Wave, 94
Friedkin, William, 57

Gaeta, Frank, 131
Gallagher, 87
Garcia Marquez, Gabriel, 80
genres, 181, 211
Ghost World, 140, 180
Giamatti, Paul, 60, 62, 64, 71, 72, 85, 111, 154, 167, 172, 188, 199, 200
Gianopulos, Jim, 203
Gilroy, Tony, 139
Girl in the Red Velvet Swing, 79
Gittes, Harry, 48
Godfather, The, 5, 65
Golden Globes, 52
Goodfellas, 165
Good, the Bad and the Ugly, The, 77
Graduate, The, 108
Greece, 202–3, 212
Greek tragedy, 163
Greer, Judy, 127, 138, 187, 188, 196
Griffith, D. W., 214
Groundhog Day, 57
Guber, Peter, 11
Guest, Christopher, 94

Hagel, Chuck, 82
Harry and Tonto, 214
Harry Potter films, 65, 68, 84, 102
Hastie, Patricia, 158
Hathaway, Henry, 124
Hawaii, 115, 118, 126, 127, 138, 143–44, 148, 156, 157, 163, 171, 176, 185–86; filming in, 130, 197; social climate of, 151
Hawaii International Film Festival, 127, 163
Hedren, Tippy, 101
Hell's Angels, 76
Helms, Ed, 132
Help, The, 121
Hemingway, Ernest, 79
Hemmings, Kaui Hart, 116, 118, 123, 126, 134, 135, 142, 150, 174, 186; involvement in film, 136, 138, 148, 173, 196–97
Holden, William, 210
Honolulu, Hawaii, 143–44, 157, 171
Hopper, Edward, 132
Horace, 140
Howe, James Wong, 218
Hud, 217–18
humor, 6, 70, 97, 104; physical, 44, 137, 165, 194; visual, 118. *See also* comedy; satire
Hung, 128, 148, 150, 157, 212

I Am Roe (McCorvey), 4
Ides of March, 141
Ikiru, 78, 108, 214
independent filmmaking, 42–43, 67
Innocents, The, 211
I Now Pronounce You Chuck & Larry, 150
Italian neorealism, 94
It's Always Sunny in Philadelphia, 128

Jackson, John, 187, 191
Jarmusch, Jim, 217
Jaws, 65, 76, 94
Jefferson, Margo, 25
Jenkins, Tamara, 150
Jennings, Peter, 58
Jeopardy, 80
Johnston, Joe, 57
Jones, Chuck, 142, 145
Jonze, Spike, 68
Joyce, James, 79
Jurassic Park III, 56–57, 73

Kazan, Elia, 112, 203
Keaton, Buster, 77, 115, 207
Keillor, Garrison, 80, 81
Kent, Rolfe, 106, 107
Kids, 12
Kilbride, Percy, 210
King Kong, 57, 77
King of California, 132
King of Hearts, 77
Klein, Chris, 103–4, 138, 164
Knife in the Water, 152
Konrad, Cathy, 19
Kotch, 214
Kramer vs. Kramer, 121
Krause, Nick, 119, 134, 196
Kubrick, Stanley, 63, 102, 109, 126, 174
Kurosawa, Akira, 78, 79, 93, 98, 108, 147, 187, 190, 209, 213, 214, 217
Kurtz, Swoosie, 12

Ladd, Diane, 19
La Dolce Vita, 46
La Follette, Robert, 81
Lai, Francis, 106
Landlord, The, 145
landscape, 69, 146
La Notte, 126

Last Detail, The, 173
Lee, Spike, 90, 198
Leigh, Mike, 70
Lewinsky, Monica, 30
Lillard, Matthew, 123, 125, 158, 185, 187
literature, 79
Little Big Man, 77, 83, 113
Lloyd, Harold, 77, 109, 207
location. *See* place, in films
London, Michael, 66
Lorenzo's Oil, 168
Los Angeles, Calif., 91
Loved One, The, 23
Lumet, Sidney, 190

Macy, William H., 73
Madsen, Virginia, 63, 64, 72, 87, 200
Make Way for Tomorrow, 145, 214
Malick, Terrence, 109, 119
Malle, Louis, 126
Manhattan, 76, 217
Mann, Anthony, 69, 112, 124, 171, 211, 219
Man on the Moon, 138
marketing, 73, 105
Martindale, Margo, 168–69
Masina, Giulietta, 210
Mastroianni, Marcello, 195
Mexicans, 69
McCabe and Mrs. Miller, 113
McCarey, Leo, 145, 210
McCorvey, Norma, 4, 11
McKee, Robert, 46
Meet the Parents, 73
Melies, George, 115
Memory Lane, 3
Mercouri, Melina, 173
Michael Clayton, 139, 186
Midnight Cowboy, 173
Midwest, 68–69, 82, 91, 219, 220

Mifune, Toshiro, 187
Miller, Amara, 123, 134, 138, 151, 154, 160, 161, 170, 191
Million Dollar Baby, 168
Minnesota Public Radio, 80
Miramax, 11–12, 20, 22, 66
Morricone, Ennio, 106
MTV Films, 29, 42, 104, 105
Murdoch, Rupert, 58
Museum of Modern Art, 56
music, 106–7
My Dinner with André, 126
Mystery of Picasso, 132

Naked Spur, The, 220
Nashville, 74
National Lampoon Radio Hour, 25
Navajo Joe, 36
Nebraska, 81–82
Nebraska, 117, 152, 170, 174, 192, 198, 202, 206, 208, 209, 210, 216–20
Neill, Sam, 73
Netflix, 121
Network, 23
news media, 58
New York, N.Y., 90, 198
New York Film Festival, 217
New York Times, 25, 99
Nichols, Mike, 68
Nicholson, Jack, 47, 48–49, 50, 52, 55, 64, 108–9, 136, 151, 159, 177, 181, 200
Nights of Cabiria, 46
Nixon, Richard, 88, 94
Norris, George, 81
novels, 63, 65, 101–2, 109
Now Voyager, 122
NYU, 93

Oates, Warren, 210

O Brother, Where Art Thou?, 186
Ocean's Eleven, 68, 186
Oh, Sandra, 64, 87, 179
Omaha, Neb., 39, 64, 69, 75, 76, 90, 91, 144, 164, 198–99, 211; setting of *About Schmidt*, 47, 48, 107
Omen, The, 78
One-Eyed Jacks, 77
One Flew Over the Cuckoo's Nest, 76
On Golden Pond, 210
On the Waterfront, 76, 112
Ozu, Yasujiro, 145, 211

Papamichael, Phedon, 131, 141
Paramount, 42, 43, 67, 105, 117
Paris je t'aime, 153, 157, 168–69, 206, 212, 219
Passer, Ivan, 3
Passion of Martin, The, 3, 7, 94, 96
Payne, Alexander: on auditions, 188–89, 191; on his career, 127; on collaborating with Jim Taylor, 7, 38, 65–66, 74, 79, 85, 97–98; controlled style of, 146; on creative process, 23, 56, 107; on criticizing society, 21; on critics and criticism, 56, 72, 100, 124, 193, 210; on editing, 13–14, 15, 17–18, 40, 104, 130, 131, 144, 146–47, 151, 155, 182–83, 210; on endings of his films, 200–201, 208; on film as a mirror, 181; on final cut, 131; on independent filmmaking, 42–43; on his influences, 8, 9, 56, 71, 77, 78, 214; on inspiration, 86; on interviews, 124; on his mother, 51, 122, 205, 217; on old movies, 51–52, 58; on post process, 130, 131; on previewing, 130; on producing films, 88, 132; on rewriting, 10–11, 200; on rhythm of film,

132, 144, 166, 185, 213; on shooting digitally, 133, 141; on shooting on location, 139; on state of American cinema, 42, 46, 58, 59, 67, 72, 73, 126, 203–4; on writing process, 7, 9, 14, 38, 39–40, 65–66, 73, 74, 79, 97–98, 117. *See also* actors; adaptation; audience; casting; characters and characterization; comedy; dialogue; emotion, in films; film school; financing; humor; satire; screening; sentimentality; voiceover
Peña, Richard, 126
Perfect Storm, The, 152
Perot, Ross, 32
Perrotta, Tom, 26, 30, 32, 148
Peters, Jon, 11
Pickett, Rex, 60, 65, 71, 79, 84, 102, 174, 179
place, in films, 143, 157, 163–64, 191, 211, 219, 220. *See also* landscape
Place, Mary Kay, 12
Playboy Channel, 107
Player, The, 23
poetry, 80
Polanski, Roman, 152
politics, 33–34, 68, 81, 82; political film, 82–83
Portrait of an Artist as a Young Man, A, 79
post-production process, 130, 131, 151
production design, 69
Proust, Marcel, 79
Pryor, Richard, 25
Psycho, 211

Raimi, Sam, 68
Ran, 78, 147
Randolph, John, 210

Rash, Jim, 116, 143, 184
Rashomon, 165
Rather, Dan, 58
Reagan, Ronald, 32
realism, 68, 91
Redstone, Sumner, 58
rehearsing, 190, 216
Reilly, John C., 132
Renoir, Jean, 128, 206
Reynolds, Burt, 12, 101
rhythm, in film, 132, 144, 166, 185, 213
Ride the High Country, 211
Rissient, Pierre, 210
Ritchie, Donald, 78
road trip movies, 61, 141, 192, 211
Rocket Gibraltar, 214
Roe v. Wade, 4
Rohmer, Eric, 212
Rota, Nino, 106
Rushmore, 36
Russell, David O., 68, 111, 215
Ryan, Robert, 220

Sabato, Ernesto, 56, 80
Sandler, Adam, 150
Santa Barbara County, 60, 61, 91, 164, 167
satire, 6, 12, 23, 25, 26, 44, 68, 116. *See also* comedy; humor
Savages, The, 150
Scarface, 76
Schell, Maximillian, 173
Scorsese, Martin, 46, 76, 83, 90, 198
Scream, 158
screening, 122, 155
Searchers, The, 76
Secret Life of the American Teenager, The, 120, 134, 173
sentimentality, 31, 78, 166
Seven Samurai, The, 93, 214

Shampoo, 25
Shea, Bob, 42
Shearer, Harry, 25, 26
Shepard, David, 93
Shimura, Takashi, 79
Shoal of Time, 186
Show People, 43
Sideways (film), 54, 60–63, 64, 71–73, 74, 75, 79, 84, 85–89, 96, 101, 102, 110–11, 113, 135, 137, 141, 145, 154, 166–67, 174, 219; casting of, 66, 111, 176, 188; ending of, 200, 201, 208; music in, 107; sense of place in, 157, 164; success of, 95, 113, 179
Sideways (novel), 65
silent films, 51, 52, 83, 106, 126, 145
Silver Linings Playbook, 204
Sister Wendy Explains Art to You, 204
Smothers Brothers, The, 25
Soderbergh, Steven, 68, 215
Solondz, Todd, 95
Sony, 67
Sorcerer, 57
Spacek, Sissy, 147
Spanish literature, 56
Spider-Man, 68
sports, 80
Squibb, June, 219
Star Wars, 76, 94
Stevens, George, 210
Stewart, James, 171
Stewart, Jane, 69, 107, 108
Stewart, Jon, 68
Sting, The, 77
studio deals, 96, 105
Sturges, Preston, 9, 64
Sullivan's Travels, 31
Sundance Film Festival, 3, 20
Sunrise, 83
Sunset Boulevard, 125, 147

Sweet Smell of Success, 218
Swift, Jonathan, 23

Tarantino, Quentin, 91, 206
Taxi Driver, 88
Taylor, Jim, 63, 64, 65–66, 71, 88, 97–98, 107, 148, 193, 207, 213; *About Schmidt*, 48; *Citizen Ruth*, 3–21, 99; *Downsizing*, 116, 150, 175, 199; *Election*, 24, 25–39, 87, 104, 165; *Jurassic Park III*, 56; *Sideways*, 71, 74, 85, 86
television, 128, 148
Tent, Kevin, 14, 18, 130, 155
Terms of Endearment, 116, 121
Thank You Masked Man, 77
That Was the Week That Was, 25
Thieves' Highway, 122
To Live and Die in L.A., 57
Topkapi, 173
Toronto International Film Festival, 124
Trip to the Moon, 115
Turner Classic Movies (TCM), 121, 199, 220
Tynan, Kenneth, 43

UCLA, 56, 58, 92, 93, 127, 163, 205
Umiliani, Piero, 106
Unforgiven, 40, 112, 211
Universal Studios, 96, 205
USC, 92–93

Van Sant, Gus, 119
Vargas Llosa, Mario, 80
Variety, 67
Viridiana, 8
visual effects, 131
voiceover, 28, 109, 147, 155–56, 165, 178, 212

Wages of Fear, The, 57
Warner Bros., 67, 93, 145
Weerasethaku, Apichatpong, 214
Weinstein, Harvey, 42, 99
westerns, 112–13, 211
What Liberal Media?, 58
Wild Bunch, 125
Wilder, Billy, 9, 64, 109, 131, 210
Wild Strawberries, 108, 214
Willis, Gordon, 145
Wilson, 140, 148, 170, 174, 212
wine, 61–62, 72, 84, 168
Winger, Debra, 172, 195
Wire, The, 123, 128
Witherspoon, Reese, 27, 38, 41, 44–45, 55, 64, 110, 164–65, 199; casting of, 44, 137, 138
Withnail & I, 71, 168
Woodley, Shailene, 115, 119, 120, 123, 134, 137, 139, 142, 154, 160, 161, 170, 172, 173, 187, 191, 195
Woods, Cary, 10, 11, 19, 99
Writer's Almanac, 80
Writers' Guild, 116
writing process, 7, 9, 14, 38, 39–40, 65–66, 73, 74, 79, 97, 117; rewriting, 10–11, 200

Yimou, Zhang, 58

Zero Dark Thirty, 204
Zorba the Greek, 168

www.ingramcontent.com/pod-product-compliance
Lightning Source LLC
Chambersburg PA
CBHW021838220426
43663CB00005B/295